AMERICA THE BEAUTIFUL
AND VIOLENT

AMERICA THE BEAUTIFUL
AND VIOLENT

Black Youth & Neighborhood Trauma in Chicago

DEXTER R. VOISIN

Columbia University Press / New York

Columbia University Press
Publishers Since 1893
New York   Chichester, West Sussex
cup.columbia.edu

Library of Congress Cataloging-in-Publication Data
Names: Voisin, Dexter R., author.
Title: America the beautiful and violent : black youth and neighborhood
    trauma in Chicago / Dexter R. Voisin.
Description: New York : Columbia University Press, [2019] | Includes index.
Identifiers: LCCN 2018058447 (print) | LCCN 2019015684 (e-book) |
    ISBN 9780231545471 (electronic) | ISBN 9780231184403 (cloth : alk. paper) |
    ISBN 9780231184410 (pbk.)
Subjects: LCSH: Youth and violence—Illinois—Chicago. | African American
    youth—Illinois—Chicago. | Urban poor—Illinois—Chicago.
Classification: LCC HQ799.2.V56 (e-book) | LCC HQ799.2.V56 V65 2019 (print) |
    DDC 303.6083509773/11—dc23
LC record available at https://lccn.loc.gov/2018058447

Cover design: Lisa Hamm
Cover image: Digital composite

This book is dedicated to my first storytellers—Irma and Cecil, my parents. My beloved Terrell, Kirk, Cheryl, and Bernice, you are always with me. I am in gratitude and awe of the youth, families, and communities that are surviving, thriving, and accomplishing greatness in the midst of the hunt. I hope I captured some of your stories.

CONTENTS

AMERICA THE BEAUTIFUL AND VIOLENT

1
THE BEGINNING

Until lions write their own history, the tale of the hunt will always glorify the hunter.
–AFRICAN PROVERB

I never intended to write a book, just as I never intended to become an academic. As a clinical social worker in the early 1990s, I worked mostly in cities, counseling clients struggling with mental illness and substance abuse. Their stories were profound, sometimes tragic, with many moments of courage, compassion, sacrifice, and pride—all deeply affecting tales about the resiliency of the human spirit. One in particular changed the path of my life's work.

In Atlanta during the winter of 1994, I was assigned a new client, a twenty-three-year-old black man, whom I will call Tim, who was just a few years younger than I. He had a slight frame, a warm complexion, and eyes that were bright and alert. His intake form noted a diagnosis of major depression and substance use, with a history of sexual abuse and trauma starting at age ten. He was now hospitalized with AIDS. In 1992, at the height of the epidemic, HIV-infected people had to take first-generation drugs, often as many as thirty pills per day. They were forced to hide their diagnosis to avoid being fired by their employers, ostracized by entire communities, or even killed. An AIDS diagnosis was often associated with increased mortality, especially for those who avoided treatment out of fear or who were in denial about their diagnosis. The time from receiving an AIDS diagnosis to rapid physical decline was often devastatingly swift.

While I was with Tim, we discussed the lack of support he received from his family owing to his diagnosis and the fact that he was gay. The following week, when I returned for my second session with Tim, the nurses informed me that he had been moved to a private room. I entered the dimly lit room and thought I had mistakenly walked in on the wrong client. Tim was now barely recognizable, a mere shadow of the man I had visited just seven days before. He had lost about fifteen pounds from his already tiny frame, his body swallowed up by the white bed sheets. His face was gaunt, his eyes protruding and his complexion darkened.

It was the first time I had encountered a hospitalized person facing death from AIDS. I was not afraid of Tim's diagnosis but was startled by the presence of death, which seemed to cast a shadow around his bed. I had experienced death up close only once before, and I was taken aback by its brazen claim on someone so young. He was afraid, and I was afraid for him. "I don't want to die alone," he said. I sat next to him and held his hand. This violated my training not to touch clients, but in that moment, I followed my instinct to reassure and comfort him. The following week, when I returned for our third session, Tim had passed away. I made several calls to his mother, but my messages were never returned. The county buried his remains.

Although Tim was my first client hospitalized with AIDS, over the years I came to understand what might lie behind his story and those of others. I heard hundreds of horrendous stories told by clients who, as children, had been physically abused, sexually violated, or both. Many began using alcohol and other drugs to treat their deep emotional pain. For some of them, self-medicating with drugs and/or having unsafe sex resulted in their contracting HIV. After hearing many such stories, I recognized the repeated connections among personal trauma, substance use, and HIV acquisition. As my clinical and intellectual curiosity about these connections grew,

I decided to enroll in a doctoral program at Columbia University to study them in more depth.

Over the course of this new academic journey, I came to realize that the scholarly literature had much to say about the connections among childhood sexual abuse, drug use, and unsafe sexual practices; however, most of this knowledge centered on white females. I stumbled across statistics documenting that urban youth, especially blacks and males, experienced homicide rates that were up to eight times higher than those of their white and Latino peers. I began wondering whether witnessing neighborhood violence might be related to the higher reported rates of drug use and risky sexual behaviors. This became my dissertation topic.

I planned to return to Atlanta after graduation to pursue counseling focused on trauma and mental health. However, several distinguished universities came knocking, and I was offered six tenure-track positions. I accepted a job offer from the University of Chicago, packed up my life, and moved, thinking that I would try academia for one year.

Now, after twenty years in the academy, I am still researching the psychological and behavioral effects of exposure to neighborhood violence and how youth and families cope with such trauma. Most of my work has focused on black youth living in U.S. cities. I have published more than 125 peer-reviewed articles on exposure to neighborhood violence and related topics, but I never intended to write a book.

However, after years of work through which I came to be considered an expert on the topic of neighborhood violence, I have grown increasingly tired of giving countless interviews on gun violence, mass murder, and senseless killings taking place in Chicago and elsewhere. While many conversations with reporters last more than an hour, the final print or television interviews are whittled down to two-minute clips to fit an American news format characterized by sound bites. I am frustrated that the complexities driving such uneven exposure to violence and its developmental consequences are diluted in this way.

These stories often refer to "the plight of black youth, especially males, with their high unemployment, poor high school graduation rates, rap sheets by age eighteen, gang involvement, teen parenthood," and so forth. These accounts, while pointing to real disparities, are grievously incomplete and often stigmatizing, especially because they are not scripted by these youth, their families, or their communities. Nor do these stories explicate the structural factors and uneven policies that uphold and fuel these disparities, although black public intellectuals, activists, and thought leaders have long attempted to broaden public awareness of these issues. Violent neighborhood enclaves grew out of decades of societal disinvestment, structural and economic violence, and inequality in U.S. social policy—including systematic residential segregation on explicitly racial grounds. Furthermore, many of these news stories do not tell the many narratives of resiliency and fortitude: stories of personal triumph, family support, neighborhood activism, and social movements, such as the globally influential Movement for Black Lives (also known by the popular slogan "Black Lives Matter").

I have often heard this quote, attributed simply as an African proverb: "Until lions write their own history, the tale of the hunt will always glorify the hunter." This maxim has been quoted by the author Chinua Achebe, the abolitionist Wendell Phillips, and many others to point to problems with colonial knowledge production. Youth and their communities lament the woefully incomplete and pathologizing narratives that often mark discourse concerning neighborhood violence and race. This book represents my attempt to elevate marginalized voices and to provide an understanding of public-space violence, often called "neighborhood violence," within the complex social context of marginalization, poverty, criminalization, institutionalized racism and sexism, commodification, invisibility and hypervisibility, and other forces that contribute to the precariousness of black life in the United States. I will discuss these concepts in fuller detail in the pages that follow.

One of the first steps in decolonizing knowledge production and bias is interrogating its terms. Therefore, while this book takes on the topic of violence, specifically neighborhood violence, I must acknowledge the assumptions embedded in those words. As many scholars and activists have reminded us, violence is a "slippery concept."[1] While the answer to the question, "What do we mean by violence?" may at first seem obvious, our notions of what constitutes violence are often governed more by linguistic convention than by conceptual rigor. The editors of one book on violence wrote in their introduction,

> Violence can never be understood in terms of its physicality—force, assault, or the infliction of pain—alone. Violence also includes assaults on the personhood, dignity, sense of worth or value of the victim. The social and cultural dimensions of violence are what gives violence its power and meaning.[2]

While most of us may agree that violence is defined in part as an assault to the bodily integrity or psychosocial well-being of a person or neighborhood, some such assaults are more likely to be classified as violence than others. Few would hesitate to call a mugging violent. However, we might find more dissent over whether welfare state cutbacks, incarceration, underfunding of schools in black neighborhoods, economic restructuring, or overpolicing and excessive arrests constitute violent acts. Yet these are all dimensions of structural violence that erode America's progress toward a more equitable and just society.

The World Health Organization's *World Report on Violence and Health* defines violence as "the intentional use of physical force or power, threatened or actual, against oneself, another person, or against a group or neighborhood that either results in or has a high likelihood of resulting in injury, death, psychological harm, maldevelopment or deprivation."[3] This definition raises the complicated question of whether intent to harm is necessary for violence to occur. For instance, in a 2009 essay on structural violence, medical anthropologist Paul Farmer shares stories of

> some of the mechanisms through which large-scale social forces crystallize into the sharp, hard surfaces of individual suffering. Such suffering is structured by historically given (and often economically driven) processes and forces that conspire . . . to constrain agency. For many . . . life choices are structured by racism, sexism, political violence, *and* grinding poverty.[4]

Farmer shares harrowing accounts from his fieldwork in Haiti of young women and girls driven by poverty into precarious employment, risky nonvoluntary sexual relationships, and deadly disease and stories of men—disproportionately poor—who were blacklisted, tormented, and tortured by military forces after the 1991 coup. Reflecting on intent, Farmer writes that "these afflictions were not the result of accident or of force majeure; they were the consequence, direct or indirect, of human agency."[5] Nevertheless, the human agency that produces this violence is spread among many people and institutions, and those who may seem most directly involved in inflicting bodily injury on others often have highly constrained individual agency, as they are themselves caught up in powerful political, economic, and historical processes and forces. Indeed, these so-called perpetrators of interpersonal violence often have far less power to produce or prevent structural violence than others—foreign investors, say, or members of international political institutions—who, paradoxically, may not even be aware of particular incidents of harm. Some have described these processes or forces of structural violence, which often produce more intimate, proximate incidents of harm, as cycles, chains, or a "continuum of violence."[6]

It is therefore essential that my treatment of violence in this book not elide the structural processes within which individual incidents of interpersonal violence are embedded. As the sociologist Sudhir Venkatesh states, "good [research] is always a mixture of close focus and long shot."[7] At the same time, I wish to be as clear as possible when defining neighborhood violence within the scope of this book. Like *violence*, the terms *black violence* and *neighborhood violence* are complicated. As many—such as the gender and race theorist Linda Alcoff[8]—have noted, writing or speaking about a neighborhood often involves the speaker taking an outside position, resulting in an "us-versus-them" dichotomy. This raises the question, What is the neighborhood being referred to in the phrase *neighborhood violence*? How is the neighborhood being defined, and how is the violence being measured? How do we define what neighborhood violence is, and how is this definition biased? All assumptions are value laden, never neutral or bias free.

The aforementioned World Health Organization report defines neighborhood violence as "violence between individuals who are unrelated, and who may or may not know each other, generally taking place outside the home."[9] In other words, the report defines neighborhood violence as interpersonal and proximate. It includes, but is not limited to, incidents of public-space violence. Yet, while by definition *neighborhood violence* could apply to a broad range of behaviors and contexts, it is most frequently used in practice to describe perceived patterns of violence in particular locations. Usually, analysts describe neighborhood violence as taking place in lower-income urban (and, increasingly, suburban) neighborhoods and highly racially segregated ones. Acts often categorized as neighborhood violence include hearing about, witnessing, or being a victim of gang- and gun-related incidents, muggings, robberies, and rapes.

I aim to draw attention to the ways in which systemic factors and forces conspire to concentrate the burden of violence on marginalized communities—after all, that is the topic of this book. I also acknowledge the sociological and political construction of neighborhood violence, which is sometimes accompanied by biased and charged public rhetoric. I offer two timely examples, both related to my adopted hometown Chicago.

First, whenever the Blackhawks (the city's professional hockey team) or the Cubs (one of the city's professional baseball team) celebrate a big victory, many of the city's wealthy, predominately white neighborhoods (especially Wrigleyville, home of the Cubs) erupt in violence, including fights, destruction of property, arson, and other acts of disorderly conduct. However, these behaviors are not considered violent acts but are seen instead as celebratory or revelatory. While arrests do occur, many residents speculate that the public rhetoric and the media and police responses surrounding the violence would be markedly different if the disorderly conduct happened in a predominately poor, nonwhite neighborhood. For example, if similar celebratory expressions occurred among black youth in Chicago's impoverished Englewood neighborhood on the South Side, the police response would likely be more muscular, and the media rhetoric more marginalizing.

The second example pertains to the "dog-whistle politics" of President Donald Trump, specifically his frequent invocations of Chicago gun violence during the 2016 presidential election and in his first year in office. Four days after his inauguration, he even tweeted that "if Chicago doesn't fix the horrible 'carnage' going on, 228 shootings in 2017 with 42 killings (up 24 percent from 2016), I will send in the Feds!"[10] Many commentators remarked on his decision to highlight Chicago—the hometown of former president Barack Obama, a frequent target of Trump's rhetoric. As the author and journalist Ta-Nehisi Coates articulated in a 2017 visit to the city, conservative politicians like Trump frequently "use Chicago as a tool—'Chicago' has become code for 'black people.'"[11] This racially coded language appeals to the antiblack attitudes and law-and-order politics of many in their voting base. And, as many have noted, although gun deaths in Chicago are a serious public health concern, data collected between 2011 and 2016 reveal that Chicago is not even among the top ten most dangerous large cities in terms of homicide rates, adjusted for population, as I discuss further in chapter 2. Later in the book, I discuss gun violence specifically, as well as the problems with analyzing gun violence at the city level and looking at short-term trends. For now, I wish simply to highlight that public rhetoric about violence is often political on many levels, frequently resulting in the detriment and further marginalization of those most burdened by neighborhood violence and the larger forces that sustain it.

In Chicago and many other large American cities, the narratives around violence are primarily crafted and owned by law enforcement officers. The perspectives of public health, mental health, education scholars, community providers and activists are largely absent. Unsurprisingly, these narratives often glorify the politics, policies, and practices of law enforcement. Look at who appears on the evening news after a tragic public shooting in a lower-income neighborhood, and note how the story begins to be framed. The public rhetoric that accompanies incidents of neighborhood violence often includes words such as "gang bangers, monsters, unintended victims, civilian casualties, war zone, criminals, illegal guns, perpetrators, violated probation, communities lacking morality or a respect for life, and criminal record." Commentators often call for stiffer sentences, additional policing, increased funding for law enforcement, and more heavily militarized forces. All too often, the narratives foreground race, drawing violent caricatures of the accused and frequently assuming guilt before due process. In short, these storytellers dehumanize the suspects—and often the victims—of neighborhood violence, and they voice the need to "arrest" or "police" the problem away. While I decidedly disagree with the myopic perspective that social problems are best fixed through the criminal justice system, it is said that "to a hammer, everything looks like a nail." I understand how police training, professional culture, and other socialization processes (including the militarization of American policing, which entrenches an "us-versus-them" mentality) have led many law enforcement officials to conceptualize and narrate neighborhood violence in these ways.

The parochial nature of these messages, which often demonize the communities besieged by tragedy and dole out simplistic labels of "perpetrators" or "victims," was driven home when a Chicago reporter contacted me after a three-year-old child became a bystander victim of gun violence in 2017. The journalist's first question was "As an expert on neighborhood violence, do you have any insights into the psyche of gang members who would kill a three-year-old child?" A veteran of such interviews, I could tell that the reporter was angling for a catchy sound bite. For almost forty-five minutes, I engaged him in a complex conversation about the structural drivers and policy inequalities underlying not only that particular shooting but also thousands of others. I shared my view that both "victims" and "perpetrators," broadly speaking, are casualties of well-documented historical processes and public policy decisions that have resulted in failing schools, scant job opportunities, racial and neighborhood segregation, and the hopelessness and anger prevailing among many youth growing up in an unequal America. Our nation is, quite literally, killing and incarcerating marginalized citizens at staggering rates, with a dangerous toll for all America. I also reminded the reporter that while large-scale social forces affect youth who find themselves entangled in violence, the tendency to generalize about the "psyche of gang members" occurs far more often when the accused and the victims are not white. As many commentators and social media activists have highlighted in recent years, too often the actions of nonwhite shooters are described as symptoms of cultural pathology (e.g., the racist "black-on-black crime" rhetoric and mischaracterizations of Islamic doctrine), whereas the actions of white shooters, including Dylann Roof, Stephen Paddock, and many others, are referred to as acts of mentally deranged "lone wolves." This time, when my thorough interview was reduced to shallow, two-minute news clips, I realized the topic merited a book-length discussion.

At its core, this book is designed to be an alternative to the sound bites, ahistorical "common sense" narratives, and detached scholarly analyses that fail to get to the heart of the matter. In it, I share the powerful stories and insights of black youth and elevate their voices, weaving their narratives through data, research findings, and historical accounts that provide further context for their experiences. In each chapter, I aim to celebrate their survival and, through their experiences, illuminate the lives of many others who have grown up in communities in which neighborhood violence is a part of daily life. At times, I draw the lens back to highlight the broad historical, political, economic, and racial factors that shape the construction, concentration, and narrative of violence in black neighborhoods. I invite readers to embrace these young people's stories and the lessons they teach us within the important context of the larger, violent social structures that influence the day-to-day experiences of these black youth, their families, and their neighborhoods.

In the first section of the book, I place neighborhood violence in the United States in context relative to other high-income countries. In chapter 4, coauthored with my longtime collaborator, professor Jason Bird, we highlight historical trends that have led to racially segregated urban neighborhoods and concentrations of poverty and violence. In chapter 5, I examine the psychological and behavioral health characteristics that researchers and practitioners have found to be associated with exposure to neighborhood violence. In the following chapters, I offer a possible concep-tual model to explain how child and adolescent development may be influ-enced by exposure to neighborhood violence. Throughout the discussion, I draw on my interviews with black youth to illustrate the broader themes.

In the second part of the book, I use interview and survey data to show how violence influences risky sexual behaviors among black youth in low-resourced neighborhoods. I devote some attention to this connection because higher rates of both neighborhood violence and HIV infection are concentrated in poorer communities. However, the existing literature has not sufficiently highlighted possible reasons for such a connection. Equally true, living in poverty and experiencing neighborhood violence are associated with lower academic achievement. I also devote some attention to this connection to illustrate that several problems experienced by youth, such as low academic achievement, involvement with "gang peers," risky sex, and illicit drug use can be linked to neighborhood trauma. I look in particular at Woodlawn, a historic neighborhood on Chicago's South Side. Illustrations of the ongoing threat of violence in impoverished communities are balanced with interviews showing caregivers' resiliency and the variety of strategies they use to protect their youth. I expand the scope of discussion of neighborhood violence to examine how positive factors, such as parental monitoring, high self-efficacy, and hopes for the future, can help protect youth living in impoverished neighborhoods.

In the final part of the book, I lay out sensible practice and policy recommendations based on the insights from the first two parts. Building on the argument that neighborhood violence results from multiple complex forces, I make the case for an integrated, multisystem approach to addressing violence in low-resourced urban communities. To illustrate this approach, I introduce the reader to several community and university partnerships working to curtail exposure to neighborhood violence and its damaging effects on youth.

When I was in the early stages of conceptualizing this book, I talked about it with a twenty-six-year-old, whom I'll call Jamal, at a Starbucks in Chicago's Hyde Park neighborhood. I told him I was interested in telling the stories of young people exposed to neighborhood violence. He asked me many questions: "Why do you want to write this book?" "Will I, and the others, be identified in it by name?" "Who are you writing it for, and will people read it or actually care?" I could tell he was wondering whether to trust me. Would I accurately convey his story and those of other people to whom he might introduce me, thereby entrusting them to my care? Would I misrepresent their stories, decontextualize them, or reduce them to stereotypes or statistics? "You know," he said, "with social media, we tell and control our own stories. Mainstream media . . . well, they tell you their version of our story."

The Beginning

I have invited these young people, their families, and their communities to share their own stories here. Yet ultimately, I am aware that I control how their stories are summarized, contextualized, transcribed, arranged, and interpreted. My own summaries of their accounts are not value free or neutral. I choose which parts to share, which details are relevant, which other texts to add to the conversation. And, admittedly, to a large extent, I do not have the power to choose at all, because of the limitations of my own perspective and my own conceptual frameworks and biases. How do I come to observe what I observe about a participant? Why do I fail to see some things while noticing others? What are my assumptions, my values, my frameworks for knowing or believing? Without question, I will misinterpret some of the meaning of my informants' messages, simply because we are different people, with different relationships to words, gestures, and ideas; different histories and experiences to draw upon; different bodies of expertise. What is more, we are dynamic: Our insights into our own experiences are ever shifting, ever incomplete. We must narrate our own pasts, which grow increasingly distant from us in time—though with passing time, we gain new insights that help us see our experiences in new ways. History is never stationary; we recast our histories by retelling them. In other words, while I aspire to convey the participants' stories in ways they would find respectful, accurate, and satisfying, this book is not "objective," nor could it ever be. It is shaped by many of the same processes and forces underlying neighborhood violence: inequality, racism, patriarchy, heteronormativity, capitalism, and many others that so powerfully pattern our society.

On top of all this is the violent, ongoing history of colonial representation: the ways that knowledge production, in the hands of powerful actors, has been used to marginalize, stereotype, silence, pathologize, commodify, and kill. As an academician, social science researcher, psychotherapist, and social worker, I take seriously my responsibility to reflect on the histories of colonial knowledge production in my own fields of expertise and to interrogate my own role in reproducing oppressive systems and structures. No matter how sincerely I wish for the lions' histories to be in the lions' hands, rather than the hunters', the histories of the young people in this book are not ultimately in their hands, but in mine, which themselves have been shaped by the systems that I critique and of which I am a part.

Therefore, this book is personal. It collects the insights and lessons I have learned over the past twenty years, in conversing with and reflecting deeply on the testimonies of youth and parents I have encountered in my research and practice, including hundreds of survey interviews and dozens of focus groups. The book is especially informed by the many hours I spent with young black youth and their guardians, who generously shared their stories with me to pass along to you. All participant names and some identifying information have been changed to protect their identities. These are actual, not fictional, people and places. Dialogue has been reconstructed from transcripts, field notes, and, in some cases, their memories and my own. I have tried to reproduce the conversations as accurately as possible. I am indebted to the youth with whom I spoke and their families for taking the time, having the courage to tell their stories, sharing their wisdom, and being willing to recall and relive the pain associated with their experiences. Moreover, I am struck by their insight and resiliency. But these stories do not start or end with me, nor with these young "lions" and their families. Their stories are a part of our larger story: of America the beautiful and violent.

2

THE TALE OF TWO AMERICAS

I love America more than any other country in this world, and, exactly for this reason, I insist on the right to criticize her perpetually.
–JAMES BALDWIN, 1955

American history is longer, larger, more various, more beautiful, and more terrible than anything anyone has ever said about it.
–JAMES BALDWIN, "A TALK TO TEACHERS," 1963

On October 16, 1963, the author James Baldwin delivered to a group of teachers a speech originally titled "The Negro Child—His Self-Image."[1] He spoke in bold, unsparing terms about the soaring myths of America, the country's brutal reality, and the weight of those contradictions upon the minds of black children:

> On the one hand, [a black child in the United States] is born in the shadow of the stars and stripes and he is assured it represents a nation which has never lost a war. He pledges allegiance to that flag which guarantees "liberty and justice for all." He is part of a country in which anyone can become president. But on the other hand, he is also assured by his country and his countrymen that he has never contributed anything to civilization—that his past is nothing more than a record of humiliations gladly endured.[2]

This child, Baldwin said, gradually will come to "discover the shape of his oppression" and, "looking at the society which has produced him, looking at the standards of that society which are not honored by anybody, looking at your churches and the government and the politicians, understand that this structure is operated for someone else's benefit—not for his."[3]

In the spirit of Baldwin's speech, in this book I examine the ongoing and present history of structural violence in the United States, amid its great beauty and opportunities. The book is premised on the understanding that America has always been a violent idea, built on the dislocation, reduction, and commodification of indigenous inhabitants and the enslavement and exploitation of black and brown people. The phenomenon of neighborhood violence cannot be disconnected from other violent processes, including settler colonialism and structural racism. In this book, I argue that what we have come to know as neighborhood violence in many of America's neighborhoods has been shaped in large part by many decades of structural inequalities and violence. Uneven social policies and practices that have contained, reduced, and led to the commodification of black youth and families who involuntarily bear the symptoms of these legacies.

An examination of neighborhood violence typically does not consider the violence that a body experiences because of structural inequities. This omission means that neighborhood violence statistics are skewed, overrepresenting acts of violence among marginalized people. Following Baldwin's advice, I endeavor to examine all facets of neighborhood violence in the United States, placing incidents of interpersonal violence within longstanding historical processes. I interrogate the very concepts we use to think about and measure violence in the first place. But in this chapter, I primarily focus on providing a snapshot of gun violence patterns in the United States. I start with gun violence because it is the most discussed form of neighborhood violence and one of the most lethal. I compare patterns of gun violence in the United States with those of other wealthy countries worldwide, demonstrating that in spite of its wealth and political prominence, the United States is particularly plagued with homicide and other types of gun violence. I offer historical, theoretical, and qualitative analyses.

But first, some personal background: My own American story echoes the dreams and narratives of millions of immigrants who came to America seeking a better life. I have achieved many accomplishments that some would consider evidence that the so-called American dream is no mere mirage. Starting as an immigrant, I became a full professor at one of America's premier academic institutions. However, I was not nested in structural disadvantage when I came to America but was embedded in systems of academic privilege. Immigrant "success" stories like mine are often disingenuously used as a wedge to cast blame on those who are not so fortunate, thereby propping up existing social hierarchies to legitimize the claim that anyone can make it in America if they just work hard and make good decisions. This rhetorical strategy, often called the "model minority myth," is used to deny the structural racism and inequality that daily affect millions of nonwhite citizens and immigrants in this country. While America's identity as "a country of immigrants" is often evoked, the narrative seldom reaches back to include the settlers' colonialism, the genocide and internal displacement of indigenous inhabitants, or the forced removal, stolen labor, torture, and subjugation of blacks under chattel slavery.

Of course, the history of this place that came, violently, to be known as the United States of America includes more than just misery and loss. As James Baldwin encouraged teachers to remind their young black students, there is much beauty in this country—beauty that cannot be stamped out or broken, beauty that was often created in defiance of oppressive systems and structures. Indeed, Baldwin's own gorgeous novels and other writings are an example of this. But, as Baldwin exhorted the young students, those who have the privilege of learning the country's violent history carry the responsibility to "find [themselves] at war with [their] society,"[4] to strive to dismantle and reformulate it into something better, more moral and just. In this chapter, I lay bare the destruction of life and well-being that lies in the wake of violent social and structural inequalities. These inequalities include social marginalization, displacement, poverty, and precarious existence, all of which fuel what is commonly referred to as neighborhood violence.

Violence in the United States: A Statistical Overview

The United States is one of the wealthiest and most powerful countries in the world. Its cultural artifacts penetrate the households and inhabit the lives of people worldwide in the form of Hollywood films, pop music, news, social media, and countless other means. Yet, symptomatic of the creative destruction that characterizes the country's economic system, its immense wealth exists adjacent—and in direct relation—to desperate poverty. Wealth inequality in the United States is pronounced and growing. According to the 2017 Survey of Consumer Finances, those Americans in the top 1 percent held 39 percent of all wealth in 2016, and the bottom 90 percent held only a 23 percent share.[5]

This deep wealth gap, which has been rapidly widening since the 1970s, is even more abysmal when broken down by race. A recent report from the Institute for Policy Studies found that the wealth of the median black household declined by a staggering 75 percent between 1983 and 2013, and the wealth of Latino households declined by 50 percent.[6] Over that same period, white household wealth increased by 14 percent. According to the Institute's analysis, if trends continue, it would take the average black household 228 years to attain the level of wealth held by the average white household and eighty-four years for the average Latino household to do the same—evidencing a veritable "racial and economic apartheid state."[7] By 2020, the median white household would hold eighty-six times more wealth than the median black household and sixty-eight times more than the median Latino household.[8] As the journalist Jamelle Bouie put it, "This isn't a wealth gap—it's a wealth chasm."[9]

These profound racial and economic inequities have motivated many U.S. thinkers and writers to describe the America of myth as "another country" from the one lived in by marginalized citizens. Indeed, this is the title of one of James Baldwin's books, and inequities also help explain how the wealthiest and most powerful country can perform so poorly on measures of national well-being. America relishes being number one, and she is. Compared with other high-income countries, the United States has the highest rates of homicide and gun-related death in the world.[10] The United States also has the highest rate of high school dropout,[11] as well as the highest rate of unplanned pregnancy among adolescents in the developed world.[12] Furthermore, 21 percent of all U.S. children live in poverty—the highest share of any age demographic in the country.[13] And the U.S. prison population rate is the highest in the world, at 716 per one hundred thousand people: six times the rate of Canada, six to nine times the rate of Western European countries, and two to ten times that of Northern European countries.[14] These facts are staggering, given that America is home to less than 5 percent of the world's population but holds 22 percent of the world's prisoners.[15] As is the case with wealth inequality, embedded within these figures are trends showing that poor and nonwhite residents disproportionately bear the heaviest burden of these social inequities.[16] The existence of the "other America" that nonwhite citizens (especially black males) experience daily might in part explain the deep cultural warfare we are experiencing in this country—as when National Football League players kneel in protest during the singing of the national anthem at games. Which citizens feel represented, protected, and afforded full citizenship under the American flag?

Gun Violence

It's everywhere. Guns and violence are in every nook and cranny of America. Many children can get a gun quicker than they can get a book out of the library. That puts us all at risk.
—MARIAN WRIGHT EDELMAN

America has more guns than any other country in the developed world. Therefore, in the remainder of this chapter, I discuss several of the tensions and complex issues related to restricting and regulating guns in the United States. This discussion is important for contextualizing the following chapters and establishing the framework for how gun violence and its aftereffects have altered developmental pathways and life chances for millions of Americans who live in neighborhoods that have not profited from the nation's immense wealth.

In recent years, few topics of public concern have featured more prominently in U.S. public discourse and media than gun violence. There have been several high-profile mass shootings, such as those at a movie theater in Aurora, Colorado; an elementary school in Newtown, Connecticut; a church in Charleston, South Carolina; a nightclub in Orlando, Florida; a country music festival in Las Vegas, Nevada; and a high school in Parkland, Florida. These slaughters have been accompanied by calls to institute "common-sense" reforms to regulate the production and sale of military-grade weaponry and limit its access by civilians. Such calls have recently been highlighted by the March for Our Lives movement composed of American school youth. However, alongside this movement to limit gun access and the presence of guns in public spaces is a well-funded antiregulatory countermovement. These efforts seek to expand private gun ownership and the presence of guns in every sphere of life, trumpeting a broad interpretation of the constitutional Second Amendment "right to bear arms."

In addition to the public debate over military-grade weaponry and mass shootings are other timely gun-related topics of public concern, occurring on larger scales and affecting victims in different ways. While the deadliness of guns is a common thread, activists have important differences in their political strategies, leadership, and objectives. One of these is the issue of police brutality and gun violence (called "officer-involved shootings" by law enforcement), which disproportionately victimizes black citizens. The Movement for Black Lives has brought heightened media attention and public awareness to this issue through a variety of strategies. Such strategies include capturing and disseminating cell phone footage of police brutality; organizing public protests and "die-ins" (a form of protest where people simulate being dead); collecting, sharing, and highlighting trends in data about police shootings; and using public platforms to raise awareness and demonstrate resistance. This movement comprises a loose affiliation of advocates who bring visibility to antiblack structural violence. Police brutality represents only one of the many issues tackled by activists who organize under the Black Lives Matter mantle.

Another topic of concern for community organizers is the ongoing public health crisis of handgun violence in poor and racially segregated neighborhoods. This crisis continues to disproportionately take the lives of poor black Americans, especially men and teenage boys. This issue is closely related to police brutality, because politicians at every level of government have cited the concentration of gun violence in poor, racially segregated neighborhoods in large cities to justify more aggressive policing strategies in cities nationwide. Finally, the epidemic of gun suicides is mostly overshadowed by media coverage of mass shootings and gun homicides despite the fact that suicides account for nearly two-thirds of all firearm deaths annually in the United States.[17]

While violence of all kinds takes a tremendous toll on victims, gun violence is of particular concern because of its lethality, immediacy, and, consequently, the ways it disrupts daily life. America's rates of gun violence and gun deaths far exceed those of other wealthy nations. Such prevalent gun deaths suggest particular historical, political, and economic reasons for why Americans, compared with citizens of other advanced and emerging countries, are far less safe from guns. In the following sections, I offer an international comparison of gun violence rates in the United States. I trace gun homicide and nonfatal shooting trends in various large U.S. cities. I contextualize this violence within historical and structural conditions that have contributed to geospatial patterns of inequality in gun violence risk. After providing an overview of the contemporary gun policy landscape, I analyze possible gun policy reform in the United States. I end with a broader discussion of the mental and public health consequences of gun violence in its historical context, drawing on both theoretical scholarship and news stories of those affected by its lived reality.

Now We See Through a Glass Darkly: Gun Violence Data and Research Gaps

The phrase "now we see through a glass darkly" was used in antiquity to describe the practice of using highly polished brass as a mirror. This practice resulted in objects appearing dark and murky. In theology, this phrase means that what we know about the divine is limited. I employ it here to indicate our limited knowledge of the prevalence of gun violence exposure and its consequences. Therefore, before presenting what are often reported as "facts," I acknowledge the glaring gaps in data and research related to gun violence. Some of the primary reasons for these gaps are congressional restrictions on funding gun violence research that effectively hamstring public health researchers at national universities, the Centers for Disease Control and Prevention (CDC), and the National Institutes of Health from studying gun violence and how to prevent it. These restrictions were passed in 1997 after some CDC officials suggested that limiting access to guns was a public health objective, leading the National Rifle Association (NRA) to successfully lobby Congress to limit use of federal funding for gun research.[18]

What is more, the CDC typically does not collect data from police departments on people killed by police officers with guns. The FBI runs a voluntary program, the Uniform Crime Reporting Program, for law enforcement agencies to submit data on what they term "justifiable homicides," defined as the "the killing of a felon by a peace officer in the line of duty,"[19] an inherently problematic framing that denies due process to the victim. The resulting lack of comprehensive data on police killings has forced many activists in the Movement for Black Lives to look outside the United States for reliable, comprehensive public health data on police killings. Many have turned to the United Kingdom–based newspaper the *Guardian* for a systematic count of the number of people killed by police in the United States. Started in the wake of the killing of Michael Brown, an unarmed teenager, by a Ferguson, Missouri, police officer in August 2014, the newspaper's project, "The Counted," documents each incident in which civilians were killed by police in 2015 and 2016.[20] As argued on the project's website, "such accounting is a prerequisite for an informed public discussion about the use of force by police."[21]

Because of these data and the resultant research gaps in the United States, it is difficult to build an evidence base for gun safety measures or gun violence intervention. Equally challenging is a study of the relationships between gun laws and violence—and the ability to hold police officers accountable for widespread and systematic abuses of power. While serving as U.S. attorney general in 2015, Eric Holder called these gaps in data "unacceptable."[22] And, as *Guardian* writers noted on the website of "The Counted," the patchwork system of data accounting "is arguably less valuable than having no system at all: Fluctuations in the number of agencies choosing to report figures, plus faulty reporting by agencies that do report, have resulted in partially informed news coverage pointing misleadingly to trends that may or may not exist."[23] The dearth of research on gun violence has led to costly and ill-informed criminal justice measures in cities nationwide that have increased surveillance, policing, and incarceration, often without meaningfully moving the needle on public safety. Recognizing these data shortfalls, here I summarize the best available research on the causes, correlates, and consequences of gun violence, drawing from diverse sources, including reputable, nonpartisan, and rigorous nonprofits and news outlets like the *Guardian*, *ProPublica*, and the *Washington Post*, among others.

Costs of Gun Violence

Gun violence rates in the United States far exceed those of other wealthy nations,[24] devastating families and communities at immeasurable human cost. Although the economic toll is difficult to fully ascertain, one study estimates that gun violence results in more than $100 billion per year in direct and indirect costs.[25] Many of these direct and indirect costs are associated with emergency treatment and health care, loss of human life, employment and productivity, mental health services, juvenile and prison involvement, insurance claims, and increased airport security. A more recent study estimates that the total cost of gun-inflicted injuries and homicides in the United States in 2015 was $229 billion—or $700 per gun.[26]

Homicides

Americans are twenty-five times more likely than citizens of other wealthy countries to be killed by a gun.[27] The United States accounts for only 46 percent of the population of high-income countries but 82 percent

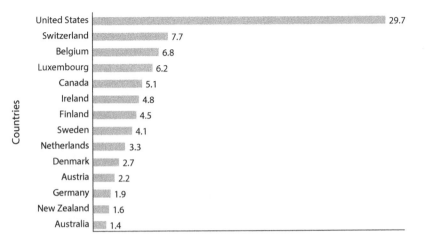

Figure 2.1

America's rate of gun homicides relative to those of other high-income countries, 2012

Source: Statista

of the gun deaths.[28] Among children in these nations aged zero to 14, 87 percent of those killed by guns lived in the United States.[29] Nearly thirty-seven thousand Americans are murdered by guns every year, a rate that has held roughly the same for more than a decade, even as the overall violent crime rate has decreased steadily.[30] That total represents more than 3.61 gun murders per one hundred thousand residents in the United States. By comparison, the United Kingdom trails far behind with 0.1 murders per one hundred thousand, the next highest gun murder rate in a wealthy nation[31] (figure 2.1).

Of the one hundred people murdered daily in the United States, on average, half are black men.[32] Black men are by one estimate ten times more likely than white men to be murdered with guns.[33] Merely 14 percent of the population, black residents account for more than 50 percent of gun homicide victims. Black men are killed at a rate of 27.6 victimizations per one hundred thousand citizens, compared with 2.8 among white men, 2.8 among black women, and 0.9 among white women. The rate of gun homicides among black men in the United States exceeds the gun homicide rate of all of Mexico, a country that also experiences high rates of gun violence.[34] Notably, the homicide rate for non-Hispanic blacks in the United States is eleven times higher than for non-Hispanic whites, with rates highest among males aged twenty to twenty-four years.[35] Figure 2.2 shows the U.S. cities with the highest homicide rates.

Women are another subgroup of the U.S. population vulnerable to gun homicide. Women in the United States are sixteen times more likely to be killed by guns than women in other wealthy nations.[36] Even children in the United States are not safe from gun murders: Seven children per day are killed by guns in the United States, with the rate increasingly dramatically among children over age thirteen. Of the 10,300 boys in the United States aged ten to nineteen who died by gunfire between 2010 and 2014, 63 percent died by homicide.[37] The risk of gun death is greater for children who are poor or nonwhite. This discrepancy led Benard Dreyer of the American Academy of Pediatrics to urge the academy to focus on both the public health issue of children's exposure to gun violence and its intersections with race and racism.[38]

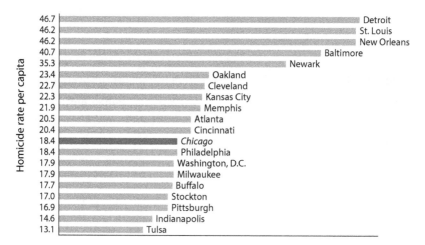

Figure 2.2

The highest homicide rates in American cities, 2011 to 2016

Source: The Trace

Nonfatal Shootings

Though data on gun-inflicted injuries are less reliable than those on gun death, nonfatal shootings appear to outnumber gun deaths by roughly five to one.[39] In 2015, 84,997 U.S. residents suffered nonfatal firearm injuries.[40]

These injuries often result in disability, chronic pain, mental trauma, increased stressful personal relationships, difficulty obtaining and maintaining work, and, consequently, financial hardships. They also often mean expensive medical treatments and health complications that persist over a victim's lifetime. Data show that the hospital cost of treating a gunshot is twice that of treating a stabbing,[41] a financial burden disproportionately borne by poor citizens and socialized through inflated insurance premiums.[42] In a recent study, anthropologist Laurence Ralph explores the textured lives of survivors of gun violence in an impoverished neighborhood in Chicago, finding that these citizens cope with mental and physical scars of this violence throughout their lives. Their injuries require them to summon deep resilience to survive and thrive in a community marginalized by unemployment, disinvestment, and structural racism.[43]

Domestic Violence

The use of guns in domestic violence incidents in the United States is of particular concern, with an average of fifty women per month losing their lives to firearm assaults by current or former intimate partners.[44] Indeed, 55 percent of women killed by guns die at the hands of intimate partners or family members.[45] According to a study of domestic violence incidents with guns in eleven U.S. cities, the presence of a gun in a domestic dispute increases by five times the likelihood that a woman will lose her life.[46] Moreover, 54 percent of mass shootings involve intimate-partner violence,[47] a fact often overlooked by media and analysts in the aftermath of these high-profile events. Another common media narrative often missed is the domestic-violence-to-prison pipeline. In America, many women are incarcerated for killing or wounding their partners (with guns) in self-defense. According to Rita Smith, the executive director of the National Coalition Against Domestic Violence, there is an implicit bias against women in self-defense cases, and "most battered women who kill in self-defense end up in prison."[48]

Suicide

One dimension of gun violence often overshadowed in the media by coverage of mass shootings and homicides is suicide, even though suicides account for 62 percent of firearm deaths in the United States.[49] Around twenty thousand Americans kill themselves with guns annually.[50] Gun suicide is the second most common cause of death among Americans aged fifteen to thirty-four and the tenth most common cause of death among all age groups.[51] Unlike homicide and nonfatal shootings, of which nonwhite men are disproportionately victims, most suicides are committed by white men.[52] Suicide rates in the United States are seven times higher than in other high-income countries, fueled by the overall gun homicide rate, which is 25.2 times greater.[53]

Accidental Gun Deaths

According to the nonpartisan research and advocacy organization Everytown for Gun Safety,[54] in 2013, there were one hundred accidental gun deaths among children under the age of fourteen, 61 percent more than were reflected in CDC data. Differences result from how the organizations characterize intent. Everytown for Gun Safety notes that accidental shootings are reported in the media every thirty-four hours on average. Children in low-income households are more likely than their peers in higher-income households to fall victim to this tragedy.[55]

Police Brutality and Militarization

A long-standing concern of nonwhite Americans, police brutality has recently gained attention among "mainstream" media outlets and public figures. This issue has been elevated in public consciousness in large part by the Movement for Black Lives. In the United States, police shootings kill around one thousand people per year,[56] a staggering figure especially considering that these citizens are killed by agents of the state without the constitutional right to due process. In the overwhelming majority of these killings, officers are not indicted or charged for their role. Despite thousands of civilian deaths at the hands of police over the past decade, between 2005 and 2017, only eighty officers responsible for these deaths were charged with murder or manslaughter, and only 35 percent of those were convicted. Some cases are still pending.[57]

These facts have led activists to challenge the culture of impunity among many police departments and districts, where a lack of accountability and oversight means that law enforcement officials regularly use excessive force without fear of meaningful consequences. Impunity on the part of law enforcement officials is a serious concern, especially in light of a long history in this country of documented and suspected police corruption and discrimination.[58] Examples include the regular participation of police in lynchings of black Americans in the early twentieth century[59] and the Chicago Police Department's notorious use of torture, under police commander Jon Burge, to elicit confessions from at least 110 (mostly black) men on Chicago's South Side.[60] In addition, a 2015 Department of Justice investigation exposed the unlawful targeting of black residents for minor violations in Ferguson, Missouri.[61] Furthermore, officers are granted a monopoly on legal force in encounters with civilians. In investigations into police brutality cases, minute noncriminal actions or reactions by civilians, such as tone of voice, posture, and speed of compliance with police commands, are often interpreted in the defense's expert testimony as signs that the civilian was "resisting arrest" and claimed to constitute a threat justifying the progressive escalation of police force. According to police codes of conduct, to justify use of deadly force, an officer must convince the court merely that he or she could reasonably have perceived that the civilian was not complying with commands and that, therefore, the civilian constituted a threat to the officer's safety.[62] In case after case, this line of defense has excused police officers for extrajudicial killings of unarmed civilians whose initial suspected offenses were as minor as failing to signal, selling single "loose" cigarettes, or having a broken taillight on their car. Compounding these accountability failures is the fact that, as mentioned previously, data on police shootings in the United States are notoriously unreliable and unsystematic.

In far too many instances in which civilians are shot and killed by police, the victims are unarmed. Several high-profile killings of unarmed civilians by police in recent years have been caught on video, often recorded on cell phones by bystanders. Many of these recordings went viral, circulated widely and rapidly on social media, particularly Twitter, and were supplemented by public commentary, analysis, and fact-checking. Often in these incidents, recordings have revealed details that directly contradict the officers' official accounts. In one widely circulated example, a white police officer in South Carolina named Michael Slager shot and killed an unarmed black resident, Walter Scott, whom Slager had pulled over for having a broken taillight.[63] Slager initially reported that Scott had taken his Taser and that he had shot Scott in self-defense.[64] Yet this account was disproved when an eyewitness shared a video recorded on his phone that showed Scott running away when the police officer fired eight rounds at him from behind, striking him five times in the back.[65]

Very seldom are the perspectives of black females solicited when exploring the effects of overpolicing black men. A 29-year-old black woman, whom I'll call Jenny, told me,

When black men are killed by police, black women are scared to love. It is terrifying that someone you love can be murdered for no valid reason and in plain sight. Black women are also traumatized because we can't save our husbands, partners, brothers, or sons. We also feel helpless even in situations where we are witnesses. We are left to pick up the family pieces. . . . Most women don't even know they are traumatized. As black women, we are taught to keep going. We have to learn to protect ourselves because we can't depend on men to protect us because they can be taken away. Black women are labeled as angry, but how many people stop to ask why? Have you ever stopped to ask a young black female how police brutality affects them?

I had not, until the day I interviewed Jenny.

Figure 2.3

Misunderstood (oil painting). This painting illustrates the traumatized black female

Source: April Sunami

Mass Shootings

A mass shooting is typically defined as an incident in which at least four people are shot by a single shooter. According to data compiled by the Gun Violence Archive (and reported by the *Guardian*), on average, a mass shooting takes place in the United States on nine of every ten days.[66] In 2015, close to one hundred metropolitan areas in the United States experienced mass shootings. In fact, no U.S. city with a population of four hundred thousand or more has *not* experienced a mass shooting since 2013.[67]

The following three paragraphs draw upon an analysis from the *Guardian*.[68] In discussions of gun policy and its impact on mass shooting occurrences, the United States is often compared with Australia. After a mass shooting in 1996, Australia passed sweeping gun policy reforms, including a mandatory buyback of nearly one million weapons. These guns were melted down, which resulted in the destruction of nearly a third of the country's total arsenal. Australia has not had another mass shooting since. By comparison, as of June 2018, the United States had experienced approximately one thousand mass shootings in the past 1,260 days. Australia's successes are laudable and informative; however, the landscape of gun ownership and policy is different in the United States. In 1995, the year before the reforms, Australia's rate of gun murders was far lower than that of the United States, with sixty-seven gun murders that year, a figure not even comparable to the rate in one of the most violent cities in the United States. Moreover, strict handgun legislation already existed in Australia leading up to the reforms. Finally, the United States has many more privately owned guns than there were in Australia at the time, leading one researcher to estimate that implementing a buyback program in the United States similar to Australia's might cost billions of dollars.

Mass shootings occur in the United States at a rate unmatched among other wealthy nations. Yet they are far outweighed by other gun murders and by gun suicides. Mass shootings account for less than 2 percent of annual gun deaths,[69] and many estimates place that figure under 1 percent. Even if all mass shootings ended today, the U.S. gun murder rate would continue to far outpace those of other wealthy countries. According to the CDC, the United States as a whole sees a firearm death rate of about 10.4 per one hundred thousand, a figure that has essentially remained steady since 1999.[70] That is around 33,500 gun deaths per year—roughly one every 15 minutes—nearly the same rate as that for automotive deaths. Approximately thirteen thousand of those are homicides, with only a tiny fraction of those homicides being the result of mass shootings.

However, media coverage of mass shootings, along with public rhetoric more generally, often overemphasizes particular threats and obscures facts. Gun control discourse has tended to focus on military-style rifles, though these were responsible for less than 3 percent of gun murders in 2014. The discursive focus on the role of mental health concerns in mass shootings also runs the risk of further stigmatizing people with mental illness. Such people are already marginalized, especially considering that those with mental illness are far more likely to be victims of gun violence than its perpetrators.[71] Also misleading is the public emphasis on expanding police presence in schools, given the *Guardian*'s report that "the typical school can expect to see a student homicide only once every six thousand years," according to the safety expert Dewey Cornell.[72] Cornell notes that there is little evidence that gun safety measures in schools reduce crime, even as the Justice Department invested almost $1 billion to put police officers in schools in the years following the 1999 Columbine High School shooting.[73] So while attention to the horrific, destructive, and distinctly American phenomenon of mass shootings is critical, it is important for policy-makers and public figures to focus proportional attention on other types of gun death and gun control policy priorities.

While mass shootings dominate public discourse about gun control, these public debates largely ignore the toll of gun violence on the lives of black Americans. Beckett writes that "as horrific as these massacres are, by most counts they represent less than 1 percent of all gun homicides. America's high rate of gun murders isn't caused by events like Sandy Hook or the shootings this fall at a community college in Oregon. It's fueled by a relentless drumbeat of deaths of black men."[74] In 2012, ninety people were killed in mass shootings, but six thousand black men were murdered with guns.[75]

Homicide Trends in the United States

Gun Types and Mortality

Guns considerably increase the lethality of violent encounters. As noted by gun violence researchers, assaults with guns are around thirteen times more lethal than assaults with knives and much more lethal than encounters without a weapon.[76] Currently, 70 percent of firearm deaths are caused by handguns, which equates to six thousand deaths per year on average.[77]

Another 21.51 percent of deaths are caused by unidentified firearms.[78] Rifles, although animating much of the gun control discourse, are responsible for only 3.55 percent of firearm deaths.[79]

Disparities in Gun Violence by City, Race, and Income

Chicago makes numerous national and global headlines for high rates of gun homicide and is often tagged as the American murder capital. Media-grabbing headlines read "Why Is Chicago a Murder Capital? Clues from a Bloody Month," "FBI: Chicago Officially America's Murder Capital," and "Murder Cases in Chicago Set to Hit the Highest Level in Twenty Years with as Many as Ninety Shootings a Week."[80] In early 2017, this narrative became even more elevated when the newly inaugurated Trump tweeted, "If Chicago doesn't fix the horrible 'carnage' going on . . . I will send in the Feds!"[81] Separating the facts from politics and media headlines, Chicago is ranked twelfth among major American cities in five-year average per capita homicide rate (see figure 2.2). In Chicago, similar to other large American cities, the highest rates of neighborhood and gun violence are clustered in a handful of communities that bear the highest burden of structural and systematic violence: economic disinvestment and poverty, educational de facto

Figure 2.4

The 2014 police murder of 17-year-old Laquan McDonald, who was shot sixteen times

Source: Insert of basketball court by Kai Wood and Patrick Lynn Rivers

ghettos, poor access to health care, joblessness, and hopelessness. These themes will be discussed in chapter 4, in which I highlight the road to concentrated poverty and neighborhood violence.

Equally accurate is the fact that there is pronounced racial and socioeconomic disparity in gun violence in the United States. According to a 2016 article in the *Guardian* on American gun violence,

> Much of America's day-to-day gun violence is concentrated in America's poorest, most racially segregated neighborhoods—places with high rates of unemployment, struggling school systems, and high levels of mistrust between police officers and community members. African Americans, who represent 13 percent of the total population, make up more than half of overall gun murder victims. Roughly fifteen of the thirty Americans murdered with guns each day are black men. Gun violence in America, as criminologist Frank Zimring put it, is another regressive tax on the poor. Some black neighborhoods have experienced so much violence that their residents report symptoms of post-traumatic stress at rates comparable to veterans of war. Because everyday gun violence is concentrated in racially segregated neighborhoods, it's easy for millions of Americans to think they won't be affected.[82]

Writing of this phenomenon, the sociologist William Julius Wilson pointed out that impoverished black Americans in 1978 were only marginally more likely than wealthier black Americans to be victims of violent crime, but, by 2008, poor black Americans were far more likely to be victimized than their wealthier black counterparts.[83] Yet, even given these socioeconomic disparities in violent crime victimhood, black Americans of all income levels are more likely to live in racially segregated and socioeconomically diverse neighborhoods with elevated levels of violent crime. Black Americans experience higher rates of racial segregation than any ethnic group throughout the nation's history. A legacy of institutional racism, including restrictive covenants, redlining (e.g., denying home insurance to black communities), and predatory lending practices, has produced concentrated disadvantages, including institutional neglect, substandard schools, reduced property values, and diminished environmental quality.[84] The public health researchers Kellee White and Luisa Borrell describe racial/ethnic residential segregation as "a spatial manifestation of institutionalized discrimination."[85] Even within a single city, violence trends may be localized to particular blocks or intersections.[86]

Because geographic inequality in homicide rates map onto racially segregated and low-income neighborhoods, some analysts and advocates have described the phenomenon as a problem of "black-on-black" crime. This framework is problematic. First, violent crimes are overwhelmingly intraracial,[87] regardless of the race or ethnicity of those involved. For example, a 2004 report using data from the Bureau of Justice Statistics found that 86 percent of white people were killed by other white people, and 94 percent of black people were killed by other black people.[88] Thus, as Garfield Hylton of *Abernathy Magazine* put it, "If there is to be a designation for 'black-on-black' crime, it would necessitate that labels were created for all races and ethnicities."[89] Instead, the emphasis on "black-on-black" crime in prominent media outlets, often without discussion of the history of systematic racial and socioeconomic segregation that contributes to high rates of neighborhood violence, creates a woefully incomplete and biased narrative. Consequently, when racially segregated, economically strapped neighborhoods experience elevated levels of neighborhood violence, the overemphasis on "black-on-black" crime can reinforce the racist assumption that black citizens are more violent and disposed to criminality than people of other races and ethnicities.[90]

Black citizens who commit a violent crime against a victim of any race or ethnicity are far more likely to face harsh sentencing by the criminal justice system than their white counterparts, controlling for severity of crime. This systemic bias partially accounts for the higher incarceration rate of black American men, who alarmingly constitute 40 percent of the jail population.[91] Research has suggested that a higher proportion of white males are victims of unarmed violence; by contrast, black males are more likely to be victimized by guns.[92] This phenomenon may be attributable to both riskier environmental conditions such as exposure to violent underground economies. Additionally, many Americans hold racist stereotypes (and archetypical images) that black men are dangerous and may therefore be more inclined to use deadly violence against them.[93]

Gun Violence and Segregation

Nowhere in the United States is the connection between gun violence and racial segregation more pronounced than in Chicago. According to Natalie Moore, although cities like Baltimore, Cleveland, and Los Angeles have areas of racial segregation, Chicago is the most starkly defined by it.[94] As the *New York Times* reporters Ford Fessenden and Haeyoun Park stated in a May 2016 feature on gun violence in the city, "While many areas have few or no killings, the South and West Sides are on par with the world's most dangerous countries, like Brazil or Venezuela, and have been for many years."[95] This geospatial pattern of violence corresponds with concentrated poverty and disadvantage in neighborhoods that were systematically racially segregated throughout the twentieth century. Black residents were kept out of some white communities through restrictive covenants, mob violence, and exclusionary zoning practices. They had their neighborhoods systematically devalued through redlining practices codified under federal law[96]; faced discrimination and predatory loan practices when trying to rent or finance homes[97]; and experienced ongoing underemployment,[98] biased policing patterns, and institutional neglect.[99]

The National Book Award winner and MacArthur Fellow Ta-Nehisi Coates used Chicago as a case example of racist housing policy in his celebrated 2014 article in the *Atlantic*, "The Case for Reparations."[100] Similarly, the sociologist Robert J. Sampson, in his book *Great American City: Chicago and the Enduring Neighborhood Effect*, explored the correlation between neighborhood characteristics and violence in the city. Sampson concluded that the major underlying causes of crime are similar irrespective of race or ethnicity. However, the intensity of the connection between social ills and violence seems more persistent in Chicago, which has a depth of segregation that surpasses that of many other American cities.[101] According to William Julius Wilson, in Milwaukee, "where 46 percent of African Americans live in high-poverty neighborhoods—those with poverty rates of nearly 40 percent—blacks are nearly twenty times more likely to get shot than whites, and nine times more likely to be murdered."[102]

By comparison, according to a *New York Times* investigation (Fessenden and Park, 2016),[103] homicides in New York City occur at higher rates in more segregated neighborhoods in parts of Brooklyn, the Bronx, and Harlem. Yet, segregation—and its attending compounded disadvantage—is far less common in New York. The longest stretch of time without a homicide in 2015 in Brooklyn, a borough of around the same population as Chicago, was twenty-two days; in Chicago, the longest stretch was five days.[104] And in New York in 2016, 58 percent of homicides were committed with a gun, whereas in Chicago, while the overall homicide rate was just a little higher than in New York when guns were not involved, shootings accounted for 90 percent of all homicides.[105] Indeed, tracking data on shootings, rather than gun homicides, has many advantages when analyzing gun violence trends. Whether a shooting ends in death often depends on chance conditions like distance from bystanders, a shooter's experience, and visibility. Sometimes cities will see the rate of nonfatal shootings trend upward while gun homicides decrease, or vice versa, as a mere result of these contingent factors.[106]

Gun Policy and Law Enforcement in the United States

In a formal statement following the mass shooting at Oregon's Umpqua Community College in October 2015, former president Barack Obama shared a telling statistic. In the decade from 2005 to 2015, in which the perceived "threat of terrorism" and "domestic security" dominated public discourse, 301,797 Americans were killed by gun violence, compared with twenty-four Americans killed in attacks classified as "terrorism."[107] Yet, the United States continues to have a complicated relationship with private gun ownership and gun policy. Although public opinion overwhelmingly supports many gun control measures, such as expanding background checks, creating a federal database to track gun sales, and banning civilian ownership of military-grade weapons and ammunition,[108] court decisions and national and state-level legislation increasingly support a more permissive gun policy regime. Steady demand has created the conditions in which there may be more guns than people in the United States.[109] However, gun ownership in the United States is concentrated among a relatively small proportion of Americans who stockpile firearms.[110]

State and Federal Policy Analysis

America has a patchwork gun control regime, in which citizens' rights to own, purchase, and sell firearms and ammunitions differ dramatically based on state laws. The analysts Patrick Blanchfield[111] and Adam Winkler[112] have written much on this topic, and I draw upon their sophisticated analysis in the sections that follows. Blanchfield describes American gun policy as

> the product of two phenomena. . . . First, a long history of skirmishes over who should be armed and how—fraught battles that pivot on questions of race, class, masculinity, and the role of law enforcement. Second, the synergy between American militarism and capitalism: a perennial entanglement that has produced a society in which there are more guns than civilians to own them.[113]

Blanchfield describes two prominent approaches to gun control in the United States. The first, most commonly associated with politically liberal, "blue" states and characterized as strict, requires citizens to pay fees and undergo training and background checks to legally own and carry firearms. Adherents to this political philosophy underscore the phrase "well-regulated militia" in the Second Amendment to the Constitution and express the belief that the right to bear arms is contingent upon citizens' fulfilling a series of "reasonable" requirements. In states typically characterized as having loose gun control regulations—often more politically conservative, "red" states— many espouse a rival political philosophy in which the right of nearly every citizen to bear arms is the foundation on which all other rights depend. These "gun rights advocates" oppose nearly all measures to limit gun ownership, even those that might appear to be modest and commonsense such as background checks, because they believe that yielding to any concessions might bring about a chain reaction of events that could lead to American civilians losing their right to own any guns.[114]

Yet, as Blanchfield and Winkler illustrate through historical review, how citizens draw political lines on this issue has generally pivoted on issues of race, class, citizenship, and belonging. At the time of the drafting of the U.S. Constitution, laws limited gun ownership by enslaved black people and black freemen, even as white men loyal to the revolution were required to own registered and regulated firearms.[115] After the Civil War, Black Codes designed to maintain white supremacy in the American South made it illegal for black citizens to own guns, and bands of white men, many of whom were Ku Klux Klan members, terrorized and seized weapons from black gun owners.[116]

Interestingly, the Black Panther Party is the unacknowledged ideological vanguard of many contemporary gun rights advocates, as well as a driving force behind the gun control movement.[117] When a group of Black Panthers organized an armed open-carry demonstration in the California State House in 1967, one leading activist, Bobby Seale, read from a written statement:

> The American people in general and the black people in particular [must] take careful note of the racist California legislature aimed at keeping black people disarmed and powerless. Black people have begged, prayed, petitioned, demonstrated, and everything else to get the racist power structure of America to right the wrongs which have historically been perpetuated against black people. The time has come for black people to arm themselves against this terror before it is too late.[118]

California's Republican lawmakers responded with legislation that is widely considered the beginning of contemporary gun control. The Republican Ronald Reagan, who was serving as California governor at the time, said, "There's no reason why on the street today a citizen should be carrying loaded weapons," and that California's gun control legislation "would work no hardship on the honest citizen."[119] Whereas previously white conservatives championed gun control measures as commonsense responses to black leftist activists, now many rural, conservative, mostly white gun rights activists are "packing heat and winning unprecedented gun rights gains in the name of 'taking [their] country back,'" against the opposition of urban progressives and white liberals, in particular.[120]

Recent events revealed the unarticulated racial undertones of contemporary gun rights advocacy. In separate incidents in different parts of the country, two black men carrying guns were killed by police on July 5, 2016. The shootings were widely publicized because in both instances, bystanders recorded the incidents on their cell phones. One of the men, Philando Castile, was complying with an officer's command to get his license and registration during a traffic stop. While reaching for his wallet, Castile alerted the officer that he had a concealed-carry permit and a gun. The officer told him not to move, and as Castile attempted to raise his hands in compliance, the officer shot and killed him. Castile's girlfriend and her daughter were in the vehicle with him at the time. His girlfriend live-streamed the harrowing video of the police encounter and shooting via Facebook. The other victim, Alton Sterling, was lying flat on the ground, and while he reportedly had a gun in his pocket, cell phone and surveillance videos of the event show that he was not reaching for the gun when he was shot multiple times and killed by the arresting officer. What is more, he was killed in Louisiana, a state that allows open carry of guns for anyone with a permit. At the time of his arrest, officers did not know whether Sterling was licensed to carry the gun and therefore whether it was legal for him to have it in his possession. Deafening silence from gun rights advocates and the NRA, which has in recent years pushed for virtually unregulated access to guns, followed both incidents. The incidents spurred public discourse, especially over social media such as Twitter, about unequal protection for black Americans of their Second Amendment rights.[121]

Municipal Policy Analysis and Case Studies

Cities nationwide have implemented municipal gun control measures. For many years, the tightest regulations were in Chicago, which banned handgun and ammunition sales, and Washington, D.C., which banned handgun possession in city limits.[122] A study of Chicago's handgun ban found that the law made it considerably more difficult for prospective gun buyers to obtain guns and ammunition within city limits, though most homicides in both cities continued to be committed with guns.[123] Researchers hypothesize that gang-affiliated people, who are responsible for the majority of shootings in the city, may obtain guns with greater ease than other citizens through trafficking and straw purchases. Straw purchasing is the practice of buying guns for individuals prohibited from purchasing or wishing to conceal their identity. However, even among gang-affiliated individuals, the gun stock tends to be rather old on average, contrary to their expressed preferences for newer guns.[124] This finding suggests that handgun regulations do make it more difficult for these individuals to obtain guns. Nevertheless, Chicago's and D.C.'s handgun regulations were rolled back when federal judges ruled that these laws were unconstitutional infringements on the Second Amendment.[125] In the *District of Columbia v. Heller* case, the Supreme Court struck down several provisions of the DC law, ruling that the Second Amendment protects an individual's right to gun ownership.[126]

The Gun Lobby

Originally created to improve the marksmanship of American soldiers and subsequently becoming a champion of anti-gun control legislation, the NRA has traveled a long way in its almost 150-year existence to its contemporary positions on gun rights.[127] For most of the advocacy organization's history, it primarily promoted "hunting, marksmanship, and responsible gun use."[128] Yet the current permutation of the NRA little resembles the organization of the first century following its founding. Claiming to broadly interpret the Second Amendment as protecting the right of almost anyone to own and carry a gun in any setting, the NRA actively fights any gun control legislation, however modest or popular. The NRA ostracizes politicians and gun industry executives who advocate for gun control. It promotes state-level legislation that increases the ease of purchasing, owning, and carrying guns. The NRA has also successfully lobbied Congress to limit public health research on gun violence and gun tracing data.[129] According to the nonpartisan Center for Responsive Politics, the NRA and affiliated organizations spent an estimated $54 million to support Republican candidates for Congress and the White House in 2016. At least $30.3 million went to support the candidacy of Donald Trump.[130]

Legal and Illegal Gun Sales

Gun transactions are regulated by the 1968 Gun Control Act, which requires gun vendors to have a federal license. According to researchers,[131] almost all guns in the United States in private hands were first sold by a licensed dealer. However, secondary gun sales are not tightly regulated. This means that guns can easily be transferred to other parties by gift, loan, informal sale, rental arrangement, or theft. A 1993 study found that only about one-sixth of the guns used in crime were obtained legally.[132]

In a 2012 study, the criminologist Anthony Braga and colleagues used Bureau of Alcohol, Tobacco, Firearms and Explosives data to explore illegal firearm trafficking patterns.[133] Key findings showed that a high number of guns used to commit crimes could be traced back to a small subset of firearm retailers licensed to sell guns. However, large-scale trafficking was not the primary way that buyers obtained guns later used in crime. New guns were disproportionately likely to be used in crime, the researchers found, suggesting the potential effectiveness of the "close-to-retail diversion of guns in arming criminals."[134] Additionally, the authors found that a considerable number of licensed firearm dealers and private sellers participated in illegal gun transfers. Illegal pathways used to obtain guns include sales from both licensed and unlicensed sellers, residential theft and theft from gun dealers, and straw purchases. Analyses also showed that about a third of the guns used in crime were obtained in the community where the crime was committed. Almost a third came from other parts of the same state, and about a third were from outside the state. Finally, established interstate trafficking routes typically transported guns from states with looser regulations to states with tighter regulations.[135]

Braga's team of researchers analyzed case studies to ascertain the effectiveness of disrupting illegal gun transfers. They found that targeting "scofflaw retail dealers" reduced illegal transfers considerably. According to the study,

> In Detroit and Chicago, the number of guns recovered within a year of first retail sale from someone other than the original purchaser was sharply reduced after undercover police stings and lawsuits targeted . . . retail dealers. In Boston, a gun market disruption strategy focused on the illegal diversion of new handguns from retail outlets in Massachusetts, southern states along Interstate 95, and elsewhere resulted in a significant reduction in the percentage of handguns recovered in crime by the Boston Police Department that were new. In Milwaukee, the number of guns recovered within a year of first retail sale from someone other than the original purchaser dramatically decreased after voluntary changes in the sales practices of a gun dealer that received negative publicity for leading the USA in selling the most guns recovered by police in crime.[136]

Background Checks

The 1993 Brady Handgun Violence Prevention Act requires licensed firearms dealers to run background checks on all people attempting to buy guns. On top of federal law, nineteen states and Washington, DC, require background checks for all handgun sales. However, thirty-one states allow unlicensed transfers with no background check required.[137] According to Everytown for Gun Safety (2018), since 1994, the National Instant Criminal Background Check System has blocked more than three million gun sales to prohibited purchasers. Even so, an estimated 22 percent of gun transfers take place between unlicensed parties who do not go through the background check process.[138]

An analysis by Everytown for Gun Safety of mass shooting data from January 2009 to July 2015 found that, controlling for population, states that require background checks for all handgun sales had 52 percent fewer mass shootings than states that did not require background checks.[139] They also found that "46 percent fewer women are shot to death by their intimate partners, 48 percent fewer law enforcement officers are killed with handguns, and there is 48 percent less gun trafficking" in states with background checks for all handguns.[140] These states also have 48 percent fewer gun suicides and 17 percent fewer aggravated assaults with firearms.[141] While this analysis does not account for interstate differences that may contribute to rates of mass shootings, it nonetheless suggests the need for further research into the relationship among background checks, illegal gun sales, and violence.

Open and Concealed Carry

The open-carry movement, led by gun rights advocates, aims to expand the legal rights of citizens to carry guns openly in public places, such as schools, colleges, and parks. Concealed-carry laws regulate citizens' rights to carry concealed weapons in such places. The gun lobby also pushes for states to allow people to carry guns in private establishments, including ones that provide alcohol, unless the establishment's owners choose to expressly ban guns. Yet, as mentioned previously, even in states with permissive gun laws, black residents carrying guns are regularly perceived as threatening and consequently arrested or killed. Alton Sterling, who was shot when an officer yelled that he had a gun in his pocket in a state that allows open carry without a permit, and Philando Castile, who alerted officers that he had a concealed-carry permit and a gun just before he was killed, are recent examples.

Online Gun Sales and Gun Shows

Thousands of websites facilitate online gun purchases, by both federally licensed firearms dealers and unlicensed "private sellers."[142] While federally licensed dealers are required by law to conduct background checks, unlicensed sellers are not. In 2011, the City of New York commissioned a study on illegal online gun sales to explore whether online gun sellers were complying with federal law by refusing to sell guns to people who had not passed background checks. Investigators found that among the study sample of 125 private vendors from fourteen states who advertised on ten different websites, 62 percent of sellers agreed to sell a firearm to a purchaser who claimed a likely inability to pass a background check.[143] Those ten websites alone offered more than twenty-five thousand guns for sale.[144]

In 2009, the City of New York commissioned a multistate study of the exception in federal law that permits private sellers to sell guns without conducting background checks or keeping records.[145] This loophole is commonly termed the "gun show loophole" because these shows, attended by thousands of Americans every weekend, are one of the largest marketplaces for private sellers to connect with buyers anonymously.[146] According to the Bureau of Alcohol, Tobacco, Firearms and Explosives, "30 percent of guns involved in federal illegal gun trafficking investigations are connected in some way to gun shows."[147] The investigation also found that 63 percent of private sellers sold to buyers who said they most likely could not pass a background check; 94 percent of licensed dealers sold to straw purchasers, who were buying guns and undergoing a background check on behalf of someone else; and thirty-five of forty-seven gun sellers approached by study investigators attempted to sell guns to people who appeared to have criminal records or be conducting straw purchases.[148] President Obama attempted to address mass gun violence following the Sandy Hook massacre by having people with known mental illness undergo background checks prior to purchasing guns, an executive order reversed by President Trump in 2018.[149]

Assault Weapons Ban

Assault weapons were first designed in the World War II era for a battlefield setting where accuracy was less important than the ability to fire rapidly on enemy soldiers at relatively short range.[150] After the December 2012 shooting deaths of twenty schoolchildren in Newtown, Connecticut, President Obama called for regulations to limit civilians' access to military-grade weapons. Yet, in 2013, legislation to ban semiautomatic assault weapons and expand background checks was defeated in the Senate.[151] Jonathan Masters of the *Atlantic* writes,

> As of 2016 [and continuing as of June 2018], there were no federal laws banning semiautomatic assault weapons, military-style .50 caliber rifles, handguns, or large-capacity ammunition magazines, which can increase the potential lethality of a given firearm. There was a federal prohibition on assault weapons and high-capacity ammunition magazines between 1994 and 2004, but Congress allowed these restrictions to expire.[152]

Stand Your Ground Laws

On February 26, 2012, in Sanford, Florida, on the way to his father's house after stopping at a convenience store for a can of iced tea and a bag of Skittles, 17-year-old Trayvon Martin was shot and killed by George Zimmerman, a private citizen who lived in the boy's father's gated community. Zimmerman was an active member of his neighborhood watch and carried a concealed handgun, and he allegedly made antiblack statements in the press in the days after he shot and killed the teenager. The night of the killing, Zimmerman called 911 to report a "real suspicious guy" in his neighborhood who looked "up to no good," and he asked the police to hurry because "these assholes always get away."[153] He told the 911 operator that Martin was running away. The operator told him to stand back and not to follow, but Zimmerman followed anyway.[154]

In the mere minutes between the end of the 911 call and the arrival of police at the scene, Zimmerman pursued and killed Martin. Police arrested and questioned Zimmerman but soon released him without filing any charges. The story spread nationally, inspiring mass demonstrations calling for Zimmerman's arrest. Many demonstrators wore hooded sweatshirts and carried canned drinks and Skittles in honor of Martin. In April 2012, Zimmerman was charged with second-degree murder, but he was ultimately acquitted of all charges.[155]

Over the past decade, dozens of states have adopted Stand Your Ground laws resembling the ones used by Zimmerman's defense to justify his killing of Martin.[156] These laws legalize the use of deadly force when a person feels reasonably at risk of serious injury—though, of course, what constitutes "reasonable" risk is highly subjective and influenced by political, social, economic, and racial biases. Studies have demonstrated that participants placed in high-stress simulations requiring them to make split-second decisions are more likely to shoot black targets, regardless of whether the targets are holding a "neutral object" like a cell phone or holding a gun. Study participants are also likely to shoot black targets more quickly.[157] Thus, Stand Your Ground laws pose a particular threat to black citizens, especially teenage boys and men. Indeed, the laws encourage vigilantism and protect shooters even when victims are unarmed, as in the tragic case of Martin's death.

Law Enforcement and Police Accountability

An analysis of gun policing by Koper and colleagues found that officers usually address gun crimes like illegal possession reactively.[158] They discover guns during routine activities, such as traffic stops, or when answering calls.[159] Because poorer neighborhoods with higher proportions of non-white residents are more likely to experience acts of aggressive policing, such as "broken windows" approaches, "stop-and-frisk" stops, racial profiling,[160] and citations for minor infractions,[161] it follows that nonwhite individuals may be more likely to be charged with gun violations, regardless of rates of offense.

Koper and colleagues detail several practical interventions that can be employed by law enforcement to curtail gun violence. Such measures include reducing the supply of illegal firearms, given that large numbers of illegal sales can be traced to a small number of sellers. Gun buyback programs remove illegal guns from the streets. Other strategies include collaborations with law enforcement, government, and community organizations to launch gun education and prevention initiatives and prosecutions.[162] In 2016, the *New York Times* highlighted one data-driven intervention used by the Chicago Police Department to monitor and target possible gun crime victims and offenders from a "nerve center" of computer analysts, where

> a dozen police officers monitor the city minute by minute. There is a map of the city overlaid with rectangles glowing red and orange to show current hot zones for gang disputes. A screen tracks the locations of the latest gunshots, capturing the sounds of shots and estimating their origin down to fifteen feet. Facial recognition software helps narrow down suspects whose images are caught on security cameras.
>
> Sometimes only minutes after the gunshots end, a computer system takes a victim's name and displays any arrests and gang ties—as well as whether the victim has a rating on the department's list of people most likely to shoot someone or be shot.
>
> Police officials say most shootings involve a relatively small group of people with the worst ratings on the list. The police and social service workers have been going to some of their homes to warn that the authorities are watching them and offer job training and educational assistance as a way out of gangs.
>
> Of the sixty-four people shot over the weekend, fifty of them, or 78 percent, are included on the department's list. At least seven of the people shot over the weekend have been shot before. For one man, only twenty-three years old, it is his third time being shot.[163]

Such approaches are touted as more efficient ways to target department resources toward addressing individuals and neighborhoods at the greatest risk of gun violence. However, they carry the risk that the complex conditions producing gun violence, now commonly deemed a public health issue, may lead to racially biased and disruptive criminal justice fixes. A common aggressive critique often leveled by many non-white activists is that social issues that disproportionately affect nonwhite people are addressed with aggressive criminal justice measures, whereas similar issues that affect white people at higher rates tend to be addressed with a softer touch. One example is the rhetoric and policies addressing the possession of crack versus powder cocaine. It has been noted that crack cocaine was more likely to be used by nonwhite people and carried much steeper penalties than powder cocaine, which was more likely to be used by white people.[164] Similarly, the "tough on crime" approach to crack cocaine use in the 1980s and early 1990s, racialized in public discourse as mostly affecting black citizens and being equated with violent criminality, contrasts starkly with the gentler "public health" approaches to the current heroin "epidemic" that mostly affects white citizens, many of whom are also relatively affluent.[165] Nonwhite and lower-income Americans are disproportionately deemed high-risk gun users and are surveilled, arrested, charged, convicted, and incarcerated at elevated rates. Therefore, addressing gun homicides primarily through the criminal justice system violates the civil rights and equal protection of black, disenfranchised, and lower-income citizens, many of whom already live on the margins of full American citizenship.

Summary and Conclusion

Gun violence and murders have become commonplace in America. In comparable high-income countries, rates are twenty-two to thirty times lower. Gun access is made easy by online distributors, private sellers, and lax evaluation practices of prospective buyers. Stand Your Ground laws broadly protect shooters who can claim, with little burden of evidence, that they feared for their safety. Such laws, against the backdrop of America's racialized history, increase the vulnerability and the number of killings of already highly stigmatized and marginalized black men and boys. Gun violence is more prevalent in racially segregated and impoverished communities, and consequently blacks bear the highest burden. Chicago, where patterns of geospatial segregation align with patterns of gun homicide, is a prime example.

Although gun violence in America has long reached epidemic proportions and is a major public health issue, a clear understanding of its larger societal impact is difficult to ascertain. Congressional restrictions restrict gun violence research. Efforts to reduce gun homicide rates are hindered by the lack of a comprehensive federal policy on gun control, a patchwork of state laws, and the influence of powerful gun lobbyists, who block any measures to limit or control gun access.

3

NOT ALL VIOLENCE IS THE SAME

Race- and Place-Based Violence

If you are attempting to study American history, and you don't understand the force of white supremacy, you fundamentally misunderstand America.
—TA-NEHISI COATES, 2017

By slow violence *I mean a violence that occurs gradually and out of sight, a violence of delayed destruction that is dispersed across time and space, an attritional violence that is typically not viewed as violence at all.*
—ROB NIXON, 2011

In this chapter, I discuss the types of violence exposure for youths and how these vary based on age, gender, and race or ethnicity. In so doing, I distinguish between "loud" traumas and "silent" traumas. Loud traumas are fatalities that often take the form of homicides, school shootings, and police violence. Repetitive examples of such loud traumas flood the twenty-four-hour news cycle. With regard to scale and repetitiveness, however, such violence represents only the very tip of the violence iceberg. Much of my research and clinical practice during the past two decades has focused on silent traumas, which commonly take the form of witnessing and being a victim of robberies, gang-related incidents, and gun violence not resulting in death. These silent traumas are devastating, costly, 120 times more frequent, and more widespread than loud traumas (e.g., homicides, mass shootings, and murders).[1] Silent traumas are present in many urban, economically disadvantaged neighborhoods and are fueled by structural violence and other social inequities in America. These inequities are deepened by race, gender, and geographic location.

The Problem with Words

Before delving into the discussion of these neighborhood traumas, I want to articulate the limitations inherent in the words we commonly use when discussing such violence. As discussed in chapter 1, how we define and measure a phenomenon like neighborhood violence is a political process that largely shapes how we view its causes and consequences, how we react to it, and how large-scale spending is directed. In addition, what we do and do not measure presents bias, as do the words and concepts we use to describe a phenomenon. Power brokers have more control over how phenomena are defined and measured. This imbalance means that those suffering from oppression and neighborhood violence are often barred from participating in the production of knowledge about it. Those who have more to gain from upholding existing systems and structures are more likely to be the ones responsible for analyzing the function and assessing the impacts of those systems and structures. Therefore, formal measurements of neighborhood violence are likely to underestimate its full extent. Rigorous analysis requires going beyond readily available data to elevate the narratives of those whose voices are silenced and whose experiences are invisible in the mainstream discussion. The construction, measurement, reporting, and, as stated earlier, analyses of neighborhood violence are never value neutral or bias free. However, the academic and research worlds impose constant pressure to standardize measurement. One consequence is that the pressure to define problems clearly and concisely sometimes flattens the complexity of an issue, so that the words we use often fail to meaningfully address the phenomena at hand. One example from my own field of social work is our discussion of individual-, policy-, or societal-scale problems and solutions. Students of the social work graduate school where I teach will ask one another whether they're more interested in individual or societal interventions, by which they tend to mean direct practice or policy, respectively.

Yet, as many social theorists have pointed out, the ways that we consider and divide the problems of social life are political and have consequences for the possibilities we imagine and the actions we take.[2] One example already noted is the way that political analysts talk about homicide rates in highly segregated and economically depressed neighborhoods. Often, they refer to homicides in segregated neighborhoods as "black-on-black" crime and call for black people to "deal with problems in their own communities." Several assumptions underlie this framing, having to do with how these analysts think about the scale of the violence and who and what factors are responsible for it.

First, analysts commonly make assumptions that such high rates of neighborhood violence are rooted in individual, cultural, moral, and community deficits. In frustration over the shooting of seventy-five people in Chicago one weekend, Mayor Rahm Emanuel blamed the violence on a "shortage of values."[3] Second is the assumption that violence among black people across different neighborhoods, cities, and regions of the United States shares the same roots and solutions, simply because the victims and perpetrators are black. This assumption is seldom supported by complex discussions of the many processes that unite to place black citizens at greater risk of living in places where violence is concentrated. Third, black "communities" are often defined in racial terms that imply that all black people are responsible for the actions of one another simply because they are black— a responsibility rarely assigned to white people. Fourth, so-called black-on-black violence is imagined as taking place face to face between black victims and perpetrators alone—erasing other forms of violence, such as environmental contamination (e.g., the Flint water crisis), unsafe workspaces, and conditions that make interpersonal violent encounters more likely. Clearly, these assumptions are underpinned by the belief that the main reason violence disproportionately affects poorer black citizens is a shared failure by black people to respond to violence appropriately. This belief is a form of racist victim-blaming. This view considers violence affecting black residents to be fundamentally the same across diverse neighborhoods throughout the country—and yet, paradoxically, a product of their individual failures and inability to take personal responsibility for their (in)actions.

In addition to ignoring the ample work done by black activists and organizers to address neighborhood violence, scaling the problem in these ways circumvents fuller insight into a broader discourse on American structural violence. It forecloses possibilities for understanding incidents of interpersonal violence in highly segregated communities as being produced by, and (re)producing, complex, violent processes that affect black residents disproportionately yet affect all black people differently. As an example, I use the action of a fist connecting with someone's jaw, which is a result of so many other actions flowing through that instant. Furthermore, other (re)actions flow from the punch itself, thereby creating ripples of consequences that often reinforce the violent act. The immediacy with which the victim experiences the punch is not affected by individual traits or societal arrangements. Similarly, the punches of white supremacy for a young person growing up in an impoverished, racially segregated neighborhood with high crime may feel exactly like hundreds of punches, never-ending hunger pangs, or a paralyzing hurt.

Other ways of thinking about violence focus on the heavily determined quality of each minute action: Agency in any instant is constrained by the weight of history. From this point of view, the factors producing any violent act may appear more like a ponderous structure than a process. For instance, the anthropologist Patrick Wolfe writes that settler-colonial, white supremacist violence in the United States is a "structure, not an event,"[4] dispensing with the conceptual bias that configures perpetrators of violence as individual actors situated around specific violent events, attitudes, or words. Thinking of violence as a structure can lead to coordinated, systemic solutions that, together, alter the violent apparatus and reconfigure possibilities. A similar misstep around framing and focus occurs when a fatal school shooting takes place in Chicago. Like actors following a script, the media, law enforcement, and the mayor's office spring into action, and they should. Grief counselors and social workers are dispatched to the school for two to three weeks to provide the affected students with what is popularly known as "trauma-informed care" until the presumed effects of the "event" have subsided or reached some state of normalcy. In reality, trauma for many of these youth is not made of singular events but is continuous, that is, interwoven in the structures of an uneven society. They cannot return to "a normal state" or even a state that approximates the opportunities and wider life chances automatically afforded to those located in neighborhoods or structures of privilege. Black youth face daily assaults related to neighborhood violence. The discordance between these two Americas presents real threats to their ability to enjoy full American citizenship and achieve their maximum human potential.

Black youth and other peers living in neighborhoods with concentrated violence are not "at risk" because of moral or behavioral deficits. Whether the media, researchers, public commentators, citizens, or policy-makers refer to these youth as "at risk," "disengaged," or "endangered" or as "opportunity youth" has significant implications for knowledge generation, the framing of solutions, and subsequent methods and targets of funding. Many black American youth reside in neighborhoods that are silently languishing because of decades of economic disinvestment, political disenfranchisement, and social marginalization. Structural weights such as substandard schools, communities plagued by decades of social disinvestment, food deserts, lack of adequate health care, and joblessness are dimensions of structural violence that give rise to high rates of neighborhood violence. Despite these hardships, members of oppressed communities continue to contribute in wide-reaching ways to our increasingly globalized and complex societies. The sociologist Sudhir Venkatesh framed it this way: "Today's champions of globalization are so busy celebrating the wondrous wealth and the charming artifacts of food and music produced by international interchange that they have little time for the plight of the invisible underclass that helps make it happen."[5] Attention to guns and sources of other fatal violence is critical. However, it is also critical for public officials to focus on the silent traumas that, though they kill more slowly and insidiously, weigh heavily on the day-to-day lives of sufferers, often fatiguing them, stifling their joy and creativity, and leading them to periods of despair. This loss is profound for them, and reason enough to prioritize reforms. Yet, it is also worth remarking on the unfathomable possibilities that go unrealized because children in disadvantaged neighborhoods too

Figure 3.1

The unfulfilled promise of a career center in the Englewood neighborhood of Chicago under Richard M. Daley, mayor from 1989 to 2011

Source: Dexter R. Voisin

Figure 3.2

The racialized capitalism of the black man in America

Source: Sean Blackwell

often do not have access to the resources they need to help them pursue their dreams. This is America's loss, whether we realize it or not.

Race- and Place-Based Violence

Homicides get the most attention from the public and media and often become sensationalized. However, rates of homicide differ significantly by gender, age, and race or ethnicity. Breaking out the data on youth neighborhood violence by various dimensions presents a complicated and sometimes incomplete picture. White high school students report higher rates of carrying a weapon on school property than both black and Hispanic or Latino students. However, a greater percentage of black and Hispanic students report being threatened or injured with a weapon on school property compared with their white counterparts. While some data indicate that overall victimization levels may be similar across racial/ethnic groups, the most extreme disparities appear in youth exposure to what many researchers term "serious violent victimization," which includes robbery, rape, aggravated assault, and homicide.[6] While so-called serious violent victimization rates have declined, disparities between racial/ethnic groups persist, with the rate of serious violent victimization for black youth aged twelve to seventeen years averaging 67 percent higher than that of their white peers.[7]

Gender disparities also exist in the forms and rates of violence victimization experienced by youth. Rates vary across and within racial/ethnic groups. Across all ethnicities, on average, boys aged fifteen to nineteen years are about four times more likely than girls to die from homicide.[8] Among black adolescents specifically, boys report exposure to interpersonal violence at consistently higher levels than girls,[9] with adolescent boys facing 50 percent more nonfatal violent victimization than their female counterparts between 1993 and 2003.[10] Additionally, in 2014, the homicide rate for black teenage boys was forty-four per one hundred thousand, nearly twenty times higher than the rate for their white male counterparts, which was two per one hundred thousand.[11] These disparate figures are reported widely in social science literature without an adequate examination. Let me pull back the lens through which we report these figures, and let us interrogate their meanings and presentations.

Looking at the Bigger Picture

More than three decades of research have shown that problems such as crime and delinquency can be traced back to neighborhood factors such as condensed need, residential volatility, dense population, and a high concentration of immigrants. These factors destabilize neighborhoods and hamper their ability to monitor and control crime. More specifically, concentrated poverty and disadvantage combined with housing and social segregation predict higher rates of youth problems.[12]

Studies have also shown that neighborhood factors are associated with residents' behaviors.[13] More specifically, youth trajectories are more positive when neighborhoods have economic, educational, and social resources.[14] In contrast, research has shown that higher levels of neighborhood violence are associated with structural disadvantage.[15] Rates of neighborhood violence are highest among the poorest, most racially segregated communities[16] and range from 75 percent to 90 percent.[17] The pattern of racial segregation is different for poor blacks when compared with their white counterparts. Impoverished blacks live in racially segregated black neighborhoods. White poverty is dispersed across different city neighborhoods except in black ones.[18] Therefore, the implications of being poor and white or being poor and black in America are vastly different. Poor whites, because they reside in socioeconomically varied neighborhoods across the city, gain wider access to better schools, supermarkets, health care, information, and other resources by mixing with residents of more upwardly mobile neighborhoods. In contrast, black poverty is concentrated in resource-poor networks or communities, leaving residents of these areas with less access to informational capital and economic opportunity.

As stated earlier, in black American communities, especially those that are low income, a long history of racist housing policies and practices, including redlining practices, restrictive covenants, and ongoing housing discrimination, has led to pronounced residential segregation. These neighborhoods are often food deserts, where residents have limited access to nutritional food.[19] Surveillance with traffic cameras and aggressive, biased policing, including racial profiling, stop-and-frisk tactics, and excessive use of force, leave residents fearful of law enforcement. Compared with their white counterparts, black Americans are disproportionately more likely to be charged with criminal activity, regardless of rates of criminal involvement,[20] and to be treated like second-class citizens by law enforcement and criminal justice systems in America. Black Americans also bear other disproportionate burdens. Limited options for high-quality, affordable child and health care, limited access to higher education, and financial and emotional stress already confront many of these families.[21] These burdens and other forms of structural violence place a heavy toll on black citizens' health and well-being.

According to statistical analyses of health inequities, an estimated one hundred thousand black Americans die every year simply because they are black.[22] A study in 2000 found 291,000 deaths attributable to poverty and income inequality, two social conditions that are closely tied to structural violence.[23] While death is the most extreme consequence of structural violence, deadly societal inequities are rarely considered violence in the minds of most Americans. This oversight wrongly absolves more privileged Americans of shared responsibility for allowing or turning a blind eye to these violent conditions and letting powerful actors off the hook.

Looking Up Close and at the Bigger Picture

As mentioned in chapter 1, the anthropologist Paul Farmer has described how wide-ranging societal and structural arrangements forces influence personal pain. He refers to these large-scale social forces as structural violence, defining them as societal forces shaped by history that circumvent and contain people from reaching their full human potential. For many people, Farmer notes, life choices are influenced by the intersection of racism, sexism, violent governmental policies, and suppressing poverty.[24] For many youth growing up in communities with high rates of violence, constraints of agency like those Farmer describes often lead to compromised well-being and mental health as a result of neighborhood trauma. Societal constraints often decrease the likelihood of youth graduating from high school. In some cases, parents are terrified to send their children to school after a deadly neighborhood shooting. In high-crime neighborhoods, some students are unable to focus on academic tasks because they are traumatized by having witnessed or experienced neighborhood violence or are fearful of the prospects of both. My research has shown that some youth may join gangs to seek physical protection, meet economic need, or feel a sense of belonging, all which might lead to higher involvement with juvenile justice systems. Such involvement can further constrain personal agency by negatively affecting their long-term educational, residential, employment, and relationship opportunities. For other youth, the erosion of safe parks and recreational centers as a result of violence might increase the amount of unsupervised time adolescents spend at home during which sexual activity might occur, increasing the risk of contracting or transmitting sexually transmitted infections including HIV and of having unplanned pregnancies. As one parent, Michelle, remarked during a focus group, "My son has book sense but no street sense. I don't let him hang outside after school because the streets are unsafe. I know he is having sex with his girlfriend after school when I am at work—but I much prefer he has sex than get killed by a bullet." These examples are merely snapshots of the ways structural violence may affect the lives of young people living under oppressive neighborhood conditions. I explore the troubling connections between large-scale structural forces and loud and silent traumas in greater detail in chapter 4.

Structural Violence

I believe it is important to draw back the conceptual lens to vigorously question our fragmented assumptions about neighborhood violence and its many roots. While doing so, we must humbly recognize that even well-meaning scholars and activists are all hamstrung and shaped by colonial and biased interpretations and by the vestiges of white, male, and class supremacy. Even among marginalized groups and activists, there are stratifications of privilege based on the multiple identities we occupy in society that obscure our own biases and limit our ability to more fully comprehend the experiences of others. To illustrate, speaking at "The Personal and Political Panel" of the Second Sex Conference in New York in 1979, the writer and activist Audre Lorde participated in the only panel of the entire feminist conference in which the perspectives of black and queer theorists were represented. The two black panelists had been "literally found at the last hour."[25] Decrying the erasure of these voices, Lorde asked her audience, "What does it mean when the tools of a racist patriarchy are used to examine the fruits of that same patriarchy? It means that only the most narrow perimeters of change are possible and allowable."[26] She famously told her audience that "the master's tools will never dismantle the master's house."[27]

A similar phenomenon often shapes knowledge about neighborhood violence and, consequently, possibilities for promoting peace and healing. Social science research, policy, and practice are hamstrung by antiliberal, antigovernment attitudes that compel researchers to neatly define problems and evaluate tidy, cost-effective solutions. The widespread belief that rampant government waste and welfare dependency exist has catalyzed the dismantling of an already anemic welfare state (compared with other wealthy nations). These attitudes are informed by racialized and gendered notions about who is deserving of social support, values built upon racist and sexist stereotypes like the "welfare queen," the "thug," and the "super-predator." Social science and policy fields are narrowing their focus on purportedly more "objective," measurable problems and technocratic interventions. The result is an ever-shrinking conceptual exploration of what is wrong and what can be done from the perspectives of communities in need, not elites. This argument has been made by social scientists, public health researchers, community leaders, and professional and lay experts from every walk of life. Throughout this book, I mostly focus on the words and writings of black thinkers, whose rich intellectual contributions are often made invisible by institutional racism, and intersecting vectors of oppression, including sexism and ableism. The ideas in this chapter come from critical race theory, anticolonial thought, black feminist and womanist studies, and the accounts of informants who shared their lived experiences, reflections, and strategies for coping and resistance. As the sociologist Patricia Hill Collins writes in *Black Feminist Thought*, the politics of the social movement she chronicles were shaped by the "dialectic of oppression and activism, the tension between the suppression of African-American women's ideas and our intellectual activism in the face of that suppression."[28] In this chapter, I seek to amplify these marginalized voices.

An Intersectional Analysis of Neighborhood Violence

Contemporary discourse often has a tendency to marginalize the recognition of social, systemic forms of oppression as identity politics.[29] Critics of so-called identity politics often misrepresent the work of those who call attention to patterns of oppression that affect a class of people, saying that such politics are divisive, that they reify categories of domination, or that they focus too much on subjective experiences and too little on systems and structures, such as capitalism. On the other hand, as the critical race theorist and legal scholar Kimberle Crenshaw writes,

> The problem with identity politics is not that it fails to transcend difference, as some critics charge, but rather the opposite—that it frequently conflates or ignores intragroup differences. . . . Feminist efforts to politicize experiences of women and antiracist efforts to politicize experiences of people of color have frequently proceeded as though the issues and experiences they each detail occur on mutually exclusive terrains.[30]

Too often this means that political advocacy by groups fails to center on, or even acknowledge, the concerns of those facing interacting dynamics of oppression. Reflecting on her research focusing on the legal challenges facing nonwhite women, Crenshaw writes that "practices [that] expound identity as woman or person of color as an either/or proposition . . . relegate the identity of women of color to a location that resists telling."[31]

In a 1989 article about black women's experiences of employment discrimination, Crenshaw proposed the concept of intersectionality to "denote the various ways in which race and gender interact to shape the multiple dimensions of black women's employment experiences."[32] In the decades since, intersectionality has become a powerful conceptual tool used by advocates and scholars to draw attention to the interacting dynamics of oppression that demonstrate how the politics of gender, race, and other factors manifest differently depending on the particularities of one's social position. These particularities shift constantly as one moves through the world. For example, with regard to her research, Crenshaw writes,

My objective there was to illustrate that many of the experiences black women face are not subsumed within the traditional boundaries of race or gender discrimination as these boundaries are currently understood, and that the intersection of racism and sexism factors into black women's lives in ways that cannot be captured wholly by looking at the race or gender dimensions of those experiences separately.[33]

Many have employed Crenshaw's concept to consider how other social dimensions, such as religion, sexuality, or (dis)ability, pattern our politics and lived possibilities.

Throughout this book, I employ the concept of intersectionality to analyze the ways that multiple processes interact to shape how violence is enacted on particular bodies and the places where they live. Focusing on black children and adolescents living in U.S. cities, in this chapter I examine different types of violence encountered by many black youth and how their lived experiences of these exposures may vary based on the particularities of their lives, such as gender, age, and class. No analysis could adequately capture the broad diversity of ways that violence manifests in the lives of black children in different neighborhoods across the country. Therefore, my goals are to highlight inequities connected with antiblack racial oppression and to flesh out some of the complexities that too often fall into the conceptual cracks in social science research, policy, and advocacy.

Measuring and Representing Loud and Silent Traumas

As a researcher, I tend to use a mixed-methods approach, bringing qualitative and quantitative data into conversation in an attempt to present different facets of whatever social phenomenon I am studying. A mixed-methods approach can draw on the strengths and complement the short-comings of each strategy included. In this chapter, I use various kinds of data to paint a picture of how silent traumas affect the lives of black youth. Estimating the full extent of exposure to neighborhood violence is challenging, and this is particularly true when attempting to capture the difficult-to-quantify concepts related to silent traumas. These include inter-nalized racism, historical erasure, and toxic stress, as well as protective factors like unity and resilience. Even more seemingly straightforward experiences, like witnessing assault, are often defined and measured differently across data sets. The World Health Organization's measurement of neighborhood violence generally relies on the following kinds of data: "mortality data (including death certificates, vital statistics registries, medical examiners', coroners', or mortuary reports); self-reported (surveys, special studies, focus groups, media); community (population records, local government records, other institutional records); crime (police records, judiciary reports, crime laboratories); economic (program, institutional or agency records; special studies); policy or legislative (government or legislative records)."[34] Some of these resources, such as crime data, are useful for capturing loud trauma, such as homicides. However, they fail to trace people who witness violent acts that go unreported because of many individuals' fear and distrust of police. Other types of data, like interviews, ethnographic data, focus groups, and agency records, may help facilitate a deeper and more textured analysis. For this reason, deep, reflexive, immersive experiences in social groups, as well as repeated interviews with study participants, are vital.

Yet, it is not enough merely to report the information shared with me by study participants—I must also be attentive to the power dynamics at play in producing knowledge that will be read by audiences who may be far removed from the experiences of those whose stories I seek to represent. This involves reflexively considering my own blind spots, habits, and assumptions that skew my perceptions in ways beyond my awareness. As my colleague, the celebrated historian Charles Payne, writes in the introduction to his history of the Mississippi Freedom Struggle, "It is still true that every way of seeing is a way of not seeing."[35] As a chronicler, synthesizer, interpreter, and producer of information, I decide which observations to include, how to portray them faithfully and with integrity, and how to render my active role in the knowledge production process visible to my audience.

Furthermore, Payne cautions, "There is a real temptation for bottom-up history to sing praises to the agency, courage, and wisdom of the poor and look no further. In fact, it is probably a good idea to assume that people are formed by the society they struggle against and carry some of its flaws within them."[36] All of us are shaped by the societies in which we are embedded, affecting how we conceptualize and explain the world around us. Tragically, this often means that we internalize the myths put forth by those who have outsized power to control what is said, heard, published, and taught. Striving to understand ourselves and our worlds apart from the conceptual instruments passed down to us—tools often devised to subjugate—is what many refer to when they speak of "decolonizing thought." In the United States, to consolidate power, slaveholders violently suppressed communication among enslaved Africans in their native tongues and the expression of their cultural customs. This resulted in suppressing their ideas, disrupting their social networks, breaking their spirits, discouraging rebellion, and imposing knowledge that reinforced white supremacy. Thus, much of the language, concepts, and national myths in the United States were designed by white supremacists to argue the subhumanity and justify the exploitation of black people. The Martinican poet and author Aimé Césaire wrote in his *Discourse on Colonialism* of the "millions of men who have been skillfully injected with fear, inferiority complexes, trepidation, servility, despair, [and] abasement" as a consequence of this colonial knowledge production and cultural genocide.[37]

Social theorists often refer to the manifold complexities described here as the "ethics of representation." When it comes to representing forms of violence experienced by marginalized people, what you say and do not say may literally have life-or-death consequences. For instance, in the 1990s, the myth of teenage "super-predators"—hyper-violent youth who were said to be remorseless, irredeemable criminals—was created by the professor John DiIulio Jr., then at Princeton, and was taken up by countless other scholars, policymakers, and pundits. The super-predator myth was used to justify harsh punishments for juvenile offenders and to explain racial disparities in criminal sentencing. In the years since, this theory has been roundly discredited, yet its impacts persist, as thousands of black and Latino men and boys languish in prisons, and their families, neighborhoods, and social networks endure their absence.

The racist stereotypes that enabled the super-predator theory to emerge and take root persist. For instance, one recent study by the psychologist Phillip Atiba Goff and colleagues found that participants were more likely to overestimate the ages of black children than those of white children, with police officers thinking of black children as four to five years older than they actually were. The police officers in the study were also significantly more likely to use force against black children: "Our research found that black boys can be seen as responsible for their actions at an age when white boys still benefit from the assumption that children are essentially innocent."[38] Another study, by researchers at Stanford, found that when participants imagined a black juvenile offender, they were more likely to view juveniles as similar to adults and expressed greater support for sentencing all juveniles who commit serious violent crimes to life without parole.[39] The consequences of such attitudes can be observed in sentencing disparities; for instance, as of 2009, in Florida— the state that has sentenced the most children and teenagers to life without parole in cases other than homicide—84 percent of juvenile offenders sentenced to life without parole were black.[40]

To return to the issue of representation, the super-predator myth illustrates the grave consequences of producing knowledge about marginalized groups that inflames bigotry and fuels oppression. "Expert" knowledge produced by powerful figures has been used to justify the racial subordination of black people in the land that came to be called the United States, starting long before the American Revolution. This has been particularly true in writings that attempt to explain away racial inequity as a consequence of cultural pathology rather than entrenched structural racism. As the historian Alice O'Connor writes in *Poverty Knowledge*, the research of liberal social scientists in the twentieth century tended to trace the problem of poverty to the individual poor, rather than see the problem as embedded within the political economy. She argues that these researchers' constructions of cultural deviance and the culture of poverty have been frequently used to stigmatize, contain, and deny help to the impoverished rather than to alleviate the conditions that produce inequity and poverty. She further points to the way that social science—and the attitudes it produced about poor people (often cast as black)—was used to justify the passage of the 1996 Personal Responsibility and Work Opportunity Reconciliation Act.[41] More commonly known as "welfare reform," this law separated caregivers, particularly mothers, from young children, forcing caregivers to meet steep hourly employment requirements to maintain eligibility for meager financial support, imposed strict lifetime limits, and plunged millions of poor families deeper into poverty.

O'Connor calls for a different approach to poverty knowledge, one that aims to

> redefine the conceptual basis for poverty knowledge, above all by shifting the analytic framework from its current narrow focus on explaining individual deprivation to a more systemic and structural focus of explaining—and addressing—inequalities in the distribution of power, wealth, and opportunity.[42]

Such an approach would eschew what some have described as "ruin porn"—descriptions of suffering that render hyper-visible some sensationalized forms of violence, such as assault, stranger rape, gun violence, and death, while obscuring other forms.[43] Instead, it would examine what Rob Nixon calls "slow violence":

> By *slow violence* I mean a violence that occurs gradually and out of sight, a violence of delayed destruction that is dispersed across time and space, an attritional violence that is typically not viewed as violence at all. Violence is customarily conceived as an event or action that is immediate in time, explosive and spectacular in space, and as erupting into instant sensational visibility. We need, I believe, to engage a different kind of violence, a violence that is neither spectacular nor instantaneous, but rather incremental and accretive, its calamitous repercussions playing out across a range of temporal scales. In so doing, we also need to engage the representational, narrative, and strategic challenges posed by the relative invisibility of slow violence.[44]

Such an approach may call for "refusal" as a research method. This is the idea that researchers, ideally in partnership with research participants, decide together whether to present particular information. Inherent in this refusal is an acknowledgment that (1) as mentioned before, representation often obscures as much as it illuminates; (2) the researchers may not have the proper understanding of context to responsibly represent sensitive material; and (3) the material may not serve to improve the conditions of life of those people and populations being studied and, in fact, may perpetuate violence and harm against them. In the remainder of this chapter, I strive to employ all of these approaches in presenting research about black children and teenagers' exposures to loud and silent trauma, contextualizing their stories within the slow violence of segregation, welfare state retrenchment, economic restructuring, and other processes.

Marcus's Experiences of Silent Trauma

The term "pornography of pain" dates back to the 1800s and was used to describe the voyeuristic excitement resulting from observing or inflicting pain.[45] This term has since been recast by critical thinkers and advocates to capture the act of peering into the suffering of others for self-interest that is devoid of empathy or a sense of how one's own privilege, actions, or inaction might contribute to such suffering. I share the story of Marcus to bring to the reader's attention the incredible strength and resilience that many of these youth demonstrate in the presence of such structural inequality and neighborhood hardship. His story is complex, as are the circumstances that shaped his silence for three years.

In 2009, I sat in my office with Marcus, a 15-year-old black male student who was attending one of the better-resourced Chicago public high schools. I was interviewing him for a study to understand how black youth on Chicago's South Side defined and mapped their communities. "What would you consider your ideal neighborhood?" I asked. Marcus hesitated, a labored pause. He then answered in a soft voice, "One where teenage girls don't get raped." Marcus went on to tell me with difficulty that his then 13-year-old sister had been walking through the neighborhood on her way home from school when she was raped by three men in an alley. Fighting back tears, he said he felt fortunate that she hadn't been killed.

"Marcus, who did you tell about this?" I asked him. He looked at me with what seemed to be a perplexed, and perhaps slightly annoyed, stare. He then said that three years had passed since the incident, and I was the first person he had told. When I asked him why, he said that he was afraid of retaliation by the men if word got out that he had told or had identified them. He also decided not to tell his mother, for her own and his family's safety. For three years, Marcus buried this event, talking about it to no one. No mental health treatment was sought or received for him—or for his sister.

I have often wondered how this horrifying event, and the secrecy Marcus felt compelled to maintain, might have disrupted his sense of self, his security, his relationships with his family. How might it have impacted his behavior, his concentration, his school performance? I wonder about the practical, philosophical, and moral questions it might have stirred in him, the existential anguish he might have felt, or the fear of and alienation from others he may have experienced in the geographical space where his life played out every day. The loneliness of being a child forced to work through all of this alone, hesitating to trust anyone with the information, is incomprehensible.

Indeed, after telling me the story, Marcus seemed to grow increasingly fidgety in his chair, in the midst of my professor's office on the imposing, Gothic-style University of Chicago campus. It was located just two neighborhoods east of his, yet worlds apart in many ways: mine the predominantly upper-middle-class, ethnically diverse enclave where private university professors and President Obama lived; his a high-poverty, racially segregated neighborhood with one of the highest rates of gun violence in Chicago and the country. He then asked me a very serious, complicated question: "You look like a professional and all that, and this is a nice office. But how do I know I can even trust you?"

To this day, I'm not sure exactly what Marcus meant. I reassured him about confidentiality, but perhaps his concerns were broader than that. Perhaps he worried about how his story might be told by me or mobilized by politicians who might someday read my words, whether it would result in more funding for his neighborhood's schools, or just more cops stopping and frisking him and other boys who looked like him. Perhaps he wondered if I "got it," if I had enough context to truly process the dynamics of his life. Maybe he wondered if I would flatten his family's tragedy and his heavy secret into some cold statistic about urban violence; maybe he considered how I might characterize the men who hurt his sister. Whatever the specific nature of his unspoken concerns, I did not take his confidence lightly.

Policing and Surveillance

In standardized measures of what constitutes neighborhood violence, hyper-policing and surveillance are rarely taken into consideration. This omission is notable, especially given what I have learned from my study participants over the decades. Many black American youth in urban cities view excessive and unjust police practices as a serious form of neighborhood violence. It has been noted repeatedly that many black and Latinx communities have had deep-seated tensions with law enforcement for centuries.[46] Modern police forces originated out of slave patrols in the 1700s, and in the ensuing years, police have often protected white supremacist violence, including the epidemic of lynching black citizens in the first half of the twentieth century.[47]

Belief in the grave risks associated with police brutality and misconduct was a common theme that emerged in a 2003 study some colleagues and I conducted on Chicago's South Side. Study participants were thirty-two black American teenagers aged fourteen to eighteen years who were attending a well-known South Side public high school. We conducted our qualitative interviews with the goal of better understanding their experiences of neighborhood violence exposure.

Six of the sixteen boys we interviewed identified policing practices and surveillance measures as a form of neighborhood violence. In the study, described in greater detail in chapter 7, boys reported feeling terrified and humiliated in their interactions with police. Such missteps add to the legacy of mistrust black communities have of law enforcement and undermine genuine police–community partnerships. This mistrust hampers the ability of police officers to be effective given that the majority of neighborhood crimes are solved with the help of community assistance.

Summary and Conclusion

What constitutes neighborhood violence is influenced by politics, perspective, and one's privilege. Most often, neighborhood violence is defined in terms of personal violence among individuals. Seldom considered is the role of structural violence, which can significantly constrain the opportunities of individuals and perpetuate the manifestation of neighborhood violence. Exposure to and experiences of neighborhood violence depend on intersecting identities that include age, gender, race, socioeconomic status, sexual orientation, and geography. In moving beyond traditional definitions of neighborhood violence and capturing its effects, it is important to consider loud versus silent traumas. Fatalities such as homicides are the loud traumas that often get the attention of the media and civic and government officials. Nonfatalities, which are silent traumas, are 120 times more common than homicides, but inadequate attention is directed toward addressing their consequences, which have damaging effects on youth and their communities. Common misconceptions about the causes of neighborhood violence in low-resourced black communities often result in misdirecting resources toward addressing and penalizing symptoms instead of root causes, thereby perpetuating other forms of structural violence on already deeply affected communities. Hyper-policing and surveillance of black communities represent a crucial form of neighborhood violence, which many social activists recognize but some researchers and public officials have been slow to acknowledge.

Within the context of reframing what constitutes neighborhood violence, I would like to revise a popular children's chant as follows: "Sticks and stones may break my bones, and words will forever hurt me." Conservative ideologies often frame the narrative around neighborhood violence as interpersonal acts taking place between individuals. When these acts are characterized as black-on-black without attention to the structural drivers and decades of inequality that often fuel them, the individuals and their communities are often blamed and framed as deficient. Such words and framing are deeply damaging to these communities. Lost in such discussions are the more prevalent forms of structural violence that exist in the lives of black youth and their families. Words are powerful because the framing of what constitutes violence by actors outside of these communities misdirects resources away from structural fixes and toward punitive, ineffective approaches. Many of these responses, such as calls for more school metal detectors or for arming teachers with guns, versus supplying books and educational resources to promote school completion and circumvent the school-to-prison pipeline, neither reduce violence rates or the effects of violence.

4

THE ROAD TO CONCENTRATED POVERTY AND NEIGHBORHOOD VIOLENCE

JASON BIRD AND DEXTER VOISIN

Slavery has never been abolished from America's way of thinking.
–NINA SIMONE

Like slavery and apartheid, poverty is not natural. It is man-made and it can be overcome and eradicated by the actions of human beings.
–NELSON MANDELA

Racial meaning and racial stratification are embedded within American societal and organizational structures. Therefore, racism operates independently of people subscribing to racial views or attitudes.[1] I have often heard it said that it is almost impossible to explain sexism, racism, or white supremacy to people when their very privilege depends on their not fully understanding it.

David, like so many of the youth I interviewed on Chicago's South Side, was growing up in a household headed by an unmarried mother. His father was involved in his life, but many of his peers' fathers were not in theirs. How did this trend of single-female-headed households become the image of the typical black American family and thus contribute to the disproportionate burden of poverty and neighborhood violence? Notably, in 1938, 11 percent of black children were born to unwed mothers; by 1994, this rate had climbed to 72 percent overall and 80 percent in some cities.[2]

The Road to Concentrated Poverty and Neighborhood Violence

In this chapter, I discuss how forms of structural violence—the Black Codes, Jim Crow laws, residential segregation policies, substandard schools, the war on drugs, the growth of the prison industrial complex, and systematic discrimination in child welfare, all within the context of entrenched racism—have paved the road to disproportionate levels of concentrated poverty and neighborhood violence among black Americans. Historically, population growth, racism, and the increasing segregation of urban black communities resulted in high concentrations of poverty and the emergence and exacerbation of urban social problems, such as neighborhood violence. In the South after the Civil War, newly freed blacks faced social and economic pressures, and a series of political, economic, and social shifts radically altered the demographics of industrialized cities in the North and Midwest. Negative reactions to these changing demographics deepened the marginalization of urban black communities and created long-term patterns of urban dysfunction and neighborhood violence that negatively affected the lives of individual residents, family systems, and neighborhood institutions. Instead of counteracting these patterns, U.S. social policy has replicated its bias in the containment, racialized capitalism, and subjugation of blacks.

Figure 4.1

The evolution of the slave in America. From left to right: Slave, Colored, Negro, Black/African American

Source: Raub Welch

Figure 4.2

Poverty as violence

"We think of violence as being conflict and fighting and wars and so forth, but the most ongoing horrific measure of violence is in the horrible poverty of the Third World . . . and the poverty in the United States as well."—Martin Sheen

Source: Dexter R. Voisin

A Paradox of Opportunity and Oppression: Prelude to the Great Migration (1865 to 1915)

The population of the United States surpassed one hundred million people in 1915, increasing from just thirty-one million in 1860.[3] Starting in the late 1800s, a growing percentage of the U.S. population began to migrate from rural towns to urban centers, drawn in by an unprecedented expansion of industrialized labor that promised increased employment opportunities and class flexibility. Concomitantly, 1915 marked the official beginning of the Great Migration. Driven by an oppressive caste system of subjugation

Figure 4.3

Oil painting of black boys
circa the late 1800s
Source: Raub Welch

in the South and a lack of economic opportunities, increasing numbers of
southern blacks migrated to northern and midwestern industrial cities.[4] The
Pulitzer Prize–winning author Isabel Wilkerson documents this decade-
long epic movement of blacks in *The Warmth of Other Suns: The Epic Story
of America's Great Migration*.[5] This was the largest movement of people in
U.S. history, with an estimated six million blacks leaving the South. By 1970,
nearly half (47 percent) of the black population lived outside of the South,
compared with only 10 percent in 1915.[6]

Southern blacks left for social and economic reasons. After the end of the
Civil War, the South experienced a period of supposed reconstruction between

1865 and 1877. A primary objective of Reconstruction was the integration of newly freed slaves into full American citizenship. It was mostly northern politicians who developed Reconstruction-era policies. Their implementation was overseen by Union troops, who were stationed in the South to ensure a smooth, orderly, and equitable process of integration for both newly freed blacks and southern whites. These policies focused on creating and increasing access to fair wage-labor opportunities for all freed slaves and aimed to protect black men as they started to engage in the political sphere as voters and elected officials. Reconstruction was also meant to strengthen the capacity and autonomy of black institutions, including family, schools, and religion.[7]

However, the Reconstruction period was rife with conflict and intractable, sometimes violent, resistance from white southerners. An entire way of life, unearned privilege, and immense profit based on racialized capitalism on the backs of blacks were threatened. In the early years of Reconstruction, southern states enacted legislation seeking to force freedmen back into forms of servitude through the manipulation of newly installed systems of wage labor.[8] For example, the sharecropping system that emerged in the South explicitly exploited black farmers. Black farmers were forced to lease land owned by whites, as they were unable to purchase land because of a lack of economic resources, the white-managed banks' resistance to extending them credit, and white property owners' opposition to selling land to them.[9] The leasing contracts often provided extremely low share wages or "standing wages," which were lump-sum amounts provided at year-end.[10] These conditions forced freed blacks back into subordinate relationships with white landowners,[11] re-creating circumstances similar to slavery with few opportunities for economic advancement.[12]

Understandably, many freedmen sought nonagricultural jobs, such as railroad and industrial work. However, these jobs were limited, and blacks were often segregated into low-paying unskilled and domestic labor. Therefore, pathways to wealth accumulation and economic stability were generally restricted, leaving southern blacks little opportunity to advance beyond their ascribed economic class.[13]

Moreover, legislation often referred to as the "Black Codes" emerged in the years directly after the Civil War to explicitly govern blacks' behavior.

These codes, or laws, restricted the freedoms and rights won through abolition and made it easier to incarcerate black men.[14] Whites often justified these types of legislation with emerging constructions of blacks as aggressive, predatory, lazy, and in need of control. For example, Black Codes in nine states targeted vagrancy in such a way that mere unemployment among black men became criminalized.[15] Once in prison, black convicts could be leased to white business owners and farmers in a system known as "convict leasing," which essentially re-enslaved them,[16] thereby re-creating the cheap labor force that had fueled slavery and white economic and social supremacy.

The influence of northern politicians helped to mitigate the impact of many of these exploitive practices; for example, Black Codes were eventually ruled unconstitutional during the Reconstruction era. However, given the South's obstinate resistance to the goals of Reconstruction, this era ended after little more than a decade without achieving equitable racial integration in the South. Among the many reasons for the failure of Reconstruction, two factors of primary importance were southern whites' significant resistance to equality for freed blacks and a lack of political will in the North to maintain a long-term occupying force in the South. In the end, southern Democrats regained their political power in the South, and the North abandoned the mission of Reconstruction, turning its focus to the Industrial Revolution driving economic prosperity in northern states.[17]

After the end of Reconstruction and the concomitant withdrawal of northern scrutiny, white southern elites were left in charge of the integration of blacks into southern society. The negative social attitudes toward blacks resulted in the reemergence of legislation in the form of Jim Crow laws that aimed to halt racial integration and equality. Like the Black Codes, the Jim Crow laws sought to suppress southern blacks by restricting their freedoms and rights. These state and local laws excluded blacks from the social and economic benefits of citizenship through physical segregation within civic institutions, including employment, housing, education, health care, and transportation. The Supreme Court's ruling against Homer Plessy in 1896 upheld racial segregation in public facilities and later become known as the "separate but equal" doctrine, allowing blacks to be segregated from whites but leaving them reliant on whites' majority power. This power imbalance and the resulting unequal access to resources created significant racial disparities and relegated blacks to second-class citizenship in the South.[18]

Furthermore, although Jim Crow laws could not explicitly deny black men their Fifteenth Amendment right to vote, southern states began to institute voter suppression laws that circumvented the spirit of voting rights.[19] These laws did not overtly create whites-only elections but achieved similar outcomes using subtle mechanisms of racial exclusion, such as poll taxes and literacy tests. These mechanisms took advantage of structural vulnerabilities for blacks (such as poverty and the lack of sufficient schools) while providing loopholes, such as grandfather clauses, for whites who might be excluded by the laws.[20] Additionally, felony disenfranchisement policies, which had been carried over from the colonial period, were used to further suppress black voters, who were subjected to unequal laws that disproportionately resulted in felony convictions and incarceration.[21] This practice was later repackaged into more contemporary approaches that have become widely known as the war on drugs, million-dollar blocks, and the prison industrial complex,[22] discussed later in this chapter.

Underlying these suppression efforts was the fundamental belief, held by many whites, in white supremacy: the belief that blacks were inferior and undeserving of equal rights. These discriminatory beliefs, used to justify blacks' social and economic subordination, were exacerbated by a deep anger about the loss of the Civil War and the early enforcement, by northern politicians, of integration policies.[23] In the context of this hostility, blacks were negatively constructed as deviant: Black men were fashioned as aggressive, violent, and predatory; black women were perceived as sexually promiscuous; and all blacks were stereotyped as lazy and untrustworthy.[24] These negative constructions were then used to justify mistreatment and a staggering rise in violence, including brutal assaults, bombings, mob violence, and lynchings, directed toward blacks by whites.[25] This campaign of violence played an important role in the decisions of many blacks to leave the South: Out-migration was greatest from counties with the highest rates of lynching.[26] The outcome of these laws and the ever-present threat of violence created a comprehensive system of suppression that relegated blacks to a state of social, economic, and political disadvantage and inequality in the South.[27] This oppressive environment and the lack of political leverage to enact meaningful change provided incentives for leaving the South, a strategy that gained momentum as the country entered the twentieth century.

The North was also subject to a radical transformation, stimulated by rapid industrialization, after the Civil War. Scientific and technological advancements affected all sectors of the U.S. economy. These advancements influenced innovation in goods and manufacturing techniques that, in turn, primed new economic markets. This rapid expansion led to an increased demand for goods and a growing need for industrial labor. The vast majority of the industries were based in cities to take advantage of concentrated labor pools, which encouraged increased migration from rural communities to urban areas in the United States.[28] Immigration also intensified during this period, and by 1910, immigrants constituted approximately 14.7 percent of the U.S. population, with more than 90 percent of new immigrants residing in cities.[29]

The dual pressure of migration and immigration shifted the population balance between urban and rural residency, resulting in nearly 45 percent of the U.S. population residing in cities by 1910, as opposed to 20 percent fifty years earlier (81 percent resided in cities in 2010).[30] This process of urbanization not only transformed the economic foundations of the United States but also contributed to a variety of urban challenges, including overcrowding, increased public health concerns, and increases in unemployment, crime, and social unrest.[31] Furthermore, it created a new era in intergroup conflict, which deepened tensions and prejudice as racially and ethnically diverse groups competed for resources in unstable urban economies.[32]

This economic growth was also accompanied by mounting social unrest as businesses took advantage of the lack of labor regulation to exploit workers as a means of increasing private profit, which manifested in poverty wages, unreasonable work expectations, and unsafe working conditions. By the early 1900s, this social unrest boiled over into a far-reaching progressive reform movement that helped rein in some of the abuses perpetuated by private industry. Therefore, by 1915, the northern states had not only experienced a fundamental economic change, becoming more urbanized and industrialized, but were also in the midst of a radical social transformation that sought to increase the rights of many vulnerable populations, including wage laborers and women.[33]

Ironically, given the contributions of immigrants to the success of industrial growth, increasingly restrictive immigration policies began to emerge in the early 1900s. These restrictions were seen as a means of decreasing labor competition and thereby increasing the power of unions and other labor groups to negotiate more favorable labor contracts.[34] These restrictive immigration laws continued to strengthen after World War I, even though this period was marked by increased manufacturing needs and growing urban economic opportunities.[35]

This economic growth and the rising focus on social reform added to the perception of northern cities as places of increased opportunity and served as an important incentive for migration.[36] Therefore, although racial discrimination existed in the North, as it did in the South, there was a belief (and a hope) that the northern cities would provide more freedom, equality, and economic stability and deliver an escape from the structural constraints of the South.[37]

The Rise of Urban Social Dysfunction (1915 to 1965)

The Great Migration provoked a profound change in the cultural and demographic landscape of northern and midwestern cities, raising new social and economic challenges. Driven away by extreme oppression, ongoing lynching practices, and entrenched segregation in the South and enticed by the promise of economic opportunity and greater freedom in the North, southern blacks began to migrate in rapidly increasing numbers to northern and midwestern cities, forever changing the demographics of these cities.[38] For example, from 1910 to 1970, the proportion of blacks in Chicago increased from 2 percent to 32.7 percent of the city's population; Detroit experienced an increase from 1.2 percent to 43.8 percent; New York, from 1.9 percent to 21.1 percent; and Philadelphia, from 5.5 percent to 33.6 percent (figure 4.4).[39]

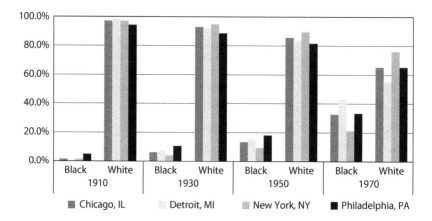

Figure 4.4

Percentage of white and black populations in four major U.S. centers, 1910 to 1970

Sources: Compiled U.S. Census data. C. Gibson and K. Junk, February 2005. Historical Census Statistics on Population Totals by Race, 1790 to 1990, and by Hispanic Origin, 1970 to 1990, for Large Cities and Other Urban Places in the United States. United States Census Bureau, Working Paper No. 76. www.census.gov/population/www/documentation/twps0076/twps0076.pdf

Southern blacks were often greeted with suspicion, hostility, and discrimination upon arrival in the North.[40] Theorists have argued that racial antagonism increases as the privileges of the majority are perceived to be threatened and that intergroup hostility grows out of a fear of competition for scarce resources.[41] This hostility is exacerbated when the groups do not share common goals or equal status; are not, or are perceived not to be, interdependent on each other; and when positive interactions are not encouraged by those in positions of authority.[42] While blacks avoided the caste-like oppression found in the South, significant racial prejudice still existed in the industrialized northern and midwestern cities. This prejudice was used to marginalize blacks as an independent outgroup that did not share common goals or equal status with whites, resulting in structures of racial inequality that generally restricted blacks to economic niches with low wages, scarce resources, and limited opportunities for advancement.[43]

Those who chose to migrate moved to a variety of cities, joining both small and large communities. Smaller and more stable black communities appeared to provide more job opportunities and be less targeted by intense discrimination, which may have been a result of the surrounding white communities' feeling less threatened.[44] However, as black communities grew, whites grew more threatened and concerned about potentially shifting balances in power.[45] As these levels of perceived threat increased, so did instances of discrimination, intimidation, harassment, and violence, dimming blacks' prospects for economic and social advancement.[46]

Southern blacks came from diverse backgrounds and locations, including both cities and rural sharecropping communities. Many of those moving into cities were unskilled in industrial labor, which sometimes complicated their adaptation to the types of work available. Furthermore, the migrants, while more likely to be educated than those who remained in the South, were often less educated than northern blacks, which may have presented a further barrier to integrating into their new communities or finding higher-wage work that required advanced training.[47]

Most southern black migrants moved into racially homogenous, predominantly black districts, which helped them acculturate and, to an extent, inoculated them against some of the racial prejudice. In choosing destinations, they looked for neighborhoods and urban enclaves where they had family members and friends. They also sought out communities that had supportive institutions, including black churches, neighborhood organizations, and established chapters of the National Association for the Advancement of Colored People (NAACP) and the National Urban League.[48]

However, southern blacks were not always welcome in their new communities. Some northern blacks were concerned that the influx of new black migrants would increase economic competition. They were afraid this would lead to fewer job opportunities and depressed wages, exacerbating economic instability and inequality.[49] Cultural differences also created tension, especially when northern blacks embraced the negative constructions of southern blacks as lazy, ignorant, or potential threats to social stability and safety. This intragroup discrimination, a perpetuation of the broader racism directed toward blacks by whites, served a similar purpose, categorizing black migrants as outsiders and thereby justifying their treatment as scapegoats for social dysfunction and their exclusion from resources and opportunities.[50]

This intragroup discrimination was likely an example of political scientist Cathy Cohen's theory of advanced marginalization: A marginalized group perpetuates discriminatory attitudes on more vulnerable subgroups to align itself with the majority.[51] The ultimate goal of such alignment is to gain greater acceptance by the majority and thereby the greater privileges associated with acceptance. In this case, some northern blacks may have adopted the constructions of southern blacks as deviant to ally themselves with northern whites who held similar beliefs about black migrants. In finding common ground with the majority, they expected to be subjected to less marginalization and gain more access to the jobs and resources controlled by whites, giving them a competitive advantage in the narrowing economic market.

However, the depth of racial prejudice precluded the reconstruction of northern blacks as equal to whites, and the "black ghetto" was treated differently from the ghettos that emerged around other (primarily European immigrant) communities in that they were not provided pathways for "assimilation" into more racially mixed neighborhoods and communities.[52] Instead, a concerted effort was undertaken to further restrict residential options for black communities by entrenching racial segregation into formal and informal policies.[53] For example, starting in the early 1900s, real estate developers, neighborhood associations, and white property owners conspired, through the use of racially restrictive covenants, to prohibit the sale of certain properties to blacks in an effort to keep communities homogeneously white.[54]

Over time, this effort resulted in an intensified segregation that restricted residential mobility and isolated black communities in increasingly undesirable, dilapidated, and overcrowded neighborhoods.[55] Disinvestment in minority neighborhoods, in favor of investment in white neighborhoods and towns, left black neighborhoods with insufficient economic or institutional resources for improvement or development.[56] Blame for the derelict condition of these neighborhoods was eventually attributed to the residents themselves, not to the structural constraints put on them. Racialized stereotypes and misrepresentations about residents' negligence, carelessness, and laziness emerged as causal explanations for dysfunction within black neighborhoods.

These mischaracterizations were used to demean black communities as a whole in the inner cities and to reinforce negative stereotypes about black "culture" as inherently deviant. These stereotypes were then used to justify residential segregation as necessary to protect white communities and their property values from black encroachment and the neighborhood dysfunction that was believed would follow. In other words, these mischaracterizations and stereotypes were used to justify the very discriminatory policies and actions that created neighborhood dysfunction in the first place.[57] Although the Supreme Court ruled restrictive covenants unenforceable in 1948, other discriminatory real estate practices, such as redlining, continued until the passage of the Civil Rights Act in 1964.[58]

While the percentage of the urban black population steadily grew throughout the early 1900s, the percentage of the white urban population slowly but steadily decreased.[59] Then, the racial composition of northern and midwestern cities radically shifted after World War II, as whites began to rapidly relocate out of the inner cities and into nearby suburban, residential towns. The development of extensive highway systems provided quick and straightforward access between these communities and their adjacent cities, which allowed residents to relocate while still taking advantage of the urban economic markets.[60]

Postwar government initiatives supported this residential mobility. The G.I. Bill helped returning soldiers obtain a college education and, in turn, provided them a pathway to higher-wage blue- and white-collar professions. Another initiative, offered through the Federal Housing Authority and the Veterans Administration, increased the availability of affordable mortgages. This higher earning potential, which provided greater economic stability, coupled with affordable mortgages, made residential mobility more viable.[61] However, these initiatives predominantly benefited white Americans. For example, the affordable mortgages extended to whites through the Federal Housing Administration were denied to blacks, cutting off a primary mechanism of residential mobility and helping to secure the suburbs for white communities.[62]

Therefore, the persistent concerns associated with a growing black population in the inner cities, the availability of government economic assistance, and the ability to self-segregate into homogenous white enclaves in the suburbs provided ample motivation for whites to leave the city in favor of suburban towns. The change was stark. Figure 4.4 illustrates the changes in population between blacks and whites in these cities between 1910 and 1970, providing a clear indication of whites' rapid abandonment of the cities starting in the 1950s.[63]

Ultimately, this rapid relocation, or "white flight," resulted in disinvestment in city infrastructure that negatively affected inner-city populations that did not have the resources to move to the suburbs. This disinvestment led to further deterioration and isolation of inner-city neighborhoods.[64] Despite the burgeoning black population in the cities, black voters continued to be disenfranchised from American political life and were generally kept from gaining a politically powerful foothold. Racism, coupled with the lack of knowledge about the political process and organizing, hampered such efforts.[65] Therefore, in the first half of the twentieth century, the population growth and concentration of blacks as a political bloc did not result in significant access to political participation or increased economic opportunities or resources for black communities.[66] Inner cities also suffered significant economic losses as industries shifted their business toward the suburbs (as well as other geographical areas), which had a growing pool of highly skilled labor and an increased demand for local jobs.[67] The growing wealth of the suburbs further shifted the balance of political power; the needs of the inner cities were often neglected as politicians sought to solidify their economic base in the suburbs.[68] This all served to increase the economic distress of the inner cities as unemployment and underemployment grew, exacerbating poverty and social unrest and leading to increased violence, crime, and family decline.[69]

Contemporary Consequences (1965 to 2018)

During the Civil Rights era and beyond, the long-standing practice of "racial capitalism" continued. Racial capitalism is "the process of deriving social and economic value from the racial identity of another person."[70] In the American context, it occurs when "white individuals and predominantly white institutions use nonwhite people to acquire social and economic value."[71] Examples of racial capitalism include chattel slavery and contemporary manifestations such as the enormous profits from the prison industrial complex that disproportionately incarcerates Americans who are considered dispensable—the poor, blacks, and Hispanics/Latinos—people with little power.

The Voting Rights Act of 1965 was intended to remove local and state barriers that prohibited blacks from voting. This bill trailed the landmark *Brown v. Board of Education* decision in 1954 that declared state laws establishing separate schools for whites and blacks unconstitutional. However, these legislative gains, while instrumental in changing some of the more blatantly discriminatory policies and constraints on blacks, did not mark the end of racial inequality or significantly change blacks' social and economic plight.[72] In the post–Civil Rights era, race and racism, neighborhood segregation, unemployment, and poverty continued to intersect in ways that constrained blacks' social and economic advancement. Speaking on the significance of race in America, Condoleezza Rice, America's first black female secretary of state, stated that racism

is a birth defect with which this country was born out of slavery; we're never really going to be race blind. . . . I think it goes back to whether or not race and class—that is, race and poverty—[are] not becoming even more of a constraint . . . because with the failing public schools, I worry that the way that my grandparents got out of poverty, the way that my parents became educated, is just not going to be there for a whole bunch of kids. And I do think that race and poverty [are] still a terrible witch's brew.[73]

Entrenched racism, coupled with extreme neighborhood segregation and economic disinvestment in black neighborhoods, thus led to the expansion of poverty and crime. These neighborhoods, or urban ghettos, became largely identified as problem communities seen not as needing economic investment but rather surveillance and suppression.

The few legislative gains of the Civil Rights era were followed by the war on drugs campaign. This campaign was advanced for thirty years by both Republican and Democratic presidents and rendered a devastating blow to black families and communities but resulted in significant economic activity and profits for some states and white rural communities. Although black communities were able to endure the assaults of chattel slavery and Jim Crow regulations, laws that were passed as part of the war on drugs, against a backdrop of race and racism in America, disproportionately targeted black males, subjecting a growing segment of the population to imprisonment, a form of state-sponsored enslavement. This contributed to higher rates of single-female-headed households, with successive generations of black youth being born into poverty and living in neighborhoods where crime and violence were pervasive. Subsequently, black youth were placed in child welfare systems at rates higher than those of their white and Hispanic/Latino peers.[74] These effects all occurred against a backdrop of poorly funded schools that remained relatively racially and economically segregated for decades, even after the *Brown v. Board of Education* ruling. Therefore, pathways for blacks to move out of poverty continued to narrow throughout the late 1900s and early 2000s. Simultaneously, neighborhoods were becoming increasingly destabilized and subject to higher rates of violence, and jobs continued to shift from these communities to the suburbs.

Schools: Still Separate and Unequal After All These Years

Education has historically been a primary path for racial minorities to obtain social and economic advancement in America. Despite the 1954 *Brown v. Board of Education* ruling, schools have remained relatively racially and economically segregated in America, which has created de facto educational ghettos, with significant disparities in funding for and resource allocation to schools based largely on race. For instance, when the Fair Housing Act was signed in 1968, 77 percent of black and 55 percent of Latino students, respectively, attended public schools in which the majority of students were minorities (i.e., nonwhite). By 2013, the percentage of minority students in schools in which most were minorities remained almost unchanged. Nationwide (except in Hawaii), property taxes fund a significant portion of district budgets. This means that poorer districts have less money to spend per child. Therefore, in low-income communities in which a higher proportion of blacks live in poverty, less revenue is available for school spending.[75]

In 1973, the Supreme Court ruled that funding public schools primarily on the basis of property taxes was not unconstitutional.[76] In reality, this practice translates into school segregation being unconstitutional but de facto school ghettos not being unconstitutional. In America, schools remain racially segregated and underfunded based on racial and economic composition, with a persistent black–white academic achievement gap.[77] The primary door for black youth to advance out of poverty is rapidly closing. The national average spent per child receiving a public education is $11,841. In Chicago schools with a majority of low-income students, approximately $9,794 is spent per child annually, whereas $28,639 is spent per child annually in nearby suburban districts.[78] Similar scenarios across America are common, and this unequal trend in spending is worsening. Between 2008 and 2014, approximately thirty-one states' spending per student decreased, and local school funding declined in eighteen states. Public low-income, majority-nonwhite schools are more inclined to experience the negative consequences of school-spending budget cuts. In some low-income districts, the school week has even been reduced to four days.[79]

The War on Drugs: Effect on Black Families

In 1971, President Nixon popularized the war on drugs. This policy was subsequently advanced over the next several decades under presidents of both major parties, and with it came the explosion of the prison industrial complex. John Ehrlichman, a top Nixon advisor, said in a 1994 interview

Figure 4.5

Slavery, Jim Crow, housing segregation, and de facto ghetto schools

Source: Carlos Javier Ortiz

that the war on drugs was really a political strategy to help Nixon win and stay in the White House:

> The Nixon campaign in 1968, and the Nixon White House after that, had two enemies: the antiwar left and black people . . . you understand what I'm saying? We knew we couldn't make it illegal to be either against the war or black, but by getting the public to associate the hippies with marijuana and blacks with heroin . . . we could arrest their leaders, raid

their homes, break up their meetings, and vilify them night after night on the evening news. Did we know we were lying about the drugs? Of course we did.[80]

In addition, the affirmative action policies of the 1960s fueled the fears and racial resentment of economically struggling whites that blacks were receiving unfair advantages in the workplace. According to the legal scholar Michelle Alexander, Nixon and subsequent presidents saw the war on drugs as an opportunity to win a significant number of votes from working- and middle-class whites, especially those from southern states.[81] It was an attempt to calm the racial fears of many whites who felt they were suddenly being forced to integrate their schools and compete with blacks for jobs, a transformation that had been incomprehensible during the Jim Crow era. Ironically, the war on drugs was launched at a time when illicit drug use in America was on the decline. Furthermore, according to Alexander, Nixon and other presidents seized an opportunity to regain the vote of this white-voting bloc by stereotyping and incarcerating blacks as drug criminals:

People are swept into the criminal justice system—particularly in poor communities of color—at very early ages . . . typically for fairly minor, nonviolent crimes. [Young black males are] shuttled into prisons, branded as criminals and felons, and then when they're released, they're relegated to a permanent second-class status, stripped of the very rights supposedly won in the Civil Rights movement—like the right to vote, the right to serve on juries, the right to be free of legal discrimination and employment [discrimination], and access to education and public benefits. Many of the old forms of discrimination that we supposedly left behind during the Jim Crow era are suddenly legal again, once you've been branded a felon.[82]

The higher rates of drug incarceration burden among blacks were not driven by use but by racism. In 2012, whites and blacks reported similar rates of illicit drug use, with whites being more likely to sell drugs than blacks.[83] However, black male incarceration rates were six times higher than those of their white male counterparts. In addition to racism advancing the higher burden of black incarceration, longer sentences were imposed for crack than for powder cocaine. As indicated earlier, this practice is widely acknowledged as racist because poor blacks were more likely to use crack than powder cocaine, which had higher usage among whites and the more affluent.[84] It has been estimated that if the rates of drug arrests for black and white men were the same, the American prison population would decline by a staggering 40 percent.[85] Notably, a large proportion of blacks are arrested for small-scale marijuana use, not drug dealing. What is considered legal or not is often driven by politics, economics, ideology, and necessity. As of 2018, the District of Columbia and nine states have legalized recreational marijuana, and it is now legalized for medical use in thirty states. It is estimated that by 2021, marijuana sales will generate $21 billion per year.[86]

The war on drugs gave rise to the rapidly expanding, and profitable, prison industrial complex. The United States accounts for approximately 5 percent of the world's population but represents more than 21 percent of the world's prisoners.[87] The United States imprisons more of its citizens than any other country globally.[88] During Nixon's presidency, about two hundred thousand people were imprisoned. Today, the U.S. prison population has grown to almost 2.2 million, with more than six million Americans under some form of correctional monitoring or confinement, including detention, jails, prison, and probation.[89]

The movement toward incarceration had devastating long-term impacts on black communities for generations. Blacks made up only 13 percent of the American population in the 1980s but represented approximately 37 percent of the correctional population.[90] As disproportionate numbers of black males were detained and/or incarcerated with longer sentences, the number of single-female-headed black households ballooned. To illustrate, in 1950, more black women were married than were white women, and only 10 percent of black children lived in a single-parent household. During the 1970s, 1980s, and 1990s, at the height of the war on drugs, these rates escalated, with nearly 70 percent of black youth residing in mostly single-female-headed households.[91] This resulted in successive generations of black youth being born to single mothers living in poverty, saddled with all the associated burdens.

Sig. 226. Sklaventransport in Afrika.

Figure 4.6

The old (*a*) and new (*b*) slavery and Jim Crow

Source: Gerald Herbert/AP (*b*)

More single-female-headed households than two-parent households live in poverty. Single, unmarried teenage mothers, regardless of race, are typically underemployed. In addition, almost 80 percent of single mothers heading households apply for welfare aid within five years after having their first child. In addition, within this demographic, significant race disparities persist. Black households headed by single females earn 36 percent as much as two-parent black households. White female-headed households earn 46 percent as much as their two-parent white counterparts. Of all black children living in poverty, 85 percent live in single-parent, mother–child homes.[92]

Poverty within the context of economically destabilized communities and families fostered higher rates of neighborhood crime and violence. Research by the notable sociologist Robert J. Sampson based on 150 American cities shows that higher rates of black male unemployment are associated with increases in black female-headed households.[93] As the number of black single-female-led households increases, youth robbery and murder rates escalate. Such changes occur even after accounting for contributing factors such as income, region, race, age, population density, city size, and welfare benefits. Sampson further argues that the results are identical for whites, indicating that family disruption is associated with youth violence involvement and exposure. Sampson argues that the high crime rates among blacks are driven by structural disadvantages linked to unemployment, economic disinvestment, and disruption of two-parent households in these neighborhoods. Arguably, high crime and violence rates would exist for any group irrespective of race/ethnicity if such structural disadvantages exists. In Chicago, five of seventy-seven neighborhoods accounted for a third of the city's homicides in 2016, with those neighborhoods having unemployment rates that ranged from 79 to 92 percent for teens and 49 to 70 percent for young adults.[94] The research data clearly show that the structure of and resources within neighborhoods predict youth involvement and exposure to violence.

The substantial abstraction of wealth from black communities through the large-scale incarceration of black fathers had devastating effects on already socially and financially stressed neighborhoods and families. Political activist Angela Davis makes several arguments with regard to extraction of black wealth.[95] Prisons extract economic capital from black communities through the exploitation of cheap prison labor. Prisons also extract social wealth by denying incarcerated parents the ability to raise their children, reset positive self-images of black manhood, participate in home ownership, and maintain neighborhood institutions such as schools and churches. In addition, given the high burden of black male incarceration, social wealth does not return to black communities. Moreover, people who have been criminally involved experience significant barriers to participating in the workforce and political process once they are released.[96] Most states place restrictions on voting for former inmates or those on parole. Most states prohibit former inmates from acquiring state driver's licenses, resulting in some job exclusions.[97] These trends advance the brutal cycle of unemployment, crime, incarceration, and recidivism. Across thirty states, the rate of recidivism within three years is as high as 67 percent.[98] For many poor and black Americans, entry into the prison system represents a door closing and the dampening of any hopes for achieving full American citizenship.

Figure 4.7

Acrylic painting entitled *Open Season*. This image depicts the effects of racialized capitalism: black men being hunted and corralled in America.

Source: Shanequa Gay

Like the West Africans who were grabbed from their homelands, they pass through the door of no return.

A Look at Chicago and Incarceration

In Illinois, the prison recidivism rate is more than 50 percent within a three-year period.[99] Prison recycling is the process of people moving in and out of prison back into the same neighborhoods, such as those on Chicago's South and West Sides. Between 2000 and 2013, incarceration had no effect on reducing crime and may have increased it, suggesting that mass incarceration targeting the structurally disadvantaged does little to reduce crime.[100]

The cycle of incarceration and recidivism weakens neighborhood collective efficacy (i.e., trust and cohesion for shared expectations of social monitoring and control), thereby contributing to greater rates of crime and delinquency, especially among youth.[101] Higher crime in black neighborhoods leads to increased rates of policing and contact with law enforcement, resulting in greater arrests and incarceration rates. These hot spots are known as "million-dollar blocks," where an estimated $1 million is spent annually on incarceration costs. According to analysts, nowhere is this phenomenon more pronounced than in highly racially segregated Chicago, where the city's most impoverished and racially segregated neighborhoods on the South and West Sides are burdened with the highest incarceration rates.[102] Million-dollar blocks, although prevalent in these Chicago neighborhoods, also exist in New York, St. Louis, and other American cities. Research has shown that the spatial unevenness of incarceration in Chicago has been consistent for more than two decades. Residents of West Englewood represented $197 million in prison spending from 2005 to 2009, and those of the Austin neighborhood, another $550 million. In 2015, despite diminishing crime rates, the Illinois Department of Corrections expenditure was $1.4 billion.[103] In some sections of Chicago's West Side, among males aged 17 to 54 years, almost 70 percent have had criminal justice involvement.[104] Many of these men are arrested for nonviolent drug-related offenses. This is in sharp contrast to wealthy white neighborhoods that are virtually untouched by incarceration. Researchers have argued that people are not just being punished for their actions but also for the poor neighborhoods in which they live.[105]

The Rise of the Prison Industrial Economy and Big Business

Growing drug arrest rates led to overcrowding of existing state and federal prisons and the need for more warehousing of prisoners. The shortage of prison beds relative to the exploding arrest rates ushered in the prison industrial complex and the establishment of for-profit prisons. Many state governments believed that private prisons could be built and operated with less bureaucracy and more financial efficiency than state- and federally run prisons. Political pressures to reduce the size of the federal government also contributed to the expansion of private for-profit prisons.[106] The imprisonment of almost 2.2 million Americans results in steady, well-paying jobs for depressed rural communities and significant financial opportunity for investors.[107] In America in 2012, the average annual cost of housing an inmate was $31,286. The highest annual rate was in New York at $31,286, and the lowest, in Kentucky, was $14,603. In Chicago, the annual cost was approximately $22,000.[108] According to journalist Eric Schlosser, what may have started out primarily as a political calculation has morphed into a colossal and unstoppable economic machine:

> The prison industrial complex . . . is a confluence of special interests that has given prison construction in the United States a seemingly unstoppable momentum. It is composed of politicians, both liberal and conservative, who have used the fear of crime to gain votes; impoverished rural areas where prisons have become a cornerstone of economic development; private companies that regard the . . . billion[s] spent each year on corrections not as a burden on American taxpayers but as a lucrative market; and government officials whose fiefdoms have expanded along with the inmate population. Since 1991 the rate of violent crime in the United States has fallen by about 20 percent, while the number of people in prison or jail has risen by 50 percent. The prison boom has its own inexorable logic.[109]

By some estimates, the prison industrial complex costs tax payers $265 billion annually.[110] This figure does not include indirect revenue (e.g., labor savings, telecommunications revenue, financial remittance costs, manufacturing, transportation). This multibillion-dollar industry now has conventions, trade shows, websites, catalogs, and direct-marketing campaigns.[111] In addition, the almost 2.2 million prison inmates in the United States are reliable customers. Phone calls, costly links to the outside world, are popular, and most are made collect. Prison calls generate approximately $1 billion dollars in yearly revenue.[112] Further, major architectural and construction firms are involved in constructing prisons. Prison bonds are traded on Wall Street, and premier universities invest significant funds in companies that build and operate prisons. According to one article, after significant student activism, Columbia University divested from prison bonds.[113] Without clear oversight and fuller transparency, it is unclear how many universities invest in companies that operate prisons.

As alluded to earlier, prisons have also been used to stabilize local economies. For instance, in several rural communities, prisons offer a middle-class income to many people with only a high school education. In addition, they provide a significant infusion of state and federal funds for construction, payroll, and operating expenditures. According to Alexander, prisons are offer solid job security and are recession proof, expanding during recessions when unemployment and crime rates converge.[114] Contrary to some popular beliefs, private manufacturing represents a small fraction of prison revenue. Most of the free or cheap labor prisoners provide goes toward the government and includes making military and police gear, providing call center operators, picking cotton, manufacturing road signs, and publishing Braille books. Prisoners also provide cheap labor and run all operating aspects of prisons (except security), including food service, commissary, maintenance, laundry, carpentry, and construction, saving the government millions annually in operating costs. Several states do not compensate prisoners for their labor, whereas others on average pay 19 to 50 cents per hour. Some prisoners learn valuable skills, but many are unable to find employment when released.

Given that blacks are disproportionately incarcerated in America, much of the revenue extracted from black households and communities comes from people who are already economically and socially burdened. Prisoners and their families are highly vulnerable on multiple levels, and, in such instances, abuses are likely. One report alleged, "When free enterprise intersects with a captive market, abuses are bound to occur. MCI Maximum Security and North American InTeleCom have both been caught overcharging for calls made by inmates; in one state MCI was adding an additional minute to every call."[115]

It has been frequently voiced that the prison industrial complex, law enforcement, and criminal justice are intertwined. Significant declines in incarceration rates could negatively impact the complex economic engine resulting from mass incarceration.[116] Few Americans would deny that violent offenders need to be held accountable and incarcerated according to the extent of their violations. However, sound logic would suggest that as rates of violent crime decrease, so would the necessity for prisons. However, some analysts have argued that incarceration is not driven simply by violent crime. According to Schlosser, "In 1980 about half the people entering state prison were violent offenders; in 1995, less than a third had been convicted of a violent crime."[117] He goes on to state,

> The enormous increase in America's inmate population can also be explained in large part by the sentences given to people who have committed nonviolent offenses. Crimes that in other countries would usually lead to community service, fines, or drug treatment—or would not be considered crimes at all—in the United States now lead to a prison term, by far the most expensive [and profitable] form of punishment.[118]

America's answer to mental illness, trauma-related youth conduct disorders, trauma-related drug use, and poverty-related circumstances is to incarcerate people. This translates into the hyper-vulnerability of poor and black Americans. According to Schlosser, approximately 70 percent of prison inmates are illiterate, and almost two hundred thousand have a serious mental illness.[119] Therefore, many people who would have been housed in mental health facilities a generation ago are now housed in the criminal justice system. According to recent data, approximately 80 percent of Americans who are incarcerated have some history of substance use. However, the resources allocated for drug treatment have steadily declined by 50 percent since 1993. Not only are poor and black American families negatively affected when fathers are incarcerated, but a significant number of women who have children are also entering the criminal justice system, deepening long-term social disadvantage for these children. Of the nearly eighty thousand women now imprisoned, 75 percent have children, and about 70 percent are incarcerated for nonviolent offenses.[120] These trends show that the lives and future trajectories of large numbers of children and youth are disrupted by the incarceration of mothers. Although U.S. incarceration rates peaked in 2008 and have declined overall by 11 percent through 2016, Americans who are poor and black continue to bear the highest incarceration burden.[121]

The multibillion-dollar prison industry is thus built on and sustained by a racialized criminal justice system that disproportionately targets blacks and the poor for incarceration. Blacks bear a disproportionate burden of poverty in the United States. This tightening connection between black and poor communities and the criminal justice system is used to further construct racist stereotypes of blacks as inherently deviant and in need of increased surveillance and greater regulation. For example, in April 2018, the arrest of two young black men at a Philadelphia Starbucks illustrates the assumption of guilt and criminality commonly thrust onto the shoulders of black men. In this instance, the two men were denied use of the bathroom and were then handcuffed within less than three minutes and detained in a police station for sitting peaceably and waiting for a colleague.[122] The burden of race in America allows black men to be vilified, deemed threatening, and often assumed guilty for simply existing in black bodies.

The 2018 Starbucks case is an example of what happens to young black men when interacting with law enforcement on a daily basis, because of the ingrained assumption of black wrongdoing and criminality. According to Schlosser,

We are not simply punishing people for the crimes they commit. We are also punishing them for the places where they live, the schools that failed them, and the employers that rejected them. And, without question, we are punishing them for the darkness of their skin. These factors work together to shape who gets portrayed as a criminal and who escapes such portrayals.[123]

This implicit bias of black guilt, "otherness," and outsider status is pervasive at every level of American society, not just in the criminal justice system. Implicit racial bias exists in hiring, in the workforce, in the child welfare system, and throughout the social fabric of America. So does implicit gender and class bias, among other dimensions. A recent example at Yale University highlights implicit bias even within the liberal bastions of America's privileged educational institutions. One of numerous such examples is an incident from 2018 involving a black female Yale University student. A white student called the campus police on her after she had fallen asleep while studying in her dorm's common area. Her legitimacy as a student and her right to exist within that space of privilege was called into question, and her black "otherness" was amplified.[124]

It has been highlighted that this assumption of black criminality inverts the American constitutional protection of "innocent until proven guilty." This expectation of guilt circumvents due process in ways that justify the disproportionate use of force by police when confronting black suspects (compared with white suspects) and, ultimately, punishments (including incarceration) that do not match the seriousness of the crimes committed. In other words, the assumption of black criminality has created entrenched segregation in the criminal justice system that subjects blacks to unequal treatment under the law.[125] This mechanism helps to explain why the rates of drug use in the black community, which correspond to the rates of use among whites, do not correlate with the higher rates of drug arrests and punishments among blacks.[126] In other words, black people are being punished for more than just the crimes they commit; rather, in the United States, the criminal justice system has become one of racial censure that entraps and imprisons blacks and their black bodies as a matter of economics as opposed to criminal action alone.

The symbiotic relationship between the prison industrial complex and the criminal justice system further isolates black communities from resources, opportunities, and pathways to full integration into American

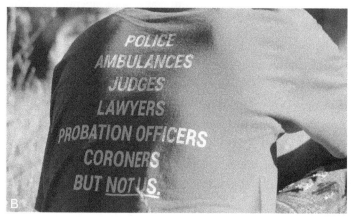

Figure 4.8a, 4.8b

Who "profits" from crime?

Source: Mashaun Ali of Trap House Chicago

citizenship. In this way, the criminal justice system in the United States has become a mechanism through which vast segments of the black population are exploited and segregated into neighborhoods with little political power, shrinking resources, concentrated poverty, decreased educational and economic opportunities, and exposure to high rates of neighborhood violence.

The Child Welfare System

One consequence of the combination of neighborhood segregation, concentrated poverty, and mass incarceration has been the overrepresentation of black youth within the child welfare system. High rates of black male incarceration not only result in the extraction of capital from black communities but also an increase in absentee-father households and a decrease in black marriage rates. Mothers in single-female-headed households often have to work multiple jobs to make ends meet. This may add to parental and family stress, triggering child welfare investigations. In America, the majority of children entering the child welfare system result from cases designated as neglect.[127] However, distinguishing neglect from the circumstances of poverty is very subjective and filtered through our own explicit biases and personal experience, making accurate assessments very difficult to render. Many years ago, at a social service agency at which I worked, several colleagues and I were discussing the clinical needs of a low-income black mother in her thirties and her eight-year-old daughter who had come to the agency for services. One white Portuguese upper-middle-income female clinician shared her opinion that the girl was being neglected. When I asked for the evidence, the clinician replied, "Well, her hair is uncombed, and her clothes are dirty and disheveled." I pointed out that the mother's clothes were also dirty and her hair uncombed. What I saw were the circumstances of poverty and a family in need of resources, not a case of child neglect. What if all the agency's staff had shared the same class and cultural interpretation of neglect? The family would likely have faced a child welfare investigation.

Being a welfare recipient has been shown to increase the likelihood of out-of-home placements for black youth compared with their white counterparts, who are more inclined to receive in-home services and remain united with their families.[128] Two studies in Texas found that race, risk, and income all influence case decisions. More specifically, black American families tended to receive lower risk scores than white families but were more likely than white families to have their cases substantiated, have their children removed from the home, or be recommended for safety services within the home.[129] Disparities also exist between blacks and Latinos. When both groups have similar incomes, Latinos are placed in foster care at rates similar to their proportion of the overall population. However, the rate for blacks is two times their representation in the general population.[130]

In Chicago, the majority of child protection cases fall within two zip codes.[131] The confluence of concentrated hardship alongside racially segregated neighborhoods, the cultural unfamiliarity between workers and families, and racial bias are likely factors contributing to the excessive monitoring and involvement of low-income blacks in the child welfare system.[132] Although black children and youth might account for a small percentage of the local population, the "visibility hypothesis" suggests that the designation of "other" might make them more vulnerable to removal from their families. Racial bias, similar to that existing at every point in the judicial process, exists in the child welfare system, in which black children face higher rates of investigations, designations of abuse and neglect, and exiting from under the supervision and care of the child welfare system.[133]

Youth with child welfare histories have more social and psychological barriers to overcome. The higher burden of child welfare involvement carried by black youth translates into greater obstacles to becoming fully functioning adults. It can also contribute to further social and economic stratification. These youth, relative to their peers with no child welfare histories, report higher rates of depression, drug use, binge drinking during adolescence, and involvement in serious fights requiring medical attention.[134] The behavioral and psychological disruptions related to maltreatment and abuse, combined with the trauma associated with out-of-home placement, can create difficult obstacles for youth to overcome even into adulthood. This trauma can therefore result in a child-welfare-to-prison pipeline that adds to the destabilization of black families and communities and contributes to higher rates of poverty and neighborhood violence.

The Case of Chicago: Structural Disadvantage

Arguably, many American cities are racially segregated. However, as many have frequently noted, Chicago is defined by racial segregation. Although no major racial group dominates the composition of Chicago's population, which is home to relatively equal amounts of blacks, Latinos, and whites, the city is hyper-segregated. Most of the majority-black neighborhoods are located on the South Side, whereas majority-white neighborhoods are mostly on the North Side.

I moved to Chicago in 1999 from New York City and set up residence in Hyde Park, just steps away from the University of Chicago campus, where I began my tenure as an assistant professor. Proudly touted as one of the most racially and economically diverse neighborhoods in Chicago and somewhat of an island on the predominantly black South Side, Hyde Park is a mix of urban mansions, high- and midrise apartment buildings over-looking the lake and downtown, student housing, and senior citizen accom-modations. Beneath this veneer, though, it is racially divided, like the city itself. Local residents know that south of 55th Street, closer to the university campus, marks the "whiter" spaces of Hyde Park, whereas the more racially diverse enclaves are north of the street.

Shortly after my move, still unfamiliar with Chicago's nuances, I needed to purchase some household supplies. I casually asked Tom, a black man in his sixties who provided maintenance for our apartment building, where the clos-est Target store was. At the time, big-box retailers were limited within the city. He replied, "The closest one is on the far North Side." Unaware of the invis-ible forces that defined Chicago's seventy-seven racial enclaves, I asked, "How far is that from here?" Tom replied, "I don't know. We don't go over there." Later, after conversations with many other white and black Chicagoans, I understood what Tom meant. Chicago has several clearly defined racial boundaries across the city that dictate perceptions of safety, desirability, and demand for housing and distinguish the city's attractive places for recreation and resource-rich neighborhoods from places where social and economic disinvestment are rampant. During the past twenty years, I have interacted with numerous whites on the near North Side who have never been to Hyde Park—a mere seven miles away. Similarly, many blacks rarely or never venture north. When I took Michael, my 12-year-old mentee who lives in the Englewood community on the South Side, to Michigan Avenue, it was only the second time he had ever ventured downtown. To him, it was "another country."

Indeed, the majority-white and majority-black spaces in Chicago differ enough that they could be separate countries: one peaceful and the other marked by high rates of neighborhood violence. The vast majority of homicide and gun-related incidents in Chicago disproportionally cluster within a handful of racially isolated and impoverished neighborhoods. In these areas, structural disadvantage—defined as concentrations of poverty, unemployment, and family disruption within geographically defined and racially isolated boundaries—stubbornly persists.[135] Many of Chicago's ecological niches have high rates of residential instability, disproportionate rates of unemployment, elevated concentrations of poverty, and high numbers of single-female-led households. These factors contribute to social disorganization[136] and low community collective self-efficacy, meaning the ability of community members to trust, monitor, and control events within the community.[137] Though some disagreement exists, many scholars have argued that the large variance in rates of crime, violence, and youth delinquency is driven by structural disadvantage and social disorganization regardless of race/ethnicity—but a higher proportion of black Americans reside in predominantly minority communities in which structural disadvantage and social disorganization persist.[138] These dynamics have been exacerbated by the factors discussed earlier, such as white flight, economic disinvestment, the loss of manufacturing jobs from inner cities, the war on drugs, and high rates of black incarceration and family disruption.

Another concept that contributes to the persistence of high racial and economic insularity is the notion of multigenerational stress, meaning the transmission and inheritance of the cumulative effects of neighborhood disadvantage.[139] When families reside in structural disadvantage for significant periods of time, children who are born and raised in such resource-poor settings experience the cumulative negative effects faced by their families, which are compounded by their own experiences. Low-income single parents may still be trying to cope with the stressful past of their own upbringing in addition to working several jobs or long hours to make ends meet. Such realities might limit the time they have to detect or monitor distress symptoms in their children, which might make it harder for them to get needed help. Contributing to the effects of structural disadvantage and social disorganization is the concept of neighborhood embeddedness. Sociologists Ruth Peterson and Lauren Krivo write, "White neighborhoods benefit from the dual privilege of low internal disadvantage as well as embeddedness within a context of other white advantaged areas,"[140] which is highly reflective of many of Chicago's low-resourced, high-violence neighborhoods:

> A common feature of many African American neighborhoods, whatever their internal character, is proximity to communities with characteristics typically associated with higher crime rates, such as high levels of disadvantage and residential turnover. . . . In contrast, white areas are surrounded by neighborhoods where crime-promoting conditions are relatively absent and factors that discourage crime, such as external community investments, are prevalent.[141]

As noted, the majority of Chicago's predominantly black neighborhoods, regardless of being impoverished, working class, or middle class, are clustered on the South Side, whereas predominantly white neighborhoods are on the North Side. Such spatial vulnerability (or embeddedness), according to Sampson, might explain why many majority-black neighborhoods face high crime vulnerability while majority-white neighborhoods do not.[142] This disadvantage can be summed up in the hardship index, a concept that combines crowded housing, poverty levels, unemployment, adults without high school diplomas, dependency, and per capita income into a single measure.[143] Figure 4.9 shows that the neighborhoods in Chicago with the highest hardship index values are majority-black neighborhoods.

Englewood, for example, is 95 percent black[144] and has a hardship index ranging from 76 to 100. Rogers Park, on the far North Side, near where the Target store was located, is 43 percent white,[145] and its hardship index ranges from 26 to 50. These statistics help to quantify the city's geographic

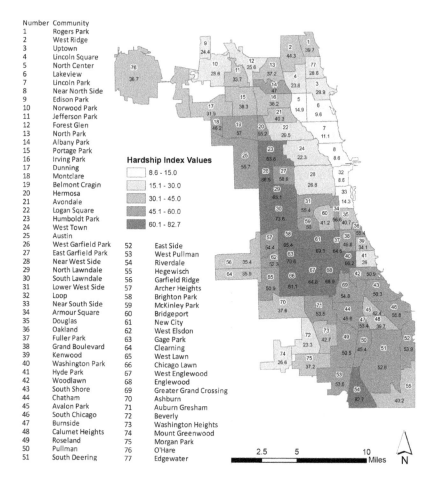

Number	Community
1	Rogers Park
2	West Ridge
3	Uptown
4	Lincoln Square
5	North Center
6	Lakeview
7	Lincoln Park
8	Near North Side
9	Edison Park
10	Norwood Park
11	Jefferson Park
12	Forest Glen
13	North Park
14	Albany Park
15	Portage Park
16	Irving Park
17	Dunning
18	Montclare
19	Belmont Cragin
20	Hermosa
21	Avondale
22	Logan Square
23	Humboldt Park
24	West Town
25	Austin
26	West Garfield Park
27	East Garfield Park
28	Near West Side
29	North Lawndale
30	South Lawndale
31	Lower West Side
32	Loop
33	Near South Side
34	Armour Square
35	Douglas
36	Oakland
37	Fuller Park
38	Grand Boulevard
39	Kenwood
40	Washington Park
41	Hyde Park
42	Woodlawn
43	South Shore
44	Chatham
45	Avalon Park
46	South Chicago
47	Burnside
48	Calumet Heights
49	Roseland
50	Pullman
51	South Deering

52	East Side
53	West Pullman
54	Riverdale
55	Hegewisch
56	Garfield Ridge
57	Archer Heights
58	Brighton Park
59	McKinley Park
60	Bridgeport
61	New City
62	West Elsdon
63	Gage Park
64	Clearning
65	West Lawn
66	Chicago Lawn
67	West Englewood
68	Englewood
69	Greater Grand Crossing
70	Ashburn
71	Auburn Gresham
72	Beverly
73	Washington Heights
74	Mount Greenwood
75	Morgan Park
76	O'Hare
77	Edgewater

Hardship Index Values

- 8.6 – 15.0
- 15.1 – 30.0
- 30.1 – 45.0
- 45.1 – 60.0
- 60.1 – 82.7

2.5 5 10 Miles N

Figure 4.9

The hardship index values of Chicago neighborhoods

Source: "Economic Hardship Index Shows Stark Inequality Across Chicago," Great Cities Institute, University of Illinois at Chicago, September 19, 2016, https://greatcities.uic .edu/2016/09/19/economic-hardship-index-shows-stark-inequality-across-chicago/

inequality, yet they are insufficient in describing the overwhelming context of racial segregation and poverty for those who experience such inequality. Perhaps more revealing is the following poem by David Flynn, a black teenage male, about life on the South Side of Chicago.[146]

South Side

White folks say the transit move better on the Southside
I don't see nothin' but food deserts on the Southside
the police make the product move better on the Southside
but then they wanna tell us do better on the Southside
they say negro stop complain'
work a job and be content
when a check from 4 jobs can barely even pay the rent
good food is miles from here
and all the kids have malnutrition
eating flaming hot for breakfast
smoking blacks and talking shit
the shorties turn cold
drop bodies at 12
the school curriculum is garbage
selling dope for retail
they playing point em out knock em out
and bones on the corner
but what the heck do you except when shorties raising themselves
they making newspaper headlines
out here roomin' blocks when it's 6 hours past their bed time
shorties poppin' pills like it's 6 hours past they med time
with deadminds
and I put that on the bible
brother hurt and they unstable
catch em out here sniffing cain
cause they didn't think that they were able

wear yo suit and go to Harvard
but you can't escape these labels
white supremacy's a demon
why you think they killin' angels
trinna cope with all this pain
that's why I always feel the need to write
out babies turn to hashtags faster than the speed of light
they upin' guns
and empty clips
and seizing rights
please get off yo knees just pleadin'
please get up you need to fight
please get on your p's and q's our babies need a decent life
the system is obese from eating blacks just like we beans and rice
then dippin' us in ethnocentric sauces so we seasoned right
add a touch of black baby blood
the lemon squeezed on ice
see once they finish eating
rub their belly and proceed to mics
to justify they actions
with a speech about our heathen life
deflecting all attention on our youth
and call us thieves and hypes
convincing us that nothin' we do good
like we aren't breathing right

Summary and Conclusion

The history of race in America means that the road to concentrated poverty and violence is a complicated story driven by multiple factors. While the Civil War ostensibly transformed race relations in the United States, it served primarily to shift the overt oppression of slavery to more covert, yet equally structural, oppression. This new form of oppression, evident in Jim Crow laws and the philosophy of "separate but equal," used the language of equality but served to ensure the social and economic marginalization of black people in the United States. The underlying racism and history of racial suppression followed blacks as they migrated from the South to northern and midwestern cities during the Great Migration, resulting in urban black communities becoming increasingly segregated. This process of segregation was exacerbated as whites increasingly migrated out of cities into the suburbs in the 1940s and 1950s. White flight shifted significant political power to the suburbs, decreasing the ability of segregated black communities to enact policies that would help to ensure greater access to resources and equality. Therefore, urban black neighborhoods and communities saw ever-shrinking resources and decreased public and private investment in educational and economic infrastructure and opportunities.

As poverty became more concentrated in segregated urban neighborhoods, a concurrent increase in social distress, including struggling schools, unemployment, violence, and crime, left growing segments of the community without sufficient economic viability. This shift was especially true with regard to opportunities for educational advancement. Post–Civil Rights era schools were, and remain, racially segregated and unequally funded. This inequality imperils the life chances of black youth and successive generations, especially in the face of capital extraction from black communities.

Governmental strategies that emerged in the 1970s to contend with this growing social unrest, including the war on drugs, disproportionately targeted and affected poor minorities, especially black males. The high levels of black male incarceration, sustained over three decades, significantly altered the composition of black families toward predominantly single-mother-led homes. The youth residing in single-female-headed households were at greater risk of being poor, thereby ensuring a cycle of concentrated poverty for successive generations. These low-income black youth, relative to their peers from other racial groups, were also more likely to be targeted for child welfare services, deepening the cycle of poverty, inequality, and disenfranchisement.

The Road to Concentrated Poverty and Neighborhood Violence

Today, among blacks in Chicago, high rates of neighborhood violence are primarily concentrated within a few designated neighborhoods. This pattern is equally present in many American cities, where poverty, high rates of racial segregation, and neighborhood disadvantage continue to exist. The convergence of racial segregation, high rates of poverty, poor school success, overpolicing, and arrests in many of these neighborhoods has resulted in youth being born into zip codes where neighborhood violence is widespread. The complicated interconnection of racial segregation, concentrated poverty, and social distress has created a deep foundation from which inner-city violence has emerged as a serious social problem, a problem that will require systemic changes in neighborhood infrastructure, governmental institutions (e.g., schools and the criminal justice system), and America's complex racial values and beliefs to adequately resolve.

5

THE SCARS OF VIOLENCE

My [American] dream is to graduate from high school and move to
the safer side of Cottage Grove and marry my girlfriend.
—JESSE, AGE 16

Nobody can "treat" a war or abuse, rape, molestation, or any other
horrendous event, for that matter; what has happened cannot be undone.
But what can be dealt with are the imprints of the trauma on body, mind,
and soul: the crushing sensations in your chest that you may label as anxiety
or depression; the fear of losing control; always being on alert for danger or
rejection; the self-loathing; the nightmares and flashbacks; the fog that keeps
you from staying on task and from engaging fully in what you are doing;
being unable to fully open your heart to another human being.
—BESSEL VAN DER KOLK, 2015

Jesse is a 16-year-old male I interviewed in 2009 for a study focused
on how black high school students in the Woodlawn community,
a South Side neighborhood adjacent to the University of Chicago,
were coping with exposure to neighborhood violence. His dreams for the
future were simple: to graduate from high school and marry his childhood
sweetheart. Crossing Cottage Grove, the major boundary avenue separating
the higher-resourced Hyde Park community from his lower-income community of Woodlawn, was a significant life goal because it would improve

his chances of surviving gun violence. He had seen several of his peers killed and knew several others who had been murdered. During the interview, Jesse stated, "I know this young girl who was sitting at her dining room table studying and was killed by a stray bullet—she was only eight years old."The precariousness and fragility of life and the harsh realities of neighborhood violence were Jesse's everyday reality.

Jesse's story, while unique, is representative of the daily struggles that countless other black youth experience on Chicago's South Side. I share Jesse's story and that of other black youth to highlight the ways in which exposure to repeated neighborhood violence alters the developmental pathways of young people living within the context of ongoing structural violence and economic disadvantage.

The Body Keeps the Score is the title of a book by the psychiatrist and trauma expert Bessel van der Kolk about the effects of childhood neglect and abuse. In Jesse's case, like that of many of his peers, his experience of violence changed his world view and the trajectory of his late teenage years. I highlight this title because although researchers, advocates, and practitioners have long acknowledged the often enduring consequences of trauma such as childhood sexual abuse and domestic violence, there is a lag and sometimes denial when it comes to recognizing and addressing the effects on the mind and body of the sustained levels of structural, racial, neighborhood violence and trauma experienced by black youth in America. Van der Kolk argues that trauma is not just an incident that took place in the past but also the scar left by that experience on the mind, brain, and body. This scar has constant consequences for how people attempt to survive in the present and changes what they think, as well as their capacity to think.[1]

For youth who have heard about, witnessed, or been a victim of neighborhood violence on a repetitive basis, the effects of such trauma can linger, sometimes interfering with their abilities to feel secure and at peace and to function in a manner that moves their lives forward. Research has shown that ongoing violence exposure can lead to neurobiological changes, mental health concerns, and strained relationships with peers, teachers, and family members.[2]A growing body of evidence also shows that such exposure is sometimes associated with increased substance use and higher rates of risky sex.[3] These stresses often co-occur, making them even harder for people to manage or disentangle. When the myriad challenges of navigating adolescence are added, it becomes clear that managing the scars of trauma is no simple task for teens. What is more, with their increased independence, adolescents, especially males, may receive less monitoring and support from caregivers, making the management of emotional and life complexities that much harder.

In this chapter, I summarize and integrate current knowledge about the ways in which exposure to neighborhood violence negatively affects youth. I draw on theories and survey data from psychology, criminal justice, social work, public health, and sociology to demonstrate how the aftereffects of neighborhood violence exposures are interrelated. I shared in the first chapter how I became an accidental academic and, prompted by my previous clinical work, began researching whether and how neighborhood violence relates to youth risky sexual behaviors. In this chapter, I highlight several studies that provide evidence linking higher rates of neighborhood violence to youth reporting higher rates of drug use and unsafe sexual behaviors, which can unfortunately render them more vulnerable to acquiring sexually transmitted infections (STIs), including HIV. Neighborhood violence and STI rates are highest among black youth. I conclude the chapter by examining how mental health distress, school difficulties, and involvement with risky peers (all influenced by neighborhood violence) might contribute to an explanation of why neighborhood violence is linked to youth drug use and unsafe sex.

The Impact of Gun Violence: Noah's Story

Even by Chicago's windy standards, it was an unusually cold winter day in 2017 when Noah and I met for an interview. Layers of packed snow lay on the ground after an accumulation of several blistery snowfalls. Noah and I sat in a small office at the University of Chicago's campus, located in the historic Hyde Park neighborhood adjacent to the Woodlawn community. The windowless office, the size of a doctor's examination room, had beige walls, two matching pictures of lilies, and a small round table around which we sat. It was not uncommon for blacks, especially males, to be aggressively policed in Hyde Park, where the university campus police seemed to find them out of place in those privileged white spaces—not uncharacteristic of similar events that happen disturbingly often in America. On rare occasions, campus security even questioned black students attending the university to ask whether they had a legitimate affiliation when entering buildings.

Noah was twenty-one years old, with a short haircut, slight frame, average height, and an olive brown complexion. He was dressed in a sweatshirt, jeans, and sneakers. He leaned forward and touched the edge of the table. I began reading the necessary statements to get his signed permission to interview him and record our talk. "Go ahead, ask me anything," he said with precision in his voice. He seemed eager to speak. His story was complex, had many layers, and provided insights into the tale of two Americas, highlighting the contrasting experiences of youth based on the intersection of race, class, and geography. I was compelled by the weight of his words and moved by the early struggles he had to endure. When he recounted his story, I learned that his slight frame carried not only thirty-odd bullet fragments resulting from a 2015 gunshot incident but also many of the mental and behavioral scars commonly associated with repeated exposure to neighborhood violence.

Noah was born and had spent most of his early youth in the three-square-mile Englewood neighborhood on the South Side of Chicago. In 1960, blacks and whites made up 69 percent and 31 percent of its residents, respectively, and had a median income of $5,579 ($46,151 today, accounting for inflation, and considered lower middle class by today's standards). The Englewood community was once vibrant; a large outdoor shopping mall, anchored by a Sears, was the second busiest shopping district in Chicago and symbolized its economic vitality. However, that Englewood was a far cry from Noah's. By 1980, the total neighborhood population had declined by thirty thousand as a result of large-scale white flight.[4] In 2012, the neighborhood's poverty rate more than doubled that of Chicago at 42 percent, and it continued to increase. The unemployment rate was 21 percent, and less than 30 percent of all residents had obtained a high school diploma.[5]

Figure 5.1

A mural in the Englewood neighborhood of Chicago

Source: Dexter R. Voisin

Figure 5.2

A block in the Englewood neighborhood of Chicago

Source: Dexter R. Voisin

Noah had nine surviving siblings ranging in age from two to twenty-three years. His tenth sibling, a sister, had been killed in a house fire, which he stated the landlord had set deliberately. She would have been fourteen years old at the time of our meeting. His mother had children in quick succession, with her first child born when she was just fourteen years old. Like many of Noah's peers, his was a single-female-headed household. His mother was the family's breadwinner, and his grandmother managed the home and helped raise the children. Noah was born when hundreds of low-skill jobs had already evaporated from the Chicagoland area and decades of uneven welfare policies and the war on drugs had decimated countless black families.

When describing his childhood in Englewood, Noah said, "In my eyes, it was fun . . . because the environment we lived in . . . we [now] see that it was bad, [but] we did not know it was bad. . . . It looked fun for us, and we wanted to do that . . . playing rough and tough . . . but we did not know it was bad." Poverty, high rates of racial segregation, and insularity often coexist. In such environments, desensitization to violence can easily occur. On a national level, as we have seen with the many deadly school shootings and other mass murders that have occurred in the United States, a certain level of desensitization has taken place, with the twenty-four-hour news cycle repeating the traumatic events and the all-too-common playbook of another large mass shooting event every few months. The abhorrent has become the American norm. Similarly, in the context of impoverished black neighborhoods, the easy access to guns and the lack of viable economic and employment opportunities, coupled with despair and desensitization, have normalized neighborhood violence. Oppressed and marginalized groups often normalize their harsh conditions as a form of survival, until, as Noah indicated, "something happens that makes you conscious."

Noah had enrolled in high school but never graduated. Dunbar High School was far from home, and some days he did not attend because he lacked the bus fare. Some weeks, he attended school just two of the five days, and much of that time was spent in detention because of fighting or late arrivals. He eventually transferred to a closer school but ended up dropping out. Noah felt that the climate of disrespect some students displayed

Figure 5.3

Differences in resources: Englewood versus Hyde Park

Source: Sean Blackwell

toward teachers stemmed from homes in which parents did not demand respect from teachers.

Noah said, "I never knew violence was bad because that was all I ever saw." This normalization of violence underscores the problem of insularity, in which youth are not exposed to a broader set of norms and are not aware of other life options. Noah's first incident with the police was in third grade, when officers chased him after getting into a fight. Fighting was the norm, but these were fistfights and occasionally knife fights. Those who had guns would put them down to fight. Guns were around, he said, "but folks were not out there just popping people. . . . It was more controlled." Noah said guns were mostly used for self-protection. He was eight years old when he first saw a gun, and he witnessed his first instance of gun violence in high school: "[My cousin] was arguing with another [girl] over a boy. They were supposed to meet up to fight. My cousin did not know the other girl came with a gun, which her uncle gave her." When his cousin opened the door, the other girl shot her point-blank, killing her. Noah went on to describe several other fatal gunfights involving kids in his neighborhood. He had personally known at least twenty people murdered by gun violence. We discussed how these gun murders affected him. He described feeling trapped in a neighborhood that was locked into a vicious cycle of violence fueled by poverty and a lack of resources. He shared that if kids had meaningful things to do, they would not be hanging out on the block, "getting their hustle on" and using or selling cigarettes—and eventually drugs.

Noah himself had been shot in 2015, on a day that began like any ordinary day. He was shot because of a "neighborhood beef," with folks from one neighborhood coming into another to settle fights and target people randomly. Two years earlier, he had been shot at but not hit. He said that he had been hanging out with a group of kids when a drive-by shooting occurred. "I was just in the wrong place at the wrong time," he said. The day he was shot became his "wake-up call," leading to a series of events that would positively alter the course of his life.

Today, Noah uses poetry and music to express his thoughts about the violence he sees in Englewood, cope with it himself, and sound the alarm for other youth to become socially conscious of the issues affecting them. In a poem entitled "My City" he writes,

They hating my city, toting guns in my city, no faith in my city, don't think I am safe in my city. Too much is going on in my city, with murders and death in my city. Too much is going on with murders and death in my city. My city is breaching. They corrupting my city. People are trying to grow up and make it out of my city.

Figure 5.4

Differences in resources: Englewood versus Hyde Park

Source: Sean Blackwell

Figure 5.5

Differences in resources: Englewood versus Hyde Park

Source: Sean Blackwell

Figure 5.6

Contrasting the promise of the "Building a New Chicago" program: Englewood versus Hyde Park

Source: Dexter R. Voisin (*a*)

Neighborhood Violence and Mental Health

Tavis is a twenty-year-old black male. In a life course similar to Noah's, he had been shot at age fourteen and shot at but not hit five times. At least twenty people he has known had been killed by gun violence, and another thirty had been shot but not killed. Regarding the time he had been shot, he said, "I kept running and running to my house; I was thirteen blocks away from home. I did not even know I was shot until my cousin grabbed me and told me to sit because I was shot." He never received any counseling after this ordeal. The violence made him paranoid about his safety. An elderly woman in his community sold her Xanax (an anxiety medication) to him for $3 a box. He explained, "Youth in Englewood use drugs to deal with not having a future. That is where the drugs come in: marijuana, ecstasy, and blue dolphin [ecstasy in pill form]." He says that when he was high on drugs as a way to cope with stress, if a cop pulled up looking for another Black guy, he could have overreacted and possibly been killed by the officer.

While David and Noah faced similar neighborhood violence, David's story exemplifies the fact that many youth do not have access to counseling or other ways to cope with the stress of constant violence; instead, they often turn to drugs and other dangerous behaviors in response to their mental distress. Serious mental distress includes depression and post-traumatic stress disorder (PTSD). Black youth are exposed to higher rates of neighborhood violence and, as a result, are 20 percent more likely to report serious mental distress, compared with non-Hispanic, white youth.[6] Moreover, black Americans living below the poverty line, relative to their same-race counterparts not living in poverty, are three times more likely to report mental distress (U.S. Department of Health and Human Services Office of Minority Health, 2014).[7] Studies of exposure to neighborhood violence—generally narrowly defined as interpersonal violence taking place outside the home or between people who are not related—have found correlations with negative mental health, including aggression and conditions such as PTSD and depression.[8] Studies have also found strong relationships between structural violence (e.g., poverty, discrimination, exposure to environmental risks) and diminished health and well-being.[9]

PTSD and Its Symptoms

Humankind's oldest texts describe experiences and emotions that can follow violence: recurring flashbacks; nightmares; and feelings of despair, horror, or guilt, among other reactions. People respond to and express the emotions and sensations associated with experiencing violence in different ways, often depending on their place and time. PTSD is a clinical diagnosis developed in the twentieth century to help categorize and treat particular symptoms associated with exposure to violence. While it is not meant to encompass all forms of violence and the ways people respond to violence in every cultural context, the PTSD diagnosis is a tool that can be used to help understand, treat, and allocate resources toward people who experience its symptoms. PTSD is commonly characterized by re-experiencing a traumatic incident, avoiding reminders or situations that may be associated with the trauma, and continuing to experience symptoms of increased over-arousal. Most studies provide some evidence linking neighborhood violence to PTSD symptoms.[10]

However, the use of PTSD as a way of understanding the consequences of traumatic exposure and stress ignores the fact that some populations do not experience single stress events but rather continuous danger, ongoing threat, and structural–economic and social containment. A more appropriate term, then, may be "continuous traumatic stress." This term emerged in the 1980s to describe mental health support provided to victims of political violence in the context of apartheid-era South Africa.[11]

Depression and Other Internalizing Behaviors

Studies have generally found associations among neighborhood violence exposure, depression, and inwardly focused negative behaviors like withdrawal, often called "internalizing behaviors," among adolescents from various racial groups.[12] A longitudinal study of urban students showed that when neighborhood violence increased over one year, and was accompanied by decreases in guardian and peer support, this led to youth using more defensive and confrontational behavioral coping styles, and their reporting higher rates of anxiety, depression, and PTSD. This pattern was more noticeable for boys than girls.[13] A study of the effects of exposure to neighborhood violence on adolescent boys living in cities found that both witnessing and being a victim of neighborhood violence were associated with anxiety and depression for one year following the traumatic event.[14]

Aggression and Other Externalizing Behaviors

Reviews of studies, including three investigations that followed participants from various racial/ethnic groups over an extended period, suggest that neighborhood violence can be associated with behaviors that often result in negative social consequences (called "externalizing behaviors"), such as aggression.[15] Two early and important studies showed that neighborhood violence over a four-year period predicted aggressive behaviors in children[16] and that neighborhood violence (i.e., witnessing violence and victimization) among black and Latino preteen boys was linked to increased aggression in subsequent years.[17] Although some findings are inconsistent, most studies show that girls report more depression and anxiety with regard to neighborhood violence exposure, whereas boys display more aggression and delinquent behaviors.[18]

Moreover, a review of 114 studies showed that neighborhood violence had the strongest relationship to externalizing symptoms such as aggression, delinquency, and symptoms characteristic of PTSD. The relationship with internalizing behaviors such as depression and anxiety, though significant, was less pronounced. Witnessing neighborhood violence had the strongest relationship to externalizing problems, followed by hearing about such violence. However, both types of violence exposure had an equal impact on internalizing problems. PTSD symptoms were equally strong among people who had been victimized and those who had witnessed or heard about neighborhood violence. Compared with children, adults reported more externalizing behaviors in response to neighborhood violence, and children reported more internalizing symptoms than adolescents did.[19]

Neighborhood Violence and Physical Health

Clearly, neighborhood violence can result in physical injury or death. Few studies, however, have examined the direct link between neighborhood violence and physical health. This challenge is complicated by the reality that poverty, neighborhood violence, and availability and access to health-related services, supermarkets, and healthy foods all influence physical health.[20] In addition, it is challenging to identify the unique effects of neighborhood violence on physical health, as mental health issues can also affect the body. For example, it would be difficult to tease out the direct health effects of neighborhood violence on hypertension or elevated cortisol levels.

Nonetheless, some studies have shown that neighborhood violence and health care–seeking behaviors are related. Based on research of youth populations from Baltimore, Maryland; Johannesburg, South Africa; and Ibadan, Nigeria, one study found that youth who had witnessed neighborhood violence were less likely to seek needed health care in all three cities. For youth in Baltimore and Johannesburg, being fearful of everyday dangers was associated with being less likely to seek needed medical care.[21] In Chicago, research has found that among young black men who have sex with men, high exposure to neighborhood violence is related to reduced adherence to HIV medication regimens.[22] It is likely that in violent neighborhoods, residents might engage in fewer outdoor activities, which might translate into poorer physical health. Indeed, the perception of neighborhood crime is associated with less adult physical activity.[23] However, a study that measured crime using city data found that a higher rate of crime was associated with more adolescent physical activity.[24] Researchers have speculated that neighborhood contexts might influence adults and adolescents in very different ways.[25] Adolescents subscribing to the myth of invincibility might respond very differently to the threats of neighborhood violence than adults who may who have witnessed or experienced the loss of someone through violence.

Neighborhood Violence and School Success

Black youth, especially males, face hurdles with regard to academic success, such as poverty, under-resourced schools, a lack of racial representation in staff and materials, racially biased discipline, and racial stigma. In addition to these factors, researchers have found direct links between neighborhood violence exposure and school success (e.g., student–teacher connections, grades, school behavior, school attendance, safety) among various racial/ethnic groups.[26] For instance, one study found that more frequently witnessing a shooting or stabbing was associated with higher rates of grade retention or lower child-reported grades, even after the known differences associated with gender, age, racial/ethnic disparities, and socioeconomic status were taken into account.[27] In a nationally representative sample of middle and high school students, participants who reported neighborhood violence or school danger had poorer attendance, more school difficulties, and lower grades than those who had not reported such violence.[28]

Participants in a different study who had witnessed neighborhood violence reported lower rates of school success (as defined by standardized test scores) over a two-year period. The youth who had witnessed violence reported higher levels of depression before their test scores dropped.[29] A more recent study of black high school youth in Chicago found that for boys, mental distress was the link that explained why youth exposed to neighborhood violence had poorer relationships with their teachers, with mentally stressed youth being more inclined to have challenging relationships with their teachers than those who were not mentally stressed. In the same study, girls who reported being exposed to neighborhood violence (as witnesses or victims) had lower grade point averages (GPAs) and worse relationships with teachers than those who had not been exposed to such violence.[30]

A clinical interaction I had two decades ago illustrates these findings well. In 1997, while completing my doctoral studies at Columbia University,

I worked part-time as a psychotherapist in the Bronx. On a Monday afternoon in early fall, I was sitting at my office desk writing client notes when
the agency got an emergency call from a nearby high school. A fourteen-
year-old black girl, Mary, needed to be seen urgently. The caller reported
that "she had single-handedly thrown her classroom and the rest of the
school into utter chaos." Mary had thrown a chair at a fellow student, physically lashed out at other students, and was uncontrollable. She was sitting
in the principal's office and was on the verge of being suspended when a
teacher who knew Mary realized this behavior was uncharacteristic of her.
The teacher advocated emergency counseling as an alternative to suspension.
I had an opening in my schedule that afternoon, so I met Mary in the waiting room and ushered her into my office.

It was difficult to imagine that this slim young girl who avoided eye contact could have caused such a frenzy in her classroom. She was calm, gentle,
and soft spoken. My mind tried to reconcile the school's narrative with my
observations in that moment. Given her shy manner, I was unsure whether
she would open up or respond to any line of inquiry. We sat less than four
feet apart, and I honored her silence. After a few minutes, I asked, "Mary,
can you tell me what happened?" She began with the prior weekend:

> We live in our apartment on the fourth floor. I was alone in the bedroom
> and looked out the window. This lady was standing on the roof of the
> building opposite mine. She had her two kids and was holding the baby.
> She pushed the kids off the roof, then jumped holding the baby. They hit
> a tree and fell to the ground.

She began and ended the story with the same calm that led her from the
waiting room into my office.

As Mary recounted this terrible trauma, I remembered the weekend television reports of a young black mother in the Bronx who had been diagnosed
with schizophrenia. The coverage stated that she had taken her three children,
dressed in their Sunday best, to the roof of their fourteen-story Section 8
housing complex, threw the two toddlers off the roof, and then jumped,
holding her months-old baby. They all died. The mother had suffered from a

lack of access to adequate mental health care—a form of structural violence. Mary witnessed this horrifying event silently and went to school the following day. At school, the reservoir of built-up feelings broke, and the symptoms of her trauma gushed into the classroom. Her symptoms, which some would call aggression, were a cry for help. Often, victims of PTSD experience not only hyper-arousal and recurring flashbacks of the event, but at younger ages they may be more likely to exhibit what is often viewed as aggression and not easily recognized as behavior stemming from trauma.

I have often wondered what might have happened to Mary if an observant teacher not already overwhelmed by the needs of the students in her many classes had not strongly advocated for Mary, recognizing that she was not acting like herself. What if suspension rather than counseling was ordered? Would school dropout and failure ensue? Without the keen intervention of a discerning teacher, increased suspensions might have been Mary's gateway to juvenile justice system involvement. Many youth labeled as aggressive are often stigmatized by teachers, bystanders, and the "cool kids" and are drawn to or recruited by youth who are commonly referred to as "high risk," "disconnected," or "problematic." In other instances, youth may miss school days after violent episodes in their communities because of safety concerns. Other youth, if they are able to stay in school, may be unable to perform well on academic tasks because of mental health difficulties. Sleep researchers theorize that sleep disruption and elevated cortisol levels, which disrupt concentration levels, could be a biological pathway through which neighborhood violence contributes to the "achievement gap" between black and white students.[31]

Without doubt, hundreds of black youth fall into these all too familiar and unfortunate craters. David, whose story opened this section of the chapter, was one of them. After being shot, he found it difficult to sit in silence, and he would keep moving around in his seat at school. He kept his struggles to himself and did not tell his mother what he was experiencing in school. He did not tell his cousins the extent of his difficulties either, because he believed his cousins would seek retaliation from his shooters. He stopped going to school for several weeks and later dropped out, eventually returning for a diploma after turning eighteen.

Neighborhood Violence and Peer Relationships

Several studies have found a direct link between exposure to neighborhood violence and the disruption of positive, health-promoting relationships. Youth who report higher levels of such violence exposure report fewer relationships with positive peer networks that would support mental health and well-being than those not exposed to violence. In youth-focused research, higher neighborhood violence exposure has been associated with reported gang membership.[32] Some youth living in violent neighborhoods may join gangs out of a desire for protection or economic security.[33] Another possibility is that youth in under-resourced communities may join gangs for social connection and belonging, particularly if youth organizations or other social opportunities are scarce or unavailable.[34]

The use of the term *"gangs"* is often oversimplified, politicized, and sensationalized. *The Chicago Crime Commission Gang Book*, published in 2012, estimates that Chicago is home to more gang members than any other U.S. city, with approximately 150,000 members.[35] The United States has an estimated thirty thousand "gangs" consisting of eight hundred thousand "active" gang members. The Chicago Police Department reports that 80 percent of all shootings and murders in the city are gang related. Nationally in 2012, Latinos/Hispanics accounted for 47 percent of all gang members; blacks, 31 percent; whites, 13 percent; and Asians, 6 percent.[36] However, what constitutes a gang and how membership is counted are subject to politics, controversy, and wide subjectivity. Not all gangs are involved in criminal or violent activity as portrayed in the media. In addition, although some youth may claim gang membership or affiliation, many are not active members or are only on the fringes of these groups. Noah, for example, said he was only nine years old when he had to decide his gang affiliation, which he reported was a common rite of passage for youth in his Englewood community. His gang affiliation was based on that of older family members.

Similarly, in 2009, I interviewed a number of black youth attending one of the academically better-performing high schools on Chicago's South Side. Curtis, a seventeen-year-old black male sat across from me. He had a tidy haircut with a side part and was wearing a reserve officer's training corps uniform. During our conversation, he disclosed that he was also a member of a local gang. I was surprised and had a hard time reconciling his boy-next-door image with his gang affiliation. For him, the gang was a group of guys he could depend on who provided him with a sense of belonging and connection. During the interview series, I also met a sixteen-year-old named Abdul. When I asked him about his extracurricular activities, he said, "I plan to try and get on the school's basketball team. If I don't make the cut, I might just join a gang in my 'hood." From these interviews, I realized that what many of these young men called gangs were not the popular stereotype of antisocial groups primarily engaging in criminal or drug activity but "crews" or a group of "road dogs" that gave them a sense of belonging and group membership. According to my interviewee Willie, some gangs offer respect, and in the tough streets it's all about respect, which keeps people from messing with you and makes you safer.

A history of gangs in Chicago shows that these groups developed along racial/ethnic lines and competed with each other for contracts with the city as volunteer fire departments during the late eighteenth century. These groups fought with each other and also organized social and civic events. When fire departments were formalized by the city, these groups disbanded or sought alternative ways of generating income.[37] Similarly, in contemporary times, some youth who are excluded from or unable to compete in the mainstream economy—because of school failure or a lack of jobs that offer a living wage—may look to gangs, which offer alternative ways to generate income.

Neighborhood Violence, Drug Use, and Risky Sexual Behaviors

David, who we met earlier in this chapter, bought someone else's prescription drugs and used them to cope with neighborhood violence and the resulting stress. The picture of substance use among black youth aged twelve to seventeen years is nuanced. Black youth, relative to peers from other racial/ethnic groups, initiate drinking at later ages and consume less alcohol.[38] However, black youth experience more negative social sanctions from drinking, report more alcohol-related illnesses and injuries, report more symptoms of alcohol dependence, and have more alcohol-related diagnoses compared to their counterparts from other racial/ethnic groups.[39] In addition, some research has shown that although their overall alcohol use is lower, their rate of past-month illicit drug use is higher for some drugs and lower for others relative to that of their counterparts.[40] Illicit drug use typically refers to the use of marijuana, heroin, cocaine, hallucinogens, and inhalants. Black youth typically have lower rates of illicit drug use than white youth during adolescence but have comparable and sometimes higher rates than whites during adulthood.[41]

Only a handful of studies have examined the association between neighborhood violence and substance use. In these studies, results indicate that when youth witnessed violence, it tripled their risk of alcohol, marijuana, and cocaine use.[42] My own work has shown that witnessing neighborhood violence among black youth was related to their alcohol and marijuana use.[43]

As I indicated earlier, the relationship between neighborhood violence and risky sexual behaviors is an area of inquiry I have devoted considerable time to researching over the past two decades. Rates of STIs are especially high among young adults aged fifteen to twenty-four years, who account for almost 50 percent of all new infections. In fact, one in four sexually active female youth among this group contracts chlamydia or human papillomavirus.[44] Partly owing to the heavy burden of structural disadvantage, black American youth bear a heavy STI burden.[45] Although unplanned pregnancy among black youth is on the decline, black youth still experience higher rates of pregnancy relative to their peers of some other racial/ethnic groups.[46] In 2013, the birth rate for black American adolescent females aged fifteen to nineteen years was 39.0 births per one thousand births. The rates for their Latina, white, and Asian counterparts were 41.7, 18.6 births, and 8.7 births per one thousand births, respectively.[47] Teen birth rates decreased from 2014 to 2015 for all racial/ethnic groups, with teen births declining 9 percent for non-Hispanic black girls; however, the U.S. teen pregnancy rate remains high compared with that of other wealthy nations.[48] Teen pregnancy may be related to factors like inadequate access to preventive health care (such as birth control) or relevant health information. Whatever the causes, studies suggest that growing up in poverty, in households with unmarried teen mothers who have low levels of formal educational attainment or in single-parent households, and poor school performance are factors associated with an increased likelihood of teen pregnancy.[49] For instance, research among low-income black youth from three high-poverty Chicago neighborhoods has shown that living in any type of married household (e.g., with biological parents or stepparents) was associated with delayed sexual debut and pregnancy. Stronger parent–child relationships were associated with delayed sexual onset, and pregnancy rates were reduced when adolescents' social networks included more working adults.[50] It has often been speculated that in impoverished communities in which mortality rates are high and youth lack the opportunities or skills to obtain sustained employment and/or attend college, youth may engage in early parenting as an alternative rite of passage into adulthood.

Collectively, an increasing number of empirical studies across various youth populations show that high rates of neighborhood violence exposure (as witnesses, victims, or both) are positively related to youth HIV risk behaviors, such as having sex without condoms, having multiple sexual partners, and using drugs during sex.[51] For instance, in terms of being a victim of neighborhood violence, a study of black American high school boys, after considering the effects of income, family composition, and social network norms, found that such exposures were associated with higher rates of sexual risk behaviors.[52] Similarly, another study of multiethnic youth aged fourteen to nineteen years, after considering the effects of poverty-related variables and household composition, found that victims of neighborhood violence were almost four times more likely to have risky sex than their peers who had not been exposed to such violence.[53]

With regard to witnessing neighborhood violence, studies have found that even after accounting for the known effects of race, gender, low socioeconomic status, and family factors, witnessing neighborhood violence was related to higher rates of risky sex. More specifically, among a racially diverse sample of youth who had reported prior juvenile justice system involvement, participants who had witnessed violence in the year before being detained were twice as likely to report having risky sex than those who had not witnessed violence in the previous year.[54]

Researchers have attempted to determine whether being a victim of or witness to violence differently affects teenagers' engagement in drug and sexual behaviors known to increase rates of HIV acquisition. Their findings suggest that being a victim of violence has a stronger relationship to these risk behaviors, compared with witnessing violence. For instance, in a study of 517 racially diverse adolescent girls seeking contraceptives, participants who had witnessed neighborhood violence were two to three times more likely to report having intercourse with a risky sexual partner and having sex after they had used drugs.[55] Participants who had experienced violence versus those who had witnessed violence were two to four times more likely to report having sex with strangers, having multiple sexual partners, and testing positive for STIs.[56] These findings show that although witnessing and being a victim of neighborhood violence are related to higher rates of drug use and risky sex, the effect of being victimized is greater than that of only witnessing violence. Additional studies that followed participants over an extended period provide further evidence that youth exposed to violence report more instances of engaging in HIV-related risky sexual behaviors than youth not exposed to violence.[57] Table 5.1 provides a summary of several studies showing linkages between exposures to neighborhood violence and higher rates of risky sex.

Given the growing number of studies showing relationships between exposure to neighborhood violence and higher rates of risky sexual behaviors among youth, I sought to investigate some of the factors that might account for this linkage. In 2009, I conducted a large survey of black youth from Chicago's South Side, most of whom lived in communities in which neighborhood violence was higher than the city average. Results showed that youth who had higher GPAs and better relationships with teachers were more inclined to report lower rates of risky sexual behaviors than their peers who had lower GPAs and poorer relationships with teachers. The link between school performance and risky sex was explained by peer factors,

Table 5.1 Selected Studies: Links Between Youth Exposure to Neighborhood Violence and Risky Sex

Authors (Year)	Purpose	Details	Results
Albus, Weist, and Perez-Smith (2004)	To examine the link between violence exposure and health risk behaviors	Number of participants: 167 Age: 10–19 years Gender: male, female Ethnicity: majority black Control variables: age, gender, ethnicity Study design: cross-sectional	Knowledge of violence was associated with substance use and sex. Victimization was associated with sex.
Berenson, Wiemann, and McCombs (2001)	To examine the link between violence exposure and health risk	Number of participants: 517 Age: 9–18 years	Girls who witnessed violence were two to three times more likely than nonexposed peers to report using drugs before sex and having intercourse with a partner who had multiple partners. Girls who were victims of neighborhood violence only were two to four times more likely than nonvictimized peers to report early sexual debut, sex with strangers, multiple sex partners, and positive STI tests.

(continued)

Table 5.1 Selected Studies: Links Between Youth Exposure to Neighborhood Violence and Risky Sex (*continued*)

Authors (Year)	Purpose	Details	Results
		Gender: female	Girls who were both witnesses to and victims of neighborhood violence were three to six times more likely than their nonexposed peers to use drugs before sex.
		Ethnicity: 25% white, 42% black, 30% Hispanic	
		Control variables: race, age, school enrollment, grade retention	
		Study design: cross-sectional	
Brady (2006)	To examine the relationship between lifetime neighborhood violence exposure and risk behaviors	Number of participants: 319	Greater lifetime violence exposure was associated with greater lifetime sexual risk taking (ever had sex, number of sexual partners, number of partners in last three months).
		Age: 18–20 years	
		Gender: male, female	
		Ethnicity: majority white	
		Control variables: gender, ethnic minority status, personality characteristics, aggression, family socioeconomic status, family support, neighborhood collective efficacy	
		Study design: cross-sectional	

Stiffman, Dore, Cunningham, and Earls (1995)	To examine the relationship between personal and environmental factors and changes in HIV risk behaviors	Number of participants: 602 Age: 16–21 years Gender: male, female Ethnicity: majority black Control variables: earlier problem behaviors Study design: longitudinal	Substance use combined with number of neighborhood murders predicted increased HIV risk behaviors from adolescence to adulthood. Childhood sexual abuse combined with number of neighborhood murders predicted increased HIV risk behaviors from adolescence to adulthood.
Voisin (2003)	To examine the relationship between violence victimization and sexual risk behaviors	Number of participants: 120 Age: 14–17 years Gender: male Ethnicity: black Control variables: socioeconomic status, household composition, family support, negative peer influences Study design: cross-sectional	Male victims of neighborhood violence were more likely than nonexposed peers to engage in HIV risk behaviors.

(continued)

Table 5.1 Selected Studies: Links Between Youth Exposure to Neighborhood Violence and Risky Sex *(continued)*

Authors (Year)	Purpose	Details	Results
Voisin (2005)	To examine the relationship between neighborhood violence and HIV risk behaviors	Number of participants: 409 Age: 14–18 years Gender: male, female Ethnicity: majority black, Hispanic Control variables: age, family composition, income, parents' education level, self-efficacy Study design: cross-sectional	Youth exposed to neighborhood violence were three times more likely to report sex without condoms, sex after drug use, and sex with multiple partners than nonexposed peers.
Voisin, Chen, Fullilove, and Jacobson (2015)	To examine the relationship between exposure to neighborhood violence and sexual behaviors	Number of participants: 7,726 (national sample) Age: 18–27 years Gender: male, female Ethnicity: black, Hispanic, white Control variables: age, gender, parental education, family structure Study design: cross-sectional	Greater exposure to violence was related to earlier sexual initiation and more sexual partners in the previous twelve months and in the participants' lifetime compared with less exposure. Greater violence exposure had stronger effects for males than females and weaker effects for blacks than Hispanics or whites.

| Voisin, Salazar, Crosby, DiClemente, Yarber, and Staples-Horne (2007) | To examine the relationship between witnessing neighborhood violence and health risk behaviors | Number of participants: 550

Age: 14–18 years

Gender: male, female
Ethnicity: 41% white, 39% black
Control variables: gender, free school lunch, religiosity, family social support, neighborhood monitoring
Study design: cross-sectional | Youth exposed to neighborhood violence in the previous twelve months prior to being detained were 1.7 times more likely to have not used a male condom, 1.6 times more likely to be high on alcohol or drugs during sex, and 2.1 times more likely to have sex with a partner who was high on drugs within the two months prior to being detained than nonexposed peers. |

Sources: Kathleen E. Albus, Mark D. Weist, and Alina M. Perez-Smith, "Associations Between Youth Risk Behavior and Exposure to Violence: Implications for the Provision of Mental Health Services in Urban Schools," *Behavior Modification* 28, no. 4 (2004): 548–64; Abbey B. Berenson, Constance M. Wiemann, and Sharon McCombs, "Exposure to Violence and Associated Health-Risk Behaviors Among Adolescent Girls," *Archives of Pediatrics & Adolescent Medicine* 155, no. 11 (2001): 1238–42; Sonya S. Brady, "Lifetime Community Violence Exposure and Health Risk Behavior Among Young Adults in College," *Journal of Adolescent Health* 39, no. 4 (2006): 610–13; Arlene Rubin Stiffman, Peter Dore, Renee M. Cunningham, and Felton Earls, "Person and Environment in HIV Risk Behavior Change Between Adolescence and Young Adulthood," *Health Education Quarterly* 22, no. 2 (1995): 211–26; Dexter R. Voisin, "Victims of Community Violence and HIV Sexual Risk Behaviors Among African American Adolescent Males," *Journal of HIV/AIDS Prevention & Education for Adolescents & Children* 5, nos. 3–4 (2003): 87–110; Dexter R. Voisin, "The Relationship Between Violence Exposure and HIV Sexual Risk Behaviors: Does Gender Matter?" *American Journal of Orthopsychiatry* 75, no. 4 (2005): 497–506; Dexter R. Voisin, Pan Chen, Robert Fullilove, and Kristen C. Jacobson, "Community Violence Exposure and Sexual Behaviors in a Nationally Representative Sample of Young Adults: The Effects of Race/Ethnicity and Gender," *Journal of Social Service Research* 41, no. 3 (2015): 295–306; Dexter R. Voisin, Laura F. Salazar, Richard Crosby, Ralph J. DiClemente, William L. Yarber, and Michelle Staples-Horne, "Witnessing Community Violence and Health-Risk Behaviors Among Detained Adolescents," *American Journal of Orthopsychiatry* 77, no. 4 (2007): 506–13.

with specific differences based on gender. Doing well in school academically and believing that teachers care about and treat students fairly are factors that can influence youth sexual behaviors. For boys, having a higher GPA was associated with having had their first vaginal sexual experience (i.e., sexual debut) at an older age and reporting lower rates of risky sex (i.e., fewer sexual partners and more consistent condom use). Also for boys, having poorer bonds or relationships with teachers was associated with higher rates of risky sex. In short, boys who had poorer bonds with teachers were more inclined to report engaging in riskier sex than boys with stronger bonds with teachers. Belonging to a gang was the pathway that explained this relationship. My colleagues and I speculated that failing in school led to some youth being drawn to or recruited by gangs, some of which endorsed more risky sexual practices. For girls, higher GPAs were associated with both sexual debut at an older age and lower rates of risky sex; this association was explained by the girls' belonging to peer networks that supported risky norms, such as drug use and sex without condoms.[58] Peers are influential in the lives of all youth, and the norms and habits that these social networks promote have a powerful socializing effect on their members. However, research has also shown that high rates of neighborhood violence are associated with decreases in parental monitoring, which are linked to youth engaging in more drug use and risky sex.[59] This finding might suggest that youth risk behaviors may escalate when parental monitoring is diminished or caregivers are distracted from these functions because of their own stress and the trauma associated with a lack of neighborhood safety.

The Role of Trauma

In this section, I focus on trauma and the ways it can affect a person's health and well-being, even long after a traumatic event has occurred. Trauma is commonly defined as "an emotional response to a terrible event like an accident, rape, or natural disaster."[60] As noted in the section on PTSD earlier in this chapter, the concept of trauma, in its clinical usage, has been used to help people understand and deal with feelings, sensations, and ways of being that may have flowed from their experience of particular traumatic events. Although they are common and predictable responses to terrible events, trauma symptoms nonetheless often create difficulties as people try to manage the day-to-day realities of their lives.

However, the concept of trauma transcends this clinical usage, and, as with almost any well-known idea, *trauma* means different things to different people. It has been used to describe people's wide-ranging reactions to diverse phenomena, including difficult experiences that are not one-time events, like a single violent attack or a deadly hurricane, but ongoing experiences such as discrimination and social marginalization. So, although a growing body of research has examined connections among difficult experiences, trauma symptoms, and other outcomes, such as susceptibility to disease or mental distress, study findings should not be generalized beyond the parameters of the studies themselves. Much of what is theorized about the enduring and sometimes harmful effects of trauma on people's bodies comes from research focused on severe instances of suffering and neglect experienced by young children, studies of sexual abuse, and even laboratory studies of nonhuman animals that simulate stressful circumstances and then monitor their responses. There is a dearth of systematic research studies on the impacts of neighborhood violence on body processes, health, and mental factors that have examined effects beyond a time frame of five years. Most of what we know about the effects of trauma is based on studies in which data were measured at a single time point. So, although the available trauma studies may help us to theorize and, in time, better predict the ways that neighborhood violence may impact people's health and well-being, their results should be interpreted only as indications that under particular stressful circumstances, people and nonhuman animals alike sometimes experience changes to their bodies that may affect their health and well-being in long-lasting ways.

Racial Problems in the Discussion of Trauma

As discussed in previous chapters, the United States has a long history of powerful actors using the myth of black inferiority to justify systemic oppression and racial inequities. Chattel slavery, Jim Crow laws, racist literacy tests as conditions of voting, racial bias in drug sentencing, and countless other oppressive structures have been created and defended by those with disproportionate power on the purported basis that black people are "different," "less than," "pathological," "dysfunctional," "primitive," or "culturally inferior." Science has always been an instrument of white supremacy, and many now-discredited studies by prominent intellectuals have been used to provide a veneer of objectivity and sophistication to widely held racist "common sense." One example is the pseudoscience of phrenology, the measurement of human skulls, which is now utterly discounted; another is scientific racism, based on the practice of separating individuals into biologically distinct, discrete races, an idea no longer considered scientific but once a dominant belief among the (at the time almost exclusively white male) scientific community. This racist logic could be found among conservatives and liberals alike. In an article on racist trauma narratives, the American author and historian Ibram X. Kendi writes,

> When racist proslavery whites in the nineteenth century claimed slavery had taken black people from the wilds of Africa and civilized them, abolitionists and scholars flipped the script in their responses. They replied that slavery (and later segregation) had degraded black people, ravishing their minds as much as their bodies. Racial reformers, whether they identified as liberal, progressive, or radical, have done the same ever since, agreeing with the racist premise of black inferiority, and then claiming the inferiority stemmed from the history of oppression.[61]

Kendi calls this the "oppression–inferiority thesis."[62] Given this history, it is important to acknowledge that the idea of black biological difference and inferiority has long existed in American society and social science and to avoid tapping into these racist currents of thought in some contemporary version of this thesis. This approach includes rejecting any attempts to generalize trauma symptoms beyond study populations or to link neighborhood violence related to trauma with mental or physical outcomes not captured by the studies themselves.

Recently, I was interviewed by the Public Broadcasting Service for a documentary seeking to understand why some blacks hold "conspiracy beliefs about HIV" and thus experience lower rates of HIV testing and health care use. In the carefully lit space, before the cameras rolled, I sat down with the producer, a thirty-something white female. She said, "I am aware that how I edit these interviews will shape how the narratives are being told and whose perspective gets privileged." I told her I understood the weight that she was saddled with based on her position of power and privilege as the producer and editor and as a white person. I mentioned a similar dilemma regarding the power of the storyteller to shape the narrative of others that I was struggling with when writing this book. I secretly wished that this preliminary discussion had been captured and would make its way into the documentary to reflect the complex challenges of telling, retelling, and constructing our own narratives and those of others.

The producer apologized for being ignorant of how these HIV conspiracies could still exist. The effects of structural trauma often get lost on privileged groups but are inescapable to people who are marginalized. One of the entitlements of being privileged is not having to be aware of one's advantage. In brief, I highlighted the health and social disparities that underscored the evidence for the existence of the "two Americas." I shared that fears of genocide in some black communities are not paranoia but are supported by a legacy of violent attacks, many of which are discussed in chapter 4 of this book: institutionalized chattel slavery, Jim Crow laws, the Tuskegee experiment, the war on drugs, biased and unevenly applied welfare policies, state-sanctioned slayings of young black males by police officers, and more. "These are survival strategies based on a rational-choice model," I explained. "Some blacks are making choices not to get HIV tested based on the documented fact that this 'America the Beautiful' has been violent toward blacks, especially those who are poor and the most vulnerable." Behind the camera, the producer nodded her head and became increasingly solemn. After the camera stopped rolling, she remarked, "There is so much collective insight from these interviews. . . . These are stories that must be told."

Findings from Trauma Studies

With this context firmly in mind, here I summarize some findings from trauma studies, which have led many health researchers and public health advocates to speculate that the enduring effects of trauma on the developing body may contribute to the health disparities facing marginalized populations, including people living in poverty. To put these health inequities in perspective, here are some facts about the relationships among poverty, inequality, and health. First, people living in poverty have demonstrably worse health than their higher-income counterparts, with health disparities showing up early in life and increasing over time.[63] On average, as income increases along the socioeconomic scale, one's health improves.[64] In the United States, past and present discrimination against racial and ethnic minority groups contributes to inequities in health care access, quality, and outcomes.[65] For instance, disparities in the development of chronic diseases often show up by the time racial/ethnic-minority children are preschool-aged, even when controlling for income and other factors, and these disparities persist over the life course.[66] Many scientific studies show that in places with greater economic and health inequalities, the overall population health is poorer, suggesting than in societies with greater inequality, the entire country suffers,[67] and answering the enduring question of why high-resource individuals should care about those who are marginalized or embedded into layers of structural violence. The answer is simple: These inequalities affect us all—economically, socially, mentally, and morally.

Biomedical research studies on trauma often seek to illuminate how experiences become encoded in the body and whether or how these biological imprints in turn affect the body's continuing development. One area of research focuses on epigenetics, the study of how experiences and exposures affect gene expression. Studies in this area have suggested that adversity in early childhood may interact with children's developing bodies to influence gene expression throughout life, affecting one's risk of developing various diseases even into adulthood.[68] Some child development experts have attempted to conceptualize the stress–health relationship using the concept of "toxic stress," defined as frequent or prolonged activation of the body's stress-response system.[69] The well-known Adverse Childhood Experiences Study surveyed more than seventeen thousand adults during the course of a medical examination, asking detailed questions about childhood exposures to stressful circumstances, such as maltreatment, neglect, food insecurity, and family mental illness. The study, which has since been replicated with a diverse range of participants, found that those with more frequent or intense early stressful exposures were more likely to experience health problems including cardiovascular disease, cancer, diabetes, depression and other mental health difficulties, and miscarriages and were also more likely to use tobacco, alcohol, and illicit drugs.[70]

These and other prominent studies have led many public health advocates to raise awareness about the social determinants of health, defined by the Centers for Disease Control and Prevention and the World Health Organization as "the circumstances in which people are born, grow up, live, work, and age and the systems put in place to deal with illness. These circumstances are in turn shaped by a wider set of forces: economics, social policies, and politics."[71] According to the U.S. Department of Health and Human Services, the social determinants of health include exposure to violence, as well as positive, health-promoting resources like "safe and affordable housing, access to education, public safety, availability of healthy foods, local emergency/health services, and environments free of life-threatening toxins."[72] The Robert Wood Johnson Foundation's Commission to Build a Healthier America summarizes the impacts of place, especially places of concentrated disadvantage, on health: "Where we live, learn, work, and play can have a greater impact on how long and well we live than medical care. Our zip code may be more important to our health than our genetic code."[73]

Studies of children who have experienced severe early trauma suggest that extreme neglect and harm can dramatically affect young children's development. Research suggests that the presence of supportive, nurturing care can provide a powerful buffer against early adversity. For instance, international studies of children raised in large, warehouse-like institutions with inadequate care and social interaction have shown that, compared with children not raised in such environments, these children were at greater risk of exhibiting neurological differences; significant delays in language development, executive functioning, and fine and large motor coordination; and learning and attention difficulties.[74] In contrast, when the children were removed from these institutions and placed in settings that provided stimulation and affection, they generally demonstrated improvements, suggesting that an early response to negative environments can have corrective effects. This finding has also been corroborated by other studies showing that among adopted orphans and children in foster care with severe neglect histories, the longer a child lives in an extremely unstimulating and unresponsive environment, the greater the chance that the child will demonstrate intellectual and social difficulties.[75] In contrast, the younger the age at which a child is removed from seriously harmful, insecure, and unresponsive circumstances and placed in a safe, nurturing, encouraging home, the greater the child's average development.[76]

While these studies do not center on neighborhood violence specifically, they do suggest what many people have long believed and reported: that experiences of great adversity can affect people long after any particular difficult events have passed and that these experiences can make them sicker, make daily functioning more difficult, and sometimes disrupt their relationships with others. Strong correlations among poverty, inequality, and diminished health and well-being have led public health organizations to conclude that eliminating these negative social determinants of health will markedly improve health and welfare. In addition, the repeated finding that responsive, nurturing relationships can buffer young children against the developmental consequences of severe early adversity suggests that society should take concerted steps to support families so that they can, in turn, have the resources to care for one another to their fullest capacities.

A Model of the Spheres Influenced by Neighborhood Violence

Several years ago, I submitted a conference abstract to a prominent international conference based on one of my earlier studies showing that youth who reported witnessing higher rates of neighborhood violence were more inclined to report higher rates of drug use and risky sex compared with peers not exposed to such violence. The conference organizers rejected my abstract submission, stating, "We do not see the link between exposure to neighborhood violence and risky sex." Ironically, insights from decades-old research showing that girls who had been victims of childhood sexual abuse were at greater risk for drug use and risky sex had been compartmentalized separately from neighborhood-related trauma. My framing of neighborhood violence as a public health concern was lost on the conference reviewers. As discussed in chapter 2, the United States faces a unique set of challenges with guns, and the vast majority of neighborhood violence witnessed and experienced by youth in this country involves guns. Similar to the conference review panel, our researchers, health care systems, and policy-makers often struggle to integrate the multiple ways in which neighborhood violence exposures affect youth behavioral health. I sought to help bridge this gap by proposing and testing a conceptual model using data obtained from black youth living in Chicago.

I reviewed the existing research, incorporated theory, and integrated my clinical observations and those of colleagues to develop a conceptual model that may explain the interaction of the various domains that research suggests are often negatively affected by exposures to neighborhood violence and how these may interact to increase the rate of sexual risk behaviors among youth repeatedly exposed to trauma from neighborhood violence. I hoped that this effort would help to challenge and reframe the often-pejorative narrative of black youth, which emphasizes pathology and deficiency without consideration of social and structural contexts. In addition, after decades of providing clinical services and conducting multiple research studies, it became obvious to me that educators, mental health and juvenile justice system workers, and public health scholars, although focused on improving youth behavioral health outcomes, did not sufficiently consider how exposure to neighborhood violence may compromise the outcomes they were concerned with (e.g., those related to mental health, education, and sexual reproductive health) or how these domains may interact to promote or curtail adolescent development.

As summarized earlier in this chapter, research and clinical evidence shows that neighborhood violence can have deleterious effects on mental health, school engagement, and the development of health-promoting peer relationships. Neighborhood violence can also be associated with an uptake in drug use and risky sex among various youth populations. However, these studies fail often to capture the full range of aftereffects associated with neighborhood violence—consequences that have been linked, in other studies, to a range of factors that can influence youth development. My conceptual model attempts to bring these findings into conversation with each other to provide a fuller picture of the potential ways that neighborhood violence can affect young people.

Figure 5.7 illustrates the interaction of social spheres (i.e., structural, community, school, peer, and individual factors) that researchers rarely include when considering the aftereffects of neighborhood violence exposure. Structural disadvantages, including racial/ethnic discrimination and inequities, poverty, unemployment, strained or disrupted social support networks, and access to health care, among others (discussed in chapter 4), are important variables that influence all domains of this model. Many of the studies summarized earlier in this chapter reflect the increasing recognition that environmental factors influence youth behaviors such as risky sex.[77] Given this, the model is based on the assumption that disparities associated with higher rates of neighborhood violence (e.g., mental, social, and behavioral health concerns; low school success; involvement with peer groups engaged in risky behaviors) result in differential rates of risky sexual behaviors such as early sexual debut, having multiple sex partners, and incorrect and inconsistent condom use, among others. A major innovation of this model is that it conceptually frames certain variables traditionally considered final outcomes in other studies, perhaps because of disciplinary boundaries, as pathways that provide a link from neighborhood violence exposures to drug use and risky sex.

Figure 5.7 shows a conceptual model explaining possible pathways linking neighborhood violence to risky sexual behaviors among youth. The solid lines represent research-based associations, and the dotted lines represent posited associations that require further testing. The solid lines indicate that

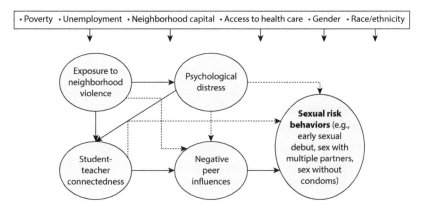

Figure 5.7

Youth neighborhood violence and youth risky sex: psychological distress, school effects, and peer influences as linking pathways

neighborhood violence exposures are related to low school success by way of psychological distress and that low school success and HIV risk behaviors are mediated by peer influence.[78] The posited relationships are based on earlier conceptual work and clinical observations and need to be further tested in experiential work.

For this proposed conceptual model to support future work in the area of neighborhood violence and its impact on youth development, several important considerations need to be acknowledged. Several of the studies supporting the model did not consider the impact of gender or poverty. Few studies have systematically explored how structural disadvantage with regard to factors like racial/ethnic discrimination, unemployment, lack of neighborhood social capital, and access to health care may influence the domains presented in this model. Because such factors are social drivers of behavioral health, these gaps in knowledge represent a major area for future inquiry. Another major consideration is that the vast majority of studies on the effects of exposure to neighborhood violence have been conducted using cross-sectional studies, meaning that they look at a sample population at a particular moment in time. Few studies have followed participants from pre-adolescence to adolescence or into adulthood.[79] More multiyear studies are needed to assess the short- and long-term effects of exposure to neighborhood violence.

Finally, measurements of important concepts such as neighborhood violence exposure, school success, and peer influence often vary across studies. Although arguments can be made for measuring these constructs in different ways, measurement differences pose significant challenges when researchers attempt to compare findings across studies. For instance, when neighborhood violence is combined into a single measure including both witnessing and being a victim of violence, it is difficult to tease out the unique effects of each. In addition, many studies of the effects and consequences of violence exposure have been conducted with racially diverse samples[80] or small sample sizes that have sometimes made it impossible to identify trends that may exist along racial/ethnic or gender lines. As noted, not all youth are affected by neighborhood violence in the same ways.[81] It is likely that factors such as personal traits, gender, age, family characteristics, and social support may moderate many of the associations in the model, suggesting the need for a large, diverse sample and an analysis of how these factors may affect outcomes differently.

Pathways Linking Neighborhood Violence Exposure to Youth Sexual Behaviors

Models of human behaviors can yield significant value in helping us understand complex forces that may influence people. The academic literature offers many such models, some of which have never been tested. As a clinician who stumbled into the halls of academia, I wanted to produce knowledge that would make a difference by connecting neighborhood-level trauma to mental health, education, and public health concerns by testing several of the relationships that I had come to observe during my years of clinical practice.

I secured permission from Chicago Public Schools (CPS) to recruit a sample of three hundred black youth attending a South Side high school.

The approval process was complicated. Interestingly, CPS did not object to questions about exposure to neighborhood violence but voiced concerns about questions relating to sexual behaviors, several of which I had to discard. The research team and I did not expect the overwhelming interest in participating that we received from students; we were approached by hundreds of teenagers. Certainly the $10 compensation was a significant incentive, but we also received feedback that many students appreciated the opportunity to tell their stories, as they felt the topics were important. We received permission from CPS and the University of Chicago's research review board to increase the number of study participants beyond our initial goal of three hundred, and we enrolled all students who expressed interest until the study funds ran out at participant number 673.

The study participants ranged in age from thirteen to nineteen years and were attending regular high school classes (i.e., non–special education classes). Over a two-week period, we asked them questions about exposure to neighborhood violence, as well as about their friendship groups, their relationships with teachers, and other things that were of importance to them. We ended up with 563 completed surveys with usable data from 219 boys and 344 girls who self-identified as black. The majority (55 percent of boys and 54 percent of girls) lived in single-female-headed households, and 61 percent of boys and 59 percent of girls reported receiving free school lunch, an indicator of socioeconomic status.

We found that participants who reported being exposed to higher rates of neighborhood violence also tended to report poorer positive connections or experiences with their high school teachers. Higher rates of exposures to neighborhood violence were also associated with having more close friends who endorsed norms of using alcohol and other drugs and having sex without condoms. In addition, youth who reported being exposed to higher versus lower levels of neighborhood violence also said they experienced more feelings of aggression, had engaged in their first sexual experience at or before age thirteen, and engaged in more risky sexual behaviors, meaning sex without condoms, sex while using drugs, and sex with more than one person at the same time.[82] Figure 5.8 shows the overall main findings of the study, which indicated that youth who

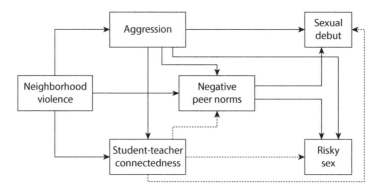

Figure 5.8

Pathways linking neighborhood violence and youth risky sex: Solid lines show statistically significant relations accounting for the effects of age, gender, and socioeconomic status

reported higher rates of neighborhood violence exposure had greater levels of aggression than their less exposed peers, which in turn was associated with having initiated sex on or before age thirteen and engaging in risky sex. Neighborhood violence was also associated with negative peer norms, which in turn were linked to sexual debut before age thirteen and risky sex. Youth who reported exposure to more neighborhood violence also reported higher rates of aggression than their less exposed peers, which in turn were related to having peers who engaged in risky behaviors such as using drugs and having sex without condoms.

Although youth who were exposed to higher rates of neighborhood violence reported poorer relationships with their teachers than their less exposed peers, poor relationships with teachers were not associated with early sexual initiation or having risky sex. Without question, however, prior research has indicated that school engagement markers, such as attendance and the quality of one's relationships with teachers, are associated with whether youth engage in risky sex.[83] Additionally, we know that exposure to neighborhood violence is a threat to positive school engagement, and this study found that youth who were exposed to higher rates of neighborhood violence experienced diminished relationship quality with their teachers compared with their less exposed peers. However, in this study, the data did not indicate that compromised relationships with teachers correlated with youth having early or risky sex.[84]

The overall findings from the study support several components of the conceptual model I have proposed, except for the teacher–student connectedness factor. The model integrates several risk domains associated with HIV risk behaviors and considers how neighborhood violence exposure might be related to psychological distress, behavioral health concerns, low school success, and risky peer influences. In later chapters, I will build on these theories and findings by suggesting potential interventions to help address the negative effects of neighborhood violence on adolescent behavior, health, and well-being.

Summary and Conclusion

Youth growing up in poor neighborhoods are often viewed from the perspective of their circumstances. Seldom are their stories seen through a complex lens that considers how being exposed to threats of neighborhood violence on a daily basis can negatively affect their mental health, challenge their abilities to perform well in school, shape the choices they make about friendships, and even influence their intimate sexual relationships. Noah's and David's stories illustrate how mental health, school success, and peer relationships can be altered by repeated exposures to neighborhood violence. Although unique, their stories share some common themes with those of many other youth born into similar zip codes, whose life trajectories and developmental outcomes have been significantly altered by neighborhood violence exposures.

In proportion to their overall population, more black Americans than white Americans live in poverty. The crushing effects of poverty combined with entrenched racial residential segregation are associated with higher rates of neighborhood violence. Compared with other types of violence (e.g., family and school violence), neighborhood violence occurs more frequently and is often repetitive. Studies have documented that youth exposed to high rates of neighborhood violence, compared with peers reporting lower rates of or no exposure, experience more mental health difficulties, poorer academic success, higher rates of gang involvement, and elevated rates of illegal drug use and risky sex. Although research from the fields of psychology, education, criminology, and public health individually show these outcomes, few studies have attempted to better understand how these factors might be linked.

I sought to test the following clinical assumptions using survey data collected from black youth on Chicago's South Side: Youth exposed to high rates of such violence are more inclined to report higher rates of depression, anxiety, aggression, and other types of mental health challenges than their less exposed peers. These youth are also at greater risk of having poorer relationships with teachers and reporting poorer academic performance, in part a result of the disrupting effects of mental stress. Failure in school, coupled with the need to belong, can lead youth who are having school and behavior difficulties to bond with other troubled youth, thereby encouraging them into behaviors such as gang involvement, problematic drug use, and risky sex.

The results from the survey data generally supported most of my speculations, with the exception of the student–teacher connectedness factor. Specifically, youth who reported high neighborhood violence exposure also reported greater levels of mental distress, shown as aggression, than their less exposed peers. Higher rates of aggression were linked to these youth having initiated sex on or before age thirteen and having sex in risky ways (e.g., not consistently using condoms and using drugs while having sex). Youth who reported high rates of neighborhood violence also reported having more friendship groups that engaged in risky behaviors (e.g., using drugs, having risky sex) than their peers who reported less or no neighborhood violence. Youth who reported exposure to more neighborhood violence also reported higher rates of aggression than their peers who reported less exposure, which in turn was related to having peers who engaged in risky behavior, such as using drugs and having sex without condoms. In the following chapter, I explore in more detail the complex ways in which violence and risky sexual behaviors are intertwined.

6

WHEN VIOLENCE AND SEX ARE ENTANGLED

[In America,] whose little boy are you?
–JAMES BALDWIN

*My son has a girlfriend, and they spend a lot at time at the house when
I am at work. I know they are having sex, but at least he is safe, and not
being shot.*
–MOTHER, AGE FORTY-NINE

In previous chapters, using mostly survey data, I showed some of the ways that neighborhood stress and trauma can affect the mental health, social behaviors, and sexual practices of adolescents. In this chapter, I introduce findings from focus group interviews with parents. These interviews explore how exposure to neighborhood violence and sex are intertwined in the lives of black youth in Chicago's South Side neighborhoods. Against this backdrop of economic and social inequality, neighborhood violence looms large. Just today, as I write this chapter, a local news anchor reported that three youth were shot in the Woodlawn community and taken to a nearby hospital.

Woodlawn

The Woodlawn community borders the University of Chicago on its northern edge and incorporates portions of Jackson Park, where President Obama's library will be built. Like many of Chicago's South Side neighborhoods, the community has changed. Until 1948, it was a white middle-class neighborhood with almost eighty thousand residents, many of whom had arrived with the influx of white families and businesses for the World's Columbian Exposition of 1893. The late 1960s and 1970s brought housing desegregation, and blacks migrated to the neighborhood, leading many whites to flee. In the late 1960s, although 63rd Street began to see economic disinvestment, it remained one of the busiest streets on Chicago's South Side, known for its rich jazz culture.[1] In 2017, 85 percent of the population was black, and the median household income for blacks was 50 percent lower than that of the City of Chicago and just 53 percent of the national average. In addition, the unemployment rate was 101 percent higher than the national rate and was 9.4 percent versus 7.3 percent for Chicago overall.[2]

Famous people who have lived in Woodlawn include the playwright and director Lorraine Hansberry, whose *A Raisin in the Sun* chronicles the increasing black and white neighborhood tensions based on shifting racial dynamics. Other notable Woodlawn residents were the boxer Joe Louis, the four-time Olympian Jesse Owens, and the musician and composer Herbie Hancock. By the late 1990s, though, much of Woodlawn's rich history and economic vitality were unknown to many of the black youth and parents I encountered and interviewed. Driving through the adjoining affluent and more racially and economically diverse Hyde Park community into racially segregated Woodlawn, one sees a stark contrast. The architecture is similar, but the physical maintenance of Hyde Park contrasts with Woodlawn's social and economic grit. In 2008, the violent crime level in this community (i.e., murder, manslaughter, forcible rape, robbery, and aggravated assault) was rated 7 on a scale from 1 (low crime) to 10 (high crime). By comparison, Chicago neighborhoods overall had an average rating of 5.5, and the U.S. average was 3, based on the total number of violent crimes.[3] As noted, crime data reflect factors including policing patterns, residents' trust in police, and the kinds of incident that are reported or not reported.

The palpable divide between Woodlawn and Hyde Park was exemplified by a series of interviews I conducted with black youth in 2009 about coping with neighborhood conditions. When asked about dreams and goals for the future, several youth indicated that their aspirations were simple: just to grow up without being killed and move to safer neighborhoods, unlike their current ones, where lives were snuffed out frequently by random, senseless acts of gun violence. As discussed in chapter 5, an established body of research has documented that youth exposed to neighborhood violence, either as witnesses or victims, are at an increased risk of poor mental health, difficult relationships with teachers, substandard academic outcomes, and worse relationships with peers than their nonexposed youth.[4] In chapter 5, I also discussed the growing number of studies showing that youth exposures to neighborhood violence are associated with higher rates of risky sex.[5]

Pathways Linking Neighborhood Violence Exposure to Sexual Behaviors

When I began investigating whether youth exposed to neighborhood violence engaged in higher rates of drug use and risky sex few scholars were researching the topic. The possibility of youth sexual behaviors being linked to rates of neighborhood violence seemed to some farfetched. When I initially posed the idea, one colleague remarked, "I don't see what neighborhood violence has to do with sex." My prior clinical experiences working with clients convinced me that such a link was probable.

However, only a few studies have investigated the many pathways by which violence might lead to higher rates of risky sex, and most of these studies are conducted by my colleagues and me. In our prior studies, which used surveys, we found that limited parental monitoring, substance use, and gang membership were pathways linking neighborhood violence exposure with sexual behaviors.[6] In another study, we found that among a sample of black teens attending Chicago public high schools, relationships between neighborhood violence exposure and both age of sexual debut and sexual risk behaviors were linked by aggression.[7] Specifically, boys who had been exposed to high rates of neighborhood violence reported higher rates of aggression than their less exposed peers. In turn, boys who reported higher rates of aggression were more likely to have had sexual intercourse at or before the age of thirteen and to report a higher number of unsafe risky sexual encounters with girls (e.g., sex without condoms, using drugs while having sex) than boys who reported lower aggression rates. For black girls in the same study, the link from neighborhood violence exposure to reporting vaginal penetration by a boy was explained by these girls having experienced high rates of aggression as well as having close friends who supported having sex while using drugs or not using condoms. These findings suggest that untreated feelings of aggression and peer influences have the power to affect the sexual behaviors of young black girls in communities with high violence rates.[8]

A Chicago study of youth in psychiatric care found that higher rates of neighborhood violence exposure were related to more substance use and sexual risk behaviors (e.g., having a high number of sexual partners and not using condoms consistently).[9] However, the mechanism linking neighborhood violence exposure to substance use and risky sex was not explained by the type of violence reported by youth or participants' motivations to cope with the violence.

Apart from this handful of survey-based studies, academic research on the pathways of exposures to neighborhood violence to drug use and risky sex is limited. However, clinicians have long suspected that when people are unable to control their emotions, risky sexual activity might be one way in which they attempt to self-regulate. Other clinicians and I have explored and observed this phenomenon with clients over the years, yet this practice-based knowledge is relatively new to behavioral researchers.

To explore this link further, I shifted from surveys to parental focus groups. Studies based on focus groups can make critical empirical contributions, in part because they can provide more in-depth, textured insights into general trends suggested by survey-based studies.[10]

In this focus group study, we explored parents' perspectives. We knew that parental figures (e.g., mothers, fathers, grandparents, aunts, uncles, older siblings who are primary caregivers) might have valuable perspectives on how the changing context of their neighborhoods' safety over time might be related to adolescents' sexual behaviors. We also envisioned potential clinical strategies to support them in reducing the effects of neighborhood violence exposure on their children's sexual behaviors. We asked the participants, "How do you think being exposed to neighborhood violence might influence sexual behaviors among youth in your communities?"[11]

Our four focus groups included fifty-four parental figures (twelve men and forty-two women). Participants ranged in age from thirty to seventy-six years, with an average age of forty-seven years. Eighteen had attended high school or had a high school diploma, twenty-five had attended college or had a college degree, and eleven had graduate degrees. Respondents lived in Chicago's South Side communities, and most lived in predominantly black communities with high rates of neighborhood violence.

We found that participants thought several dynamics might link exposure to neighborhood violence with youth sexual behaviors in their neighborhoods. They believed that neighborhood violence (1) influenced youth sexual interests and opportunities for having sex; (2) shaped the sexual identities of youth; (3) was related to gang involvement and sexual initiations; and (4) resulted from conflicts on behalf of or because of romantic partners. In the following section, I present the major themes that emerged in our conversations.

Violence, Sexual Interests, and Possibilities for Sex

Parental participants, both male and female, stated that violence, specifically the threat of violence, altered youths' sexual behaviors in two ways. First, they thought the fear of neighborhood violence increased the likelihood that youth would have sex at home when parents or guardians were at work, because traditional recreational spaces were unsafe, thus limiting opportunities to engage in activities other than sex. Second, they said that the trauma and fear often associated with exposure to neighborhood violence left some boys uninterested in sex and more inclined to hang out with other boys and use alcohol and other drugs, especially marijuana. Then, when these boys eventually did have sex, they were more likely to engage in unsafe "sexual binging."

Many focus group participants noted a direct link between neighborhood violence exposure and sexual behaviors. One woman said, "Sex is violence, first of all. . . . When there isn't enough for kids to do, sex and violence are heightened." Several focus group participants said they encouraged or required their adolescent children to travel directly from school to home, avoiding social activities within their neighborhoods, because of the constant threat of physical attacks and gun violence. Comments such as "He won't go outside anymore [because of violence, so] they call him a houseboy," "I don't let my kids walk down the street or get on the bus," and "My kids go to school and go home," surfaced in each focus group. This sheltering strategy, according to some participants, minimized the risk of their children being shot but created situations in which their children were left unsupervised at home, possibly engaging in sexual behaviors.

One facilitator in the last focus group took up this theme, asking, "What about the boys or the girls who are just staying at home, or going from school to home because the community is rough? Do you think it sets them up, when they are at home unsupervised, to get into sexual stuff?" This question elicited an overwhelming yes from the group. Several focus group participants thought that for their youth, having recreational sex at home was a better option than socializing in the community and thereby placing themselves at risk of gun violence.

By contrast, some participants believed that neighborhood violence exposure lowered some boys' interest in sex or in having a steady romantic, sexual partner. One man explained, "I know a group of boys that are so out in the streets, a girl is not even on their mind—they [are] thinking about getting some money and drugs." In these instances, exposure to neighborhood violence, the participants suggested, led these boys to replace their interest in romantic partnering (a common adolescent milestone) with a preoccupation with money to buy drugs. When these boys were interested in having sex, because they did not have a steady romantic partner or any interest in finding one, they were having "hookups or jump-offs," casual sexual encounters that placed them at high risk of STIs.

In summary, participants thought that exposure to neighborhood violence led some youth to have more sex, others to become uninterested in sex, and some to engage in casual sex with multiple partners because they did not have steady romantic partners. All of these situations increased these teenagers' risk of STIs.

Violence and Social Status

Many participants saw gendered patterns in the ways that sexual behaviors raised the social status of teens in their neighborhoods. Several participants identified having sex as a marker of the transition from boy to man. "You ain't really no man until you can bust a cherry," one stated. Such statements showed that sex was not only a symbolic rite of passage into adulthood but provided important "street credibility, proving to their friends that they were a man and no longer a boy," as one participant put it. As for girls, some traded sex for material goods, which conferred status and thereby provided them with friends and protection from neighborhood violence by peers. Arguably, these dynamics might be prevalent in many communities, not just those with high levels of neighborhood violence. However, in low-income communities saddled with high rates of neighborhood violence that threaten personal safety, compounded by racial segregation, a lack of jobs and economic opportunities, and significant distrust of the police, the link between violence and these social and sexual dynamics might become more pronounced.

Several parent participants also suggested that credibility from sexual behavior could reduce boys' likelihood of being viewed as weak, thereby protecting them from being targets of peer violence. One woman stated, "[If other boys] think you are not having sex, that sets you up to be punked . . . beaten up, and you become a target by other boys who [are] looking for the weakest one in the bunch." Women far outnumbered men in the focus groups, and viewpoints like this tended to be expressed by women, but some men in the group had similar perspectives. In comments like these, focus group participants seemed to suggest that in communities in which neighborhood violence is high, not conforming to conventional notions of manhood and not "being tough" could place teenage boys at risk of being victimized. Several focus group participants stated that in prior generations, not having sex might have left these young men vulnerable to social embarrassment or isolation. In the current environment of gangs and guns, being known as not sexually active was a risk factor for becoming a target of neighborhood violence by peers.

Many parental figures stated that, especially for boys, participating in sexual activity not only conformed to peer norms but also increased boys' social status and popularity, especially when broadcasting their sexual stories to peers. Several focus group participants identified one's reputation as significant because what was considered a good reputation translated into a larger group of friends, which for some youth meant more protection from violence.

However, many parents suggested that although being perceived as sexually active may protect some boys, it could also leave them vulnerable to violence by the family members (especially brothers) of rumored female sexual partners. As Anthony explained, "If people think the kids are having sex, then the girl's family can get involved, and the boy can get hurt." He illustrated this point by describing how his thirteen-year-old son, Tim, created a false story about having sex with his girlfriend to be seen as "grown" and to avoid being picked on by other boys. Tim went so far as to book a hotel room for his girlfriend and himself to create the image of being sexually active. Paradoxically, his girlfriend's older brother heard the story that Tim had bragged about to other boys and beat Tim violently. This example illustrates boys' predicament: attempting to live up to peer expectations regarding sex, which would allow them to be seen as grown and manly and avoid being a target of peer violence, could paradoxically put them at risk of violence once again.

As mentioned, according to some participants, some girls used transactional sex to acquire status symbols (e.g., popular cell phones or handbags), which provided them with more friends, whom they believed offered them greater protection from violence. One woman in a focus group said, "Girls these days are sleeping with boys for cell phones and stuff. They get bragging rights and show off to their friends what these guys, and sometimes older men, are buying them. They think it makes them popular . . . and with that [popularity], less likely to be picked on and beaten up by other teens." Another said,

> The whole world is a marketplace; let's keep it real, people are buying and selling. . . . Boys and girls figure out early on what they have that is valuable and desired. . . . Girls learn their beauty, youth, and bodies are desirable by older men . . . who have more money than boys their age and can buy them things that have value and make them feel valued by their friends.

Focus group participants roundly endorsed this theme.

Violence, Gangs, and Group Sex

Some teenagers, the focus group participants said, had sex in part to demonstrate loyalty and reinforce relationships. Relatedly, some parental figures believed that some girls become active gang members because it offers them protection from being targets of violence. The pressure to join gangs for physical protection was high for both boys and girls, but the cost for entry into the gangs for girls sometimes involved engaging in sex with male gang members. Girls joined gangs and had sex with the boys to prove their loyalty to the gang members. One parent stated, "One girl told me if they are going to get raped anyway, better they have sex with fellas who would protect them, and they get some benefit from that than being taken advantage of by a stranger."

A handful of parental figures said that in some of these instances, teenagers were making difficult decisions regarding how to prioritize their overall physical, emotional, or sexual safety. For some who sought security in gang affiliation, sexual or physical violence at the hands of fellow gang members was preferable to facing other forms of neighborhood violence. Some parental figures offered firsthand examples of the difficult choices that gang-affiliated teenagers faced. One woman offered an example shared with her by a female adolescent who reported being encouraged by peers to engage in sex to demonstrate loyalty or to solidify social ties: "You got to prove yourself that you love me [her male gang boyfriend said]; go 'F' my friend." In another focus group, a participant described a similar phenomenon reported by teens: "If you want to be in our gang, you have to have sex with five guys to get in; if you don't, we'll beat you up anyway . . . or you can end up getting beaten up by strangers in the street." As comments like these showed, the threat of neighborhood violence placed some teenagers in the dangerous and challenging position of deciding whether to endure sexual risk in exchange for other forms of protection.

Romantic Partners and Violence

Conflicts between girls were a theme linking violence and sex. These conflicts sometimes escalated when male sexual partners were brought into the disagreement. Other fights, usually between boys, occurred because they shared the same sexual partner. Several focus group participants, mostly women, noted that relatively small disagreements between girls often erupted into severe violence when they brought boys, and especially their sexual partners, into the arguments. These parents said that when boys got involved, conflicts could intensify to the point of physical beatings and even gun violence.

Two female focus group participants noted that severe violence often erupted when a girl had multiple male sexual partners. According to these parents, conflicts over sexual rivalries or perceived romantic betrayals often erupted into severe violence, sometimes involving guns. Several other participants stated that they had not heard of such scenarios but added that they did not find them unlikely. Participants also described differences in how boys and girls understood and managed their feelings about sex, differences that could sometimes result in boys engaging in physical violence out of affection and loyalty.

Romantic and sexual partnering is a typical adolescent milestone, as are these dynamics. However, in neighborhoods with high rates of violence, where some boys and girls are involved in gangs and may have access to guns, ordinary adolescent rivalries and jealousies that might otherwise fade can tragically evolve into deadly violence. Conflicts in the presence of guns are thirteen times more deadly than conflicts involving knives.[12]

Ways to Reduce Risky Sexual Behavior

This study was the first to examine relationships between sex and neighborhood violence, particularly in neighborhoods with relatively high levels of public-space violence, by asking parents in racially segregated and economically depressed neighborhoods about their perceptions of the issues and how the problems are linked. Only a handful of survey studies had previously examined factors linking exposure to neighborhood violence with sexual behaviors among youth, and few focused on black American youth. This study provided new insight into these dynamics among black teenagers in a cluster of Chicago neighborhoods.

Parents in the focus group recounted wide variations in the experiences of their children, even within a relatively small geographic area, depending on the diverse factors shaping their children's lives. Nevertheless, identifying patterns can help us design solutions that address the shared concerns of teenagers exposed to structural violence. Given the history of racism that has shaped risk patterns among black teenagers nationwide, research studies must examine how this structural racism influences the lives of black teenagers, even as it affects each adolescent in slightly different ways.

Previous studies have shown ways that parenting can reduce the links between neighborhood violence exposure and negative youth outcomes, including those related to sexual behaviors.[13] Our study illuminated that parents' important functions can be compromised when significant safety concerns prevent youth from participating in typical recreational activities outside of school. Our interviews revealed that teenagers are often required to go straight home to avoid public-space violence. At home, many are unsupervised because parents are still at work. Several parents we interviewed thought that this made their teens more likely to engage in sex.

Factors that may increase unsupervised time at home include a lack of funding for social and after-school educational programs in under-resourced communities, irregular work hours in low-income service-sector jobs that make childcare arrangements difficult, a lack of funding to support parenting and/or childcare services for older children, a shortage of youth job opportunities, particularly among black and lower-income teenagers (both in Chicago and nationwide), and the reality that a majority of black households are headed by single females.[14] Challenging parental scenarios like these may help explain why black youth experience their sexual debut at earlier ages than youth in other racial/ethnic groups, on average.[15]

Several strategies might reduce the risk of teenagers engaging in risky sexual activity. Training should be offered to parents and legal guardians on ways to educate youth about making good decisions about reproductive and sexual health when parents are not present. Policy reforms that would bolster parental supervision include eliminating harmful welfare work requirements; compensating parents for the invaluable, society-building labor of childrearing; and expanding after-school programs and childcare subsidies to include care for children of all ages.

Additional measures might include expanding youth employment opportunities, and a slew of social programs could help make neighborhoods safer by reducing economic inequality and social marginalization. Among these programs, sexual health initiatives should target girls and boys in ways that are responsive to gendered differences in sexual behavior patterns and risks. Few partner-based programs are available to address the ramifications of violence for young women's sexual decisions and safety, and ones geared toward the experiences shared by many black American girls are notably scarce. However, one example is Horizons, aimed at both girls and their male sexual partners, which has been shown to reduce rates of risky sex.[16] An intervention working in parallel to Horizons, directed at parents and legal guardians, sought to enable parents and legal guardians to support and reinforce the program's goals.

The heightened stakes in low-resourced communities call for particular interventions aimed at helping teens define positive masculinity, hold appropriate sexual and romantic expectations, and learn effective conflict resolution strategies. One example is the highly successful "Becoming a Man" (BAM) program, which offers group mentorship to teenage boys at high risk of dropping out of school. BAM addresses social norms of manhood, highlighting actions like completing high school, finding a job, and attending college.[17] The findings about parents' strong protective role in preventing their children from engaging in risky sexual behaviors suggest that value could be gained by supplementing successful programs like BAM with parental components designed to reinforce the program's beneficial effects. Ideally, such social programs would be accompanied by structural reforms to improve the violent conditions in the first place.

Summary and Conclusion

Regardless of youth race/ethnicity, growing up in impoverished neighborhoods where gun violence and homicides frequently occur changes how youth see their self-worth, what they can achieve and become, and how fast they grow up. The black parents' voices we heard illuminated the ways in which neighborhood violence alters youth social relationships and how adolescents experience sexual development and romantic relationships. Our study also showed that exposure to neighborhood violence may be associated with increased adolescent drug use, as well as tendencies to have sex with multiple partners. A prior study of a multiethnic sample of juvenile justice system–involved teenagers indicated that substance abuse was one pathway linking exposure to neighborhood violence with sexual behaviors, reinforcing earlier research, but that study did not address nuances, including how drugs affect the connections between neighborhood violence and sexual behavior.[18] Some parents in our focus groups believed that some drugs (e.g., marijuana) may reduce teenagers' desire for sexual activity, a finding that needs further exploration. Some participants suggested that some boys preoccupied with securing drugs had less interest in developing romantic partnerships than boys not interested in drugs, leading them to instead participate in higher-risk casual sexual encounters. These frequent, casual partnerships place these boys and their sexual partners at higher risk of STI acquisition and transmission. More research on the frequency of casual sex among youth in neighborhoods with high rates of public-space violence, and how substance use plays a role in these sexual contacts, is needed.

Another important theme emerging from this study is that neighborhood violence and gang involvement can have serious ramifications for young women's sexual decisions and safety. More research is needed to determine how parents and legal guardians could be more closely involved in sexual safety programs for girls, especially girls navigating the difficult choice of whether to engage in sexual behaviors in the hope of keeping themselves safe from other dangers, such as neighborhood violence.

Our findings shed light on participants' notions of how sex fits into teens' mental and social development, and how love, loyalty, sex, and violence are entangled. Sexual growth and exploration are normal parts of adolescent development. In neighborhoods with violence, though, as several parents in our focus groups expressed, the presence of gangs and guns turned typical adolescent skirmishes, which are generally harmless in other neighborhoods, into dangerous or deadly conflicts in theirs.

7

LIVING AND PARENTING IN THE PRESENCE OF EVERYDAY DANGERS

In America, they are building graves for us to go down into. We already have an X on our backs, but I would prove them wrong.
—MALCOLM, AGE FOURTEEN

Every parent wants to see their child grow up. . . . No parent should have to live through the murder of their child.
—PARENT, AGE FORTY-FOUR

Media-grabbing headlines like "More Than Sixty Shot, Nine Dead in Chicago's Bloody Holiday Weekend"[1] and "Homicides in Chicago Outpacing Last Year After Deadliest Day So Far in 2017"[2] have fueled discourse about public-space violence in Chicago. Overlooked in these headlines and subsequent conversations are the variety of ways that black youth cope with the threat of everyday neighborhood trauma. When such stories are absent or rare, inaccurate assumptions often fill the void. During one of my many conversations with reporters about neighborhood violence in Chicago, I was asked, "Aren't most youth living in high-crime communities using violence to battle violence?" Lost are the nuances of the experience—the factors that affect an individual teen's chances of overcoming the harsh influence of neighborhood violence. Equally absent from the social science literature are the narratives of black parental figures who engage in child-rearing and protecting their children in the face of commonplace neighborhood violence. In my studies, I have found black youth and their parents are eager to share these narratives.

How Youth Cope with Violence

Coping refers to approaches people use to control stress.[3] The little we know about neighborhood violence and coping among youth comes from survey studies.[4] Findings from one study of multiethnic sixth graders showed that behavior coping approaches generally clustered around avoiding, reducing, or tolerating violence.[5] These studies have illustrated that youth who were victims of neighborhood violence and had strong social support from parental figures were less inclined to engage in delinquent behaviors (e.g., joining a gang or using illicit drugs). Confrontational coping strategies (i.e., doing things to improve one's reputation or gain the respect of others) were a greater risk factor for delinquent behaviors for boys than for girls. Avoidant coping strategies (i.e., avoiding dangerous places or people) placed girls, but not boys, who witnessed neighborhood violence at higher risk of delinquent behaviors. Another study of a multiethnic youth sample showed that "negative coping" (e.g., criticizing, blaming others, wishful thinking) was related to participants' reporting higher rates of PTSD symptoms.[6] A qualitative study of coping styles among black Chicago women residing in public housing showed that many respondents used avoidance, acceptance, and self-protection approaches to cope with neighborhood violence exposure.[7]

Existing research on coping, though useful, did not use in-depth interviews to describe how black adolescents, specifically, cope with neighborhood violence. Findings based on youth samples comprising various ethnicities that do not tease out potential group differences may mask important findings. For example, patterns in black teenagers' experiences and coping strategies may have been shaped by the long history of racist housing policies in the United States, which for decades restricted black citizens to highly segregated and overcrowded neighborhoods, depreciated their home values, and made it more difficult for them to obtain affordable home loans and to accumulate equity. Though these policies have changed, they still profoundly shape neighborhood demographics and economic disparities.[8] Mistrust of police officers and judicial systems, fueled by the numerous acquittals of police officers after brutal and unjustifiable murders of black citizens, may also influence the specific coping strategies of black youth. Indeed, black families and social networks have developed various practices to deal with the intersections between antiblack structural racism and violence, and these trends may not be visible in studies that rely on numeric or less richly descriptive qualitative data or that include adolescents of a variety of racial/ethnic groups and socioeconomic levels. In addition, little research has explored whether coping patterns among black teenagers may differ by gender.

My research team and I sought to address this gap by conducting a qualitative study in which we interviewed thirty-two black high schoolers (sixteen boys and sixteen girls) in Woodlawn, a low-income, racially segregated neighborhood in Chicago.[9] We used an approach called grounded theory to discover themes or patterns that emerge from interview data. Using this approach, we identified the nature and types of public-space violence to which these black adolescents were exposed, explored these teenagers' various approaches to coping with neighborhood violence, and examined whether gendered patterns appeared to exist in how girls and boys in our sample coped with violence. We conducted semistructured, one-on-one interviews with the teens in a private, conveniently accessible location. I, a black West Indian man interviewed all the male participants, and a black American woman interviewed the female participants. We omitted one female participant from our analysis because some inconsistencies and gaps in her answers led us to question our ability to analyze her responses accurately. Rather than risk misrepresenting her experiences and insights, we decided to exclude her data. Participants were between the ages of fourteen and seventeen years, with sixteen years being the average age.

Most participants (67 percent) lived in single-female-headed households, and 25 percent lived in homes with both parents. In terms of education,

38 percent reported that their mothers had some college education, 12 percent said their mothers had a college degree, 12 percent indicated that their fathers had some college education, and 16 percent reported that their fathers had a college degree. Slightly more than one-third of the youth reported that they received or would qualify for free school lunches, and 16 percent reported that someone in their household had received welfare assistance (e.g., Section 8 housing assistance or Temporary Assistance for Needy Families) during the previous twelve months. Most participants (77 percent) had lived in their neighborhoods for one year or more, whereas 16 percent had lived in their neighborhood for less than six months. There were no differences between boys and girls with regard to age, household composition, parent educational attainment, or socioeconomic status.

Types of Violence Exposure

For all youth, neighborhood violence exposures took the form of hearing about, witnessing, or becoming a victim of violence. Physical attacks, fighting, incidents involving police officers, gun violence, and murders were the five most common forms of neighborhood violence exposure. Boys were exposed to more "extreme" forms of neighborhood violence than were girls. Direct victimization was considered the most extreme exposure, followed by witnessing violence and then hearing about violence secondhand. More boys reported witnessing and being direct victims of neighborhood violence than girls did, while both boys and girls said they heard about neighborhood violence secondhand at roughly the same rate.

Physical Attacks The boys in the study seemed to have heard more detailed accounts of physical attacks that had occurred in their neighborhoods than had girls, and the attacks described to them were often more violent. These findings are consistent with those of other studies showing that males are exposed to higher rates of neighborhood violence as victims, compared with females, who report more experiences of violence as witnesses.[10] Roughly 40 percent of the boys said that they had heard graphic stories of local violence, whereas 66 percent of girls reported hearing such stories, albeit in less detail. One girl shared the following account: "There [are] a couple girls that get raped and stuff. Someone had got raped down the street from my house. She used to live above me. And there's a boy that got raped, somebody I know. . . . I never witnessed that; I heard about it."

One girl and one boy also reported having witnessed physical attacks. The girl described how she had seen a fellow gang member "clock this one girl, bust her head" one day at McDonald's, using a padlock with shoestrings tied to it. Although none of the female participants reported direct involvement (as either a victim or perpetrator of violence), 38 percent of the boys reported having been attacked by two or more people. These attacks included being pushed in front of moving vehicles; having objects, such as bicycles, thrown at them; and being beaten with baseball bats. Another participant was robbed and stabbed at age eleven, an incident that continued to haunt him.

Fighting Fighting differed from physical attacks in that fights involved retaliation, whereas physical attacks were what a few participants called being "jumped on." Fighting was more prevalent than physical attacks and was more common among boys than girls. A handful of participants reported hearing about fights; 13 percent of girls and 25 percent of boys said they had witnessed fights. The fights that the girls had witnessed were primarily between girls and involved no firearm injuries. The boys who had witnessed fights also reported seeing mostly girls getting into sporadic altercations, ranging from occasional fistfights to more extreme violence. Fighting involving extreme violence, such as stabbings, took place mostly among boys, with four boys reporting having been involved in fights individually or in groups. Among the three girls who had experienced violence directly, two had been in fights, and all three altercations involved girls victimizing other girls.

Police Incidents Six boys (37 percent) identified surveillance measures by police as a form of neighborhood violence. These boys reported being made to feel "humiliated," "terrified," and "like a criminal" in their encounters with police. Several boys had seen police officers chase individuals through the neighborhood, and one participant experienced officers entering his home to arrest an older brother, which ended in a fight between the police and several of his family members, including his mother. He said that the police were "just tearing our whole house up . . . fighting."

Gun Violence and Murders Gun violence exposure was prevalent among participants, with more boys than girls being firsthand witnesses of such violence. More than half of the girls (60 percent) had heard about gun violence in their neighborhoods. Participants reported hearing accounts of incidents in which people were victims of gun violence or were murdered. The stress that the gun violence caused was evident in the participants' descriptions. "When that boy got shot down the street," said one girl, "it affected me. . . . I go to school, I do all my work. But then I go to sleep in the class." It is not uncommon for traumatic stress occurrences to lead to sleep problems. Female participants who had heard secondhand accounts of gun violence were deeply affected by these traumatic stories, a finding supported by prior studies showing that both firsthand witnesses and those who hear about violent events report mental health difficulties (e.g., depression, anxiety, and PTSD symptoms). Among the boys, 38 percent reported hearing about gun violence in or around their neighborhoods, with one participant reporting that he knew several people who had been shot.

Several girls reported hearing about murders but were unsure of the weapon used in the killings. For instance, four girls (27 percent) had heard about murders in their neighborhoods. One said that a woman had been murdered in an alley next to her home; as a result, the girl was frightened to go outside. Another girl described the psychological effects that these accounts of violence could have on residents: "[You're] always spacing out. . . . I mean, every time you go around, it's like somebody['s] getting killed."

Four girls said they had been firsthand witnesses of drive-by shootings, and 63 percent of boys reported having seen people shot at or killed by gunfire. One boy had seen the manager of a currency exchange shop shot during a robbery attempt. Another recalled a time when he and his girl-friend had seen a young man in his neighborhood get gunned down:

> These boys shot him. He never got to see his baby born. He was like, "I love my baby, and tell my baby when it's born that I tried to stay here to see it, but I can't hold on no more." And he left. Because he had been shot so many times . . . he couldn't take all them gun wounds or anything.

One girl had seen her mother murdered by random gun violence while she was buying cigarettes at a corner store. She had told her mother several times, "Ma, you have to stop smoking cigarettes; that stuff is going to kill you." She never expected her mother, at thirty-nine years old, would be killed by a stray bullet.

In addition to witnessing gun violence against others, 38 percent of boys reported having had a gun pulled on them or having been shot at unintentionally. One boy reported having been shot at six times, including twice in the previous year. He attributed these incidents to his being in "the wrong place at the wrong time."

Coping with Neighborhood Violence

On the basis of prior studies of coping,[11] we grouped the strategies employed by these youth to cope with neighborhood violence into four domains:

- "Getting through," which included putting up with neighborhood conditions or working toward leaving permanently, given that violence exposure in the neighborhood was inescapable.
- "Getting along," which included self-defense techniques (e.g., being more careful about one's surroundings, conversation partners, and choice of words).
- "Getting away," which included avoidance coping strategies (e.g., avoiding certain places).
- "Getting back," which consisted of confrontational coping strategies (e.g., learning to fight or carrying weapons as a means of defense).

Getting Through "Getting through" was the most common strategy for coping with violence, employed equally by girls and boys. It entailed enduring the crime that plagued some communities in the neighborhood, trying not to think about it, or using school as a way to cope or get out of the neighborhood. This strategy was illustrated by one boy's words indicating the randomness of violence:

> I don't know what could happen to me. I could probably be walking out the building in the morning, going to school . . . something might happen . . . you could just get shot for no reason at all . . . because crazy stuff is all around you . . . and you have nothing to do with it [provoking violence].

For some respondents, getting through the violence involved making meaning of the violence and how it had shaped their world views. For them, violence was a reminder of how quickly life could "be taken away" and that "life is precious." One male participant recounted advice his uncle had given him to "just be strong."

Another strategy several teenagers shared for getting through the violence was doing well in school, in hopes of being able to leave their neighborhood. One teenage girl explained that doing well in school was a means to "achieve more and get off of Cottage Grove," the main street in her neighborhood. One boy commented that "getting a bachelor's or a master's degree would really help you get away." Another girl used school as an outlet to express the emotional trauma she felt after she had been caught in a drive-by shooting in which she had not been the intended target, stating, "I expressed myself in what I wrote. So as I wrote, it got deeper and deeper, to the point where it made the teachers like, 'Oh, she really feeling this.' "

Getting Along The second coping mechanism, getting along, was a widely used strategy among both girls and boys. For some, it meant becoming well known in the local neighborhood or associating with those they called "the right people," which often, but not always, meant either gang members or positive, influential or well-respected people in the neighborhood who, by association, could offer them a greater level of reverence or personal safety. For several boys, establishing their standing in the neighborhood by getting along with as many people as possible was one way of circumventing neighborhood violence. As one boy described, "I'm more like an idol on that block. It's like, since I been on that block the longest now. . . . So, it's like everybody look[s] up to me now. I ain't in no gang or nothing; they just look up to me." According to a number of boys, the strategy of having a wide network of friends and acquaintances came in handy when another person sought to "come at you," or target an individual with violence.

This strategy was also examined in a recent study of black sixth graders.[12] In that study, researchers found that in high-violence neighborhoods, friendship formation was based more on strategy than fondness. When considering friendships, children often sought friends who had the ability to protect them. Some avoided forming deep friendships as a way of avoiding conflict that might lead to violence. Another strategy was selecting friends only after carefully determining whether they could be trusted.[13]

Getting Away The third strategy, getting away, entailed avoiding situations in which violence might erupt, often by isolating oneself from other neighborhood members. Girls commonly reported avoiding situations in which violence might occur, whereas boys reported this strategy less frequently. One girl described avoiding the park where she had once hung out "because there be drug dealers up there." Another girl chose to stay home "most of the time. . . . [I] watch TV or read a book." Some boys shared similar responses. One said, "I just walk quickly, straight in the house, don't say nothing to nobody." Some respondents said they tried to avoid crowds or gatherings at which violence seemed likely to erupt.

Getting Back The final coping strategy, getting back, represented active resistance, such as learning to fight or defend oneself or carrying a weapon. This was the least-used coping strategy, according to respondents, with only three boys discussing this option. For them, however, learning to defend themselves was almost a necessity because they had found that efforts to avoid violence, get along, or accept violence as a fact in their neighborhood was not working for them, given that they could not escape being targets of violence. "I used to be a little punk," said one participant. "You know, running from all types of fights. But then I got to realize that no matter how much I run, I'm still going get into these things. . . . [Now] if I have to get into a fight, I'm just ready. I'm not going to be scared." Another participant said he realized he was stronger than he thought after he had been attacked by a group: "Hey, it took seven of them to whup me. [I] learned how to fight better, learned how to defend myself more." As for many boys, regardless of neighborhood, learning to fight can become a necessity if the boy is small or perceived as weak. However, in violent neighborhoods, the stakes are much higher, and learning to fight or defend oneself may be necessary for safety or survival. This study showed that for the male participants who reported it, getting back was a form of self-defense in response to violence. This narrative is very different from the one often promoted about black males in the media. Prior studies have not included this confrontational approach as a coping strategy, perhaps because of the ages of study participants or because of societal views of physical aggression as acceptable or permissible for adolescent boys.

Patterns of Coping Strategies

This study revealed several notable gender differences with regard to violence exposure. On average, boys were exposed to a greater number and more severe forms of violence than girls, as both victims and witnesses, especially with regard to gun violence. These findings align with prior survey research.[14] By contrast, girls were more likely than boys to report having heard about violent events.

One explanation for these gender differences could be that girls in violent neighborhoods may be subject to greater parental monitoring than boys, which could make girls less likely than boys to be in situations in which violence emerges. Another is that gender-patterned behaviors (e.g., socializing in pairs versus larger groups) might help girls avoid crowded situations in which violence may be more likely to erupt.[15] Notions of gender also may have broader implications. For example, the fact that boys are more likely to experience direct exposure to violence may cause them to be seen as inherently more dangerous to the neighborhood than girls in the eyes of many, which could consequently exacerbate fears and expectations of violence from male adolescents. On the other hand, since we studied a relatively small convenience sample of adolescents, these trends could merely be features of our sample, not indications of any broader trend in the neighborhood where they live. Further research, such as in-depth ethnographic inquiry, would be necessary to gain greater insights into the dynamics at play. Additionally, because rates of witnessing versus directly experiencing violence may differ by gender, researchers may need to refine their neighborhood violence exposure measures to consider a broad range of exposures, given that current measures of victimization and witnessing may not adequately capture girls' exposure to violence.

Gun violence was the most common form of violence reported by both boys and girls, a finding supported by prior data.[16] This may suggest that youth are more likely to use guns than to engage in less lethal forms of fighting or simply that respondents remember or talk about gun violence more than other forms of violence because it is dramatic and traumatic. Finally, it could reflect a ready availability of firearms in some neighborhoods where gun violence is relatively common; additional research would be necessary to shed light on this possibility.

A noteworthy finding, alluded to earlier in this book, is that many teenagers consider common police encounters to be a form of neighborhood violence. This aspect of neighborhood violence is not evaluated or identified in traditional measures of neighborhood violence.[17] This finding is significant because law enforcement is used as a primary means of addressing violence in neighborhoods with high crime rates, yet aggressive police action may actually enhance the trauma experienced by many adolescents rather than increasing feelings of security or safety. Therefore, aggressive law enforcement may unintentionally deepen the impact of both experienced and perceived neighborhood violence, thereby exacerbating adolescents' general concerns about their safety and the negative outcomes associated with neighborhood violence. Neighborhood-building activities between law enforcement and neighborhood residents may therefore be beneficial to address neighborhood violence through a more nonviolent approach. Other strategies may include increasing oversight of police and accountability of police who engage in brutality or other forms of misconduct—or, as some activists advocate, envisioning new neighborhood safety strategies that replace traditional policing methods altogether. These strategies, many of which have been developed and advocated by Chicago-area activists, could include deploying trained, unarmed mediation and intervention teams; decriminalizing many behaviors now classified as crimes, such as marijuana use, panhandling, and sex work; replacing courts and jails with restorative justice alternatives; implementing policies aimed at reducing gun violence, such as manufacturer regulations; and, as mentioned, simply improving the economic and general well-being of residents, thereby eliminating many variables associated with violence.[18]

Findings from this study and prior research indicate that many participants used multiple coping strategies. Some participants in our study used these strategies concurrently and strategically, such as avoiding dangerous situations while also building supportive personal attachments with key neighborhood members. Other participants progressed from what they saw as a less useful to a more useful strategy. For example, one girl initially associated with gang members for safety but over time realized that such affiliations exposed her to more danger "because people get hurt like that . . . so I just keep to myself."

Many coping styles were reported by both boys and girls. Strategically making connections with influential people in their neighborhoods was a common strategy for "getting along" that could take either beneficial or dangerous forms. For some, it meant associating with people who had status and respect within their neighborhood or who might be able to offer physical protection, including gang members. For others, it meant growing and strengthening their social networks, gaining respect from other residents, and having a network of supportive friends and acquaintances.

The strategy of "getting away" or avoiding violence was common for girls but not for boys. This finding may be related to differences in physical vulnerability or in the tendency to address conflicts directly with violence. Avoidance may protect girls from coming into contact with more severe forms of violence, but it may also fuel feelings of isolation when girls go directly from school to home and avoid socializing with peers. Such isolation in the presence of trauma may exacerbate mental distress and advance other problems, such as depression, substance use, and risky sexual behaviors, especially when youth have unsupervised time at home.

In our study, only boys discussed the strategy of confrontation, which in prior literature has not been viewed as a coping mechanism.[19] Thus, what is often seen as perpetration of interpersonal violence may actually be a form of self-defense for some boys, for whom the perception of weakness may increase their vulnerability to becoming a victim.

Some coping strategies, though effective in the short term, may have negative long-term consequences for the mental and social development of these youth. For instance, the use of physical aggression by some boys to cope with neighborhood violence exposures may also place them at greater risk of victimization, and, as noted, isolation as a means of coping may increase girls' susceptibility to depression.

Because this study involved a relatively small sample of black teens from a geographically clustered, low-income neighborhood, we cannot generalize about the broader pattern of coping among black teenagers from these findings alone. Although the patterns in our study are simply suggestive, the findings regarding unique gender differences in coping strategies suggest that neighborhood-level interventions may need to be more gender responsive, taking into account both the gender differences in the degree and type of violence teenagers are exposed to and the mechanisms they use to manage the risks of neighborhood violence.

Interestingly, while other researchers have documented that parents of middle school children of various ethnicities adopt measures to protect their children from violence, such as serving as confidants, heightening their parental monitoring, and screening their children's friends,[20] the participants in our study did not mention their parents as a source of coping. Perhaps adolescents may be less inclined to report experiences of neighborhood violence exposure to parental figures because they fear getting in trouble, because they do not want to upset or worry their parents, because such exposures have become so commonplace that discussion seems unnecessary, or because they simply were not asked. In fact, one participant who reported witnessing a murder in an alleyway on his way to school several years earlier stated, "I told no one because I was scared and no one asked me." Other research has shown that neighborhood violence exposures are similarly underemphasized by service providers (e.g., social workers, counselors) working with inner-city youth.[21]

Implications for Policy and Practice

Collectively, these findings suggest that greater attention needs to be paid to neighborhood violence exposure within school systems and other systems serving black youth in high-violence neighborhoods. In addition to developing measures that would better identify teenagers exposed to neighborhood violence, trauma-informed approaches are needed within classrooms and organizations that serve youth and their families, such as schools, social clubs, and churches.[22] The Cognitive Behavioral Intervention for Trauma in Schools program is one initiative that has shown some effectiveness in reducing youth distress related to neighborhood violence. This intervention is typically offered in a small group format. It educates youth about trauma symptoms, normalizing common reactions to violence and helps them develop positive coping and problem solving skills in relation to trauma.[23]

Coordinated neighborhood initiatives that address structural factors are also vital. Such approaches may seek to curtail gang activity, reduce the flow of guns to minors, improve youth supervision, address joblessness and poverty, and teach alternatives to violence. One example of a neighborhood initiative is the Partnership to Reduce Juvenile Gun Violence in Oakland, California. This intervention provides counseling to juvenile youth victims of gun violence at their hospital bedside to prevent further retaliation by the victim or the victim's friends and family members.[24] Such approaches may be especially pertinent to a subpopulation of boys who seek to cope with violence by physical retaliation. Project FIRE, which is modeled after this program, is discussed in chapter 9, along with several other programs.

From a policy perspective, the prevalence of gun violence exposure among teenagers suggests the need for policies and programs designed to limit teens' access to and use of guns. Chicago has the fourth strictest gun access laws in the United States, but neighboring states Wisconsin and Indiana have some of the most lax laws, and various studies have traced gun sales across state and city lines.[25] This situation calls for uniform nationwide gun violence laws that apply across states and municipalities, as well as the policy approaches discussed in chapter 2.[26] Of course, all these programs and interventions require resources, and unfortunately, as I have discussed at length, many of the teenagers at greatest risk of exposure to neighborhood violence live in some of the lowest-resourced neighborhoods in the country. True investment in these teenagers' well-being and safety would require changes in the ways that schools and organizations are funded and more equitable resource allocation within cities.

Factors That Protect Youth from Violence

I noted in earlier chapters that narratives matter, whether they are factual or not, because they drive public opinion, program types, funding, solutions identified (if any), and how communities and their potential are represented with regard to neighborhood violence. The portrayal of Chicago is one such example: The city is often portrayed by the media as having one of highest homicide rates in America. In fact, Chicago ranks twelfth per capita, behind New Orleans, Cleveland, Memphis, Atlanta, and several other cities. This misperception affects home purchases, tourism, and other factors. A similar scenario occurs when a lopsided narrative is constructed about the challenges facing black youth in Chicago. It is accurate that black youth, especially those who reside in impoverished and segregated neighborhoods, bear a heavy burden of violence. However, not all youth living in low-income black communities are exposed to the same levels or types of neighborhood violence. In addition, youth are significantly influenced by their close friends, and these influences can be both positive and negative. Expanding the narrative has important implications for how black youth are viewed by society and themselves, the opportunities that are afforded them, and their future life prospects.

Driven by this approach, my colleagues and I collected survey data from more than six hundred black youth residing in mostly low-income Chicago South Side neighborhoods. We aimed to determine what factors might distinguish youth living in low-income communities with regard to low versus high neighborhood violence exposure rates and low versus high delinquent peer associations.[27] These questions are important because the often random nature of neighborhood violence can leave these youth feeling less hopeful about the future and less concerned about the long-term consequences of risky behaviors.[28] In addition, black youth experience greater social and legal sanctions for behaviors similar to those of their white peers. Thus, identifying factors that protect youth from delinquent peer associations and neighborhood violence can help inform the development of programs that can support these youth even when faced with structural disadvantage.

Our analyses revealed variation in both exposures to neighborhood violence and affiliations with delinquent peers. The majority of youth fell into the low neighborhood violence exposure and low peer delinquency category. Peer delinquency was assessed by the degree of illegal, norm-violating, and aggressive behaviors in the previous twelve months (e.g., hurting someone badly enough to require bandages or medical attention). However, this measure is complex and does not always capture context, such as hurting someone in self-defense. The results suggest that although the overall rates of neighborhood violence in Chicago South Side communities are higher than the city average, only a subgroup of youth in these communities face high exposure to violence. Low versus high neighborhood violence exposure rates were distinguished by belonging to delinquent peer networks. More girls than boys belonged to the low violence exposure and peer delinquency group. This finding indicates that associating with peers who subscribe to positive norms may have implications for reducing rates of neighborhood violence exposure even in low-income neighborhoods.

The results also showed that youth in the low neighborhood violence and low peer delinquency group had higher levels of self-esteem and future orientation than peers in the high neighborhood violence and peer delinquency group.[29] This finding suggests that youth with low self-esteem may seek deviant peers as an alternative source of self-worth if they are unable to form meaningful relationships with less deviant peers.[30] Youth who experience lower levels of neighborhood violence may see themselves and their potential future in a more positive light than youth experiencing high levels of chronic violence exposure, which could influence the ways in which they select and associate with peers. We also found that higher levels of future orientation were related to lower rates of reporting neighborhood violence, delinquent activity, illicit substance use, and engaging in risky sex. In addition, stronger future orientation was associated with more positive behaviors, such as school bonding and better student–teacher relationships. One approach to promoting future orientation would be for youth programs to expose youth from low-income neighborhoods to job opportunities, culturally responsive mentoring programs, and initiatives that promote positive black youth development. A black parent from Chicago's South Side said,

> We live in Englewood, and every so often I would take my son on the bus to downtown Chicago on Michigan Avenue and the North Side to show him that there are very different places than where we live . . . to show him that he [could] have some of that someday and have a different type of life.

Exposing youth to opportunities not limited by their circumstances may be an effective strategy for fostering a sense of hope and future orientation.[31]

A similar pattern emerged when we examined the protective effects of high self-esteem. After we accounted for differing levels of poverty, black youth with low self-esteem reported rates of delinquency, drug use,

Figure 7.1

A young girl picking fruit in the Englewood neighborhood of Chicago

Sources: "I Grow Chicago" (left); Dexter R. Voisin (right)

and risky sexual behaviors two to seven times higher than those of peers reporting high self-esteem. Youth with low self-esteem were substantially less connected to teachers or invested in school. These characteristics are also common aftereffects associated with exposure to neighborhood trauma.

For the youth in this study, more complex relationships exist between parental resources and their personal resources of self-esteem and future orientation. Those who reported high levels of parental monitoring (i.e., caregivers knowing their friends and their whereabouts) reported less delinquency. When parents monitored their youth, the children had a greater sense of a future for themselves, which correlated with youth engaging in fewer delinquent behaviors. These findings also suggest that in communities of high economic need and neighborhood violence, parental monitoring has a significant positive effect on children.[32]

Figure 7.2

Children's workshop: elementary school children writing words that help them deal with neighborhood stress

Source: Carmellia Boyd

Figure 7.3

The children turned their paper and words into origami art

Source: Carmellia Boyd

Parents' Protective Strategies

In black communities facing insufficient mental health services, school closings, funding shortfalls, a mistrust of police officers, and inequitable resource allocation, parenting strategies might evolve in particular ways to compensate for these structural and social challenges. The role of parents and parental figures in supporting positive youth development is widely corroborated by practice evidence and decades of research, but few studies have examined how parenting strategies may vary within the context of high rates of neighborhood violence. Existing studies have primarily been based on surveys, which provide useful but limited insights.

One study surveying parents of middle school children found that many caregivers encouraged their teenage children to confide in them, provided increasing parental monitoring, and screened their children's friends to protect them from neighborhood violence.[33] Another parental survey showed that parents were less likely to advise their teenagers to use conflict to address violence when they believed that the neighborhood included people whose role was to intercede to help their children. This finding suggests that parents took into consideration the context of their neighborhood environment before advising their children how to resolve conflicts.[34] However, these studies neither focused on samples of black parents specifically nor explored whether parenting strategies depended on the child's gender.

We sought to address this research gap by exploring the protective strategies employed by parents to keep their youth safe.[35] To recap, in this study, we recruited parents or legal guardians of black youth aged fourteen to eighteen years who resided on Chicago's South Side. We posed the following questions to parent participants regarding their roles in mitigating their children's exposure to violence:

- What are some things parents can do to help reduce the amount of violence children experience outside the home?
- Do these approaches differ for boys or girls, and if so, how?

- What are some things parents can do to protect children from the negative effects of being exposed to violence outside the home?

As earlier mentioned, we interviewed fifty-four parental figures (twelve males and forty-two females) who ranged in age from thirty to seventy-six years, with an average age of forty-six years. Eighteen parental participants had attended high school or had a high school diploma, twenty-five had attended college or had a college degree, and eleven had a graduate degree.

Parents' Perspectives

Three general themes emerged related to neighborhood violence: (1) There were no "safe havens" or violence-free places, though some places were perceived as safer than others; (2) no one was entirely safe from violence, even elderly individuals or religious leaders; and (3) parents used both general and gendered strategies to protect their youth from neighborhood violence exposure and its effects. The most common parental strategies included sheltering, chauffeuring, removing their children from violent communities, and attempting to rebuild community protective factors by using schools to enhance or re-create "the village," a concept I will explain in greater detail later in this chapter.

No Safe Havens One common theme that emerged in all focus groups and was threaded throughout the areas of discussion was the belief that few, if any, places within the neighborhood could be considered safe from violence. One participant, Sonia, stated, "There are no safe havens," and referred to the city's violent side using the popular epithet "Chiraq" (combining *Chicago* and *Iraq*). Participants across the groups expressed common notions that many places in their neighborhoods that had previously been considered safe (e.g., churches, schools, and homes) were increasingly becoming dangerous, although some still named these sites as locations of relative sanctuary. This theme resonated across all groups: "It's everywhere," one participant asserted. "There's no safe neighborhood in Chicago anymore," said another. In another group, the comment "There aren't any safe zones" elicited widespread agreement, indicated by head nods and murmurs of assent. Many parents expressed a belief that violence can occur "downtown," in "nice areas," or near "million-dollar homes" as easily as in neighborhoods at the other end of the socioeconomic spectrum. Regardless of how widespread violence was in each of these settings, what stood out was that parents strongly felt that no place was safe for them or their loved ones, and they asserted that this reality was not limited to their own neighborhoods but was a condition of life for people across the city and socioeconomic spectrum. Perhaps the latter point made by many parents was an attempt, in part, to counter narratives that locate violence only within racially segregated and lower-income enclaves of the city, with parents seeking to highlight forms of violence that occur in other parts of the city but are sanitized from those areas' narratives. Alternatively, it may have reflected the prevailing sense of a lack of safety that for many was an existential condition of daily life and therefore felt boundless.

Although the focus group participants seemed to consider violence widespread throughout communities, several identified places where they thought violence was particularly likely to occur. Participants in a number of focus groups referred to schools as sites of violence, particularly shootings, and referenced certain schools by name. Public transportation, such as buses and trains, especially during school hours, was mentioned as a place where violence is likely to erupt, with one participant exclaiming, "Have you *been* on the bus lately?" This point elicited enthusiastic reactions of agreement from many others in her focus group. In addition, although viewpoints were mixed, participants also mentioned recreational public spaces, such as parks and basketball courts, as other neighborhood spaces where youth could be exposed to neighborhood violence.

In summary, although several participants cited churches and certain schools as safe places, others said that even these traditionally safe sites had become unsafe, offering examples of gun violence against preachers in the pulpit or during funeral services and of people being robbed while at church. Despite the widely expressed feelings of insecurity within their neighborhoods, several participants indicated that they still felt relatively safe within their homes, although this viewpoint was decidedly mixed.

No Safe Groups Similarly, many participants commented that neighborhood members who had historically been "safe" from violence, particularly the very young, the elderly, and members of the clergy, had become increasingly vulnerable. Long-held neighborhood traditions of protecting young children, the elderly, and the sacred were seen as being undermined by widespread neighborhood violence.

Several participants further emphasized that violence was often random, senseless, and could occur anywhere, to anyone. Some participants recounted incidents in which babies had been killed by random gun violence. Helen recalled,

> This mother was sitting on the porch holding her baby, and someone passed by and started shooting up the house, and the baby took several bullets and died. These people have gone crazy; imagine, they are shooting and not caring who gets killed. An innocent baby murdered who has not done nothing to anyone and not even gotten a chance to live, or even learn to walk.

Other participants reported that the elderly were also commonly victims of neighborhood violence, a violation of long-held community norms. Evelyn said,

> A boy somewhere around thirteen to fifteen attacked and robbed this old lady. There was a time when old people were off limits and respected by young people. Young people would have their beef, and rob and steal from each other, but they knew not to put their hands on old people. That [old person] could be their mother or grandmother. . . . They should know better; they would not want anyone to rob or harm their own people.

Across all groups, several participants reported that ministers and other clergy were increasingly becoming victims of neighborhood violence. Melissa recounted an incident of a priest being shot inside a church:

> This whole thing is crazy. It is like the wild, wild, west, gangster style. This one priest was shot inside the church—people are shooting in churches.

Imagine, on church doors they have stickers saying "No guns allowed"— crazy you have to put that on church doors. That is all so crazy. Back in the day, church was a respected and sacred place . . . not anymore."

In summary, several participants endorsed the theme that neighborhood violence did not spare anyone, even those who had been protected from it in the past. One participant said, "These people come together anywhere and take it [violence] anyplace and everywhere, like it's a job."

Common Protective Parenting Strategies

The three most prevalent parenting strategies described by focus group participants in response to neighborhood violence exposure can be roughly summarized as "sheltering," "chauffeuring," and "removal." Sheltering consisted of limiting children's activities within the neighborhood; chauffeuring involved driving children between school, home, and recreational sites; and removal meant enrolling children in schools outside of the neighborhood.

Participants expressed a general sense that there was a lack of safety within Chicago's schools, and many reported removing their children from the Chicago Public Schools system altogether. A number of focus group participants indicated that they believed that suburban schools, private schools, and/or charter schools outside their neighborhoods were safer alternatives to the public school system. Many participants also believed that some black families choose to live in the suburbs for this reason, though there was disagreement as to whether the suburbs—or any place—were safe.

The protective parenting strategies most often mentioned were sheltering and chauffeuring, with little variation between male and female participants on these points, regardless of whether their children were boys or girls. Many participants said they limited their teenagers' activities, insisting that they go directly from home to school, staying away from playgrounds and public recreational spaces. One participant described parents acting as their teens' "private chauffeur services, taking them to and from school, to the mall, and avoiding public transportation because those are the places where violence is likely to jump off." Another participant said, "If I don't have enough gas that day—and I'm going to be honest to you—to take them to school, they not going," to which many in the group responded with a chorus of "Amen." Indeed, such strategies were often seen as having their own negative trade-offs.

One drawback to sheltering and chauffeuring that parents brought up was their concern that, without experience in the neighborhood, children are less able to build social ties and navigate their own communities. One parent explained, "The consequence is that they don't know anybody in the neighborhood and are less safe as a result." Several participants suggested that having a limited number of friends in the neighborhood meant that teenagers would have less protection against neighborhood violence. One participant, whose children lived in the south suburbs but stayed with him every other weekend in the city, said,

> I don't feel comfortable letting them [go] to the park. [I tell them,] "Y'all don't know anyone over here." They don't understand the mentality that the suburban kids have and the inner-city kids have. They don't experience none of the violence directly. I just don't feel comfortable letting them go out there.

On top of this, some parent participants said that attending an institution outside the neighborhood can create a stigma that the child "thinks they are better than" local kids or is "not as street smart," inadvertently setting the child up to become a target of violence. Some parents went on to explain that neighborhood youth often targeted those they perceived as feeling superior to other adolescents in the neighborhood, which often resulted in "high-minded youth becoming targets and victims of peer violence," in the words of one parent. Allison said that her son was attacked because of this stigma: "My son was jumped because he attended a charter school, and the other kids thought that he felt he was better than them."

These protective strategies entail financial, time, and other costs. Chauffeuring, for instance, means financial costs associated with transportation (e.g., gas and public transportation costs), and removal requires a large investment of time and money. One participant described how sending her child to school on the North Side meant that she was either commuting or in school from 6:15 AM to 5:15 PM. She said, "We attach an hour and a half of travel time onto our kids' days and still expect them to get the same amount done."

Finally, sheltering, removal, and chauffeuring may get in the way of particular milestones of child development and maturation within communities, such as developing autonomy by learning how to navigate public transport. One participant said, "I don't let my kids get on the bus or walk down the street . . . [but] that's not the answer, though, because it hinders their maturation." Another said, "Something else has to happen, because that's not a good fix . . . because you'll end up with eighteen-, twenty-one-year-olds who've never been on a bus." Roma said that her "son is relatively safe, because he really does not go anywhere other than home and school," but that "he is a pussycat because he has book sense but no street sense and does not know how to survive or handle himself on the streets, because he is so sheltered."

Many focus group participants saw rebuilding community networks and institutions as a solution to the challenge of neighborhood violence exposure among their children. Several participants echoed this notion, with one parent articulating that "it really does take a village," and another saying, "I know that sounds like a cliché, but that's where we have lost." One participant described the need for strong neighborhood institutions:

The reason why some areas have a higher propensity for violence is because in some neighborhoods, they have YMCA, they have BAM ["Becoming a Man"] programs like my child is in, they have after-school programs, [and] they have neighborhood programs . . . when you have other neighborhood[s] that have kids that are just as good and just as smart [who don't have access to such neighborhood supports]; that is where the greater violence is.

There seemed to be a consensus that both the problem of youth violence and its solution depended on the entire community—that to effectively curtail violence, the local community would need to engage in "rebuilding the village." However, participants recognized a paradox, with one summarizing, "We need the village, but we don't trust the village." This belief was a common theme across all groups: that trust or cohesion was undermined among neighborhood members in sectors where violence was prevalent.

Differences in Parenting Boys and Girls

A number of participants' parenting strategies differed according to the biological sex of their children, and they identified gender-specific approaches to coping with neighborhood violence. None of the participants raised issues related to gender-nonconforming youth, possibly because facilitators did not pose such questions. Most participants agreed that boys were more likely than girls to experience severe forms of violence in their neighborhoods because men and boys were often more physically threatening than women and girls. As Noreen explained, "Violence is just on a much more dangerous level, because men are more of a threat, which can result in someone getting killed."

Consequently, the gendered strategy of de-escalating aggressive and potentially violent male-to-male encounters emerged from the discussion. Some parents spoke of teaching their boys to, in the words of one participant, "walk away, try and cool down the situation," in order to stay alive. One father, Michael, recounted walking down the street with his fifteen-year-old son and being aggressively approached and shoved by four teenage boys. He described how he moved aside and modeled for his son the act of walking away, because he believed that retaliation might result in him or his son being shot. He said that although he fought the urge not to "get punked in the eyes of [his] son, it was more important that his son had a father who was alive than dead." Several focus group participants said they tried to teach their sons to "walk away and then get help." A common theme across all groups was that boys were more aggressive than girls, and, as a result, in the words of one parent, "things can quickly go really wrong, and sometimes deadly, when boys get into it."

Many participants indicated that boys were doubly at risk, as targets of both neighborhood violence and the criminal justice system. This was another reason some parents taught their sons not to use aggressive force. Jacquie stated that the "police are looking for boys more; they are looking for any reason to put our sons away. You have more black boys in prison than in college." This, by the way, is a common misconception: There are actually more black men in college than in prisons in the United States, though the number of incarcerated black men is troublingly high.[36] Several participants said they had told black boys that they were in a double bind: They could not trust police to protect them, and, even if they did report incidents of violence to the police, others in the neighborhood might retaliate. Within one focus group, many participants echoed a popular maxim: "Snitches get stitches." Participants discussed how young men in particular must manage daily threats from within their neighborhood, as well as the external threat of sometimes being unfairly targeted by police.

By contrast, many participants said that girls experienced greater physical and sexual vulnerability than boys. Participants consistently stated the need to protect their daughters from gender-based and sexual violence. Parental strategies included discussing what clothing their daughters wore. Shirley explained, "I tell her, don't wear certain types of clothes, because it incites certain types of problems." Neighborhood violence faced by boys and girls alike was, in the words of Monica, "both physical and psychological," with violence being used by "people that try to control them." Participants discussed the challenge of modeling positive communication behaviors, especially for girls, who may be vulnerable to negative or violent interactions with their male partners. One parent described a need to "talk with girls respectfully, so they can recognize when they aren't being treated well."

The distinct challenges faced by women and girls led several parents to reinforce the need for their daughters to carry weapons for defense. Shirley described women carrying weapons as a way to "put ourselves on equal footing [with] a man," and a majority of participants agreed that women needed to be "packing extra to put them on the same level." Eunice lamented the need for young girls to carry weapons, saying,

It's because I don't want [my daughter] to be like me; I don't want her to be afraid of everything. When I get on the train, I got a Taser, I have a knife, and I have mace. Why do I have all of this? I don't want her to be like me, I want her to be able to live free—[to] protect herself but live free at the same time.

Several parents indicated that they had forthright discussions with both their sons and daughters about neighborhood violence, and they often watched the local evening news together as a way to "talk about the topic and explain to them the need to be careful on the streets, given that someone was continuously getting shot in Chicago, and the news [was] always happy to report it." On the other hand, one mother reported that she did not allow her daughter to watch the local news for this very reason and only watched it with her son because she did not want her daughter to walk around in terror as she did. This strategy differed from the general consensus expressed by several other parents, who indicated the need to have both sons and daughters be well informed about the conditions of violence within their communities.

Summary and Conclusion

Numerous reports have established that black youth are exposed to higher rates of gun violence and murder relative to their white peers, a burden driven by the higher poverty rates they experience in America. However, few studies have investigated the coping strategies they use to navigate such violence. In the studies that my colleagues and I have conducted, boys reported more incidents of witnessing or being a victim of violence than girls did. Most of the violence reported by youth involved gangs. Coping styles ranged from "getting through," which included both an acceptance of community conditions and efforts to avoid thinking about one's situation or to overcome it; "getting along," which included self-defense techniques; "getting away," which included avoidance strategies; and "getting back," which consisted of confrontational strategies. Boys reported using confrontational coping styles more often than girls, who more often used avoidance approaches. These coping styles, despite being protective in some circumstances, can have unintended negative consequences.

On the other hand, studies of youth have also pointed to positive protective factors. Although the grinding effects of poverty and structural disadvantage are entrenched in American hierarchies, we can identify that having or being able to develop certain positive factors or characteristics, such as high self-esteem, having hope for the future, and more positive engagement with teachers and schools, can help youth avoid the harshest effects of inequality and neighborhood violence, even in the face of such hardships. Some of these factors are associated with lower levels of risky behaviors (e.g., delinquency, problem drug use, risky sex).

In this chapter, I also examined how black parents help their teenage children navigate violent neighborhoods and the strategies they use to protect their kids in the face of such dangers. Prior qualitative studies have revealed strategies that parents use to protect their teenagers from neighborhood violence, such as fostering open dialogues based on trust, increasing parental monitoring, and screening their children's friends.[37] Our study extended that research, finding that parents attempted to protect their youth primarily by sheltering and chauffeuring their children—both forms of active parental monitoring. However, many parent participants in our study indicated that these protective strategies sometimes made their children susceptible to other vulnerabilities. This study also extended earlier findings[38] by documenting that parents believed that exposure to neighborhood violence was pervasive, often random, and unpredictable, and that unlike in earlier times in their communities, no places or people were completely safe from violence.

Among our study participants, some parents' protective strategies depended on their children's gender. In general, boys were told to use less aggressive strategies to avoid or de-escalate potentially violent conflicts, whereas girls were encouraged to use more aggressive protective strategies because they were more physically vulnerable than boys. Many parents expressed the concern that boys in particular might become targets of the police and criminal justice system if they engaged in physical violence. Establishing a sense that parents working together could make a difference in the community was a priority expressed by many of the parents in our study, who also identified important obstacles to strengthening "the village," or the community. As several participants pointed out, while many stated their desire for enhanced connections and community institutions, many also indicated that they did not trust all fellow neighborhood members. The "removal" strategy that several parents employed—taking their children out of local schools and forbidding them from visiting local parks and recreational areas—also disrupted neighborly interactions, community-building routines, and the potential of local institutions to serve as social anchors for neighborhoods.

Noah, whom we met in chapter 5, mentioned that youth felt trapped in his neighborhood, which lacked resources and meaningful activities for them to engage in, leading youth to hang out and eventually use or sell drugs. In his words,

> I [am] thinking about the way the city and our life set up . . . the segregation in the city; if we all in one area, there are no resources and only negative energy to feed off from . . . then people would end up killing each other. In our environment, we are bored, we have to find things to entertain each other. . . . If there were resources in Englewood for people to get into after-school programs and positive things, we would not have so much violence.

Noah referenced the Salvation Army on 63rd Street, saying that it was doing its best without enough resources for all the people in the community who needed it. This Salvation Army operates a number of after-school, mentoring, and summer enrichment programs for youth. As he prophetically stated when talking about the root causes of being exposed to or participating in neighborhood violence, "for black youth . . . it's all about resources . . . having access to it or not." Therefore, giving young people in disadvantaged neighborhoods access to programs and resources that support positive youth development is critical for efforts to combat the causes and effects of neighborhood trauma. I discuss several of these programs in chapter 9.

8

JOINING THE BROKEN PIECES

Practice and Policy Solutions and
Systems Integration

America's health care system is neither healthy, caring, nor a system.
—WALTER CRONKITE

Walter Cronkite, the iconic newsman once called "the most trusted man in America," uttered this phrase describing our nation's disjointed system of care. The epidemic of neighborhood and gun violence in the United States is linked to our mental, physical, economic, and public health. Unfortunately, the ways in which the effects of and responses to neighborhood violence are addressed are uncaring and often haphazard. The lack of adequate treatment is worsened by factors such as race, poverty, and location. The responses, or nonresponses, often depend on the narrative in question, including the type of violence, who commits it, and in what public spaces it occurs.

In previous chapters, I highlighted how race affects policy, power, and access to full American citizenship. I traced the importance of understanding how knowledge is produced in our society and how power influences what we frame as or consider to be violence. I showed how neighborhood violence in impoverished black neighborhoods is in large part the result of decades of America's racialized history and uneven social policies. Finally, on the basis of my clinical practice and research, I amplified the narratives of youth and their parents to show that neighborhood violence is not merely an event but also an ongoing state of existence. Violent acts are perpetuated by humans but also by city, state, and federal structures and policies. Understanding the historical and ongoing trauma that youth in a racially and economically segregated America experience as continuous traumatic stress is a valuable foundation for assessing how well existing neighborhood violence programs or practice approaches respond to the needs of these youth.

As noted, the far-reaching effects of neighborhood violence among youth are not routinely assessed or treated with approaches that span the fields of mental health, education, juvenile justice, and public health. Social science literature often treats these overlapping domains as separate. Many of the negative behavioral health factors that mental health specialists, educators, juvenile justice systems, and public health professions are attempting to ameliorate in their own fields have root causes that can be attributed to neighborhood violence exposure. These multiple systems often work in isolation and tend to focus on one outcome while neglecting others. Consequently, practitioners and policy-makers do not adequately consider how deficits in one domain, resulting from neighborhood violence, might compromise the prospects of youth success in other areas. For example, education systems often try to improve academic outcomes by improving teacher training or reducing class sizes. This approach ignores the threats to academic success posed by ongoing neighborhood trauma, mental health difficulties, substance use, and sexually transmitted infections. In chapter 6, I used survey data to show how neighborhood violence, mental health problems, school deficits, juvenile justice system concerns, sexual risk behaviors, and drug use are all connected. I also shed light on these connections using youth narratives from interviews I have conducted over the years.

Social scientists increasingly recognize that neighborhood trauma is connected to mental health problems, educational difficulties, and juvenile justice system involvement. However, this understanding has not been effectively communicated and applied in the practice and policy domains. Consequently, many youth residing in low-resourced communities affected by neighborhood trauma are not routinely assessed for such violence exposure when they come into contact with the educational, child welfare, social service, and juvenile justice systems. Left unrecognized and unaddressed, the negative mental and behavioral aftereffects of neighborhood violence can culminate in huge social, human, and financial burdens. The price paid for this neglect is extended over time: When youth behavioral needs go untreated, these needs become more difficult and costly to treat in adulthood and have broader negative effects on the individual's partners and children, their community, and society overall.

In 2007, I published an article entitled "The Effects of Family and Community Violence Exposure Among Youth: Recommendations for Practice and Policy." The article shared several practice and policy recommendations aimed at reducing the far-reaching effects of such violence exposure among youth. Most of those recommendations come from the *Report of the Surgeon General's Conference on Children's Mental Health: A National Action Agenda*, published in 2000, which focused on improving mental health services for youth.[1] However, I specifically addressed service delivery for youth exposed to neighborhood violence—a natural area of focus, given that mental health difficulties are often associated with exposure to neighborhood violence, especially repetitive exposure.

In this chapter, I revisit and update these 2007 practice and policy recommendations. To frame the discussion, I briefly remind readers that approximately half of the neighborhood violence that youth experience is never reported.[2] The five proposals for addressing and reducing the effects of neighborhood violence are as follows: (1) increasing public awareness of exposure to neighborhood violence; (2) improving the detection and assessment of such exposure; (3) increasing the provision of evidence-based programs addressing violence; (4) locating mental health services in other vital youth systems; and (5) improving the coordination of services and interagency collaboration (figure 8.1).

Increasing Public Awareness of Exposure to Neighborhood Violence in America

The limited and biased ways in which violence in black neighborhoods is covered and black men are portrayed in the media restrict public

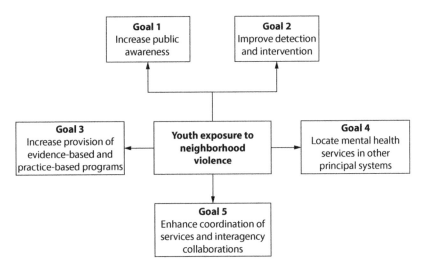

Figure 8.1

Recommendations for addressing the effects of youth exposure to neighborhood violence

awareness of the complex issues and the true extent of violence in America. This in turn has a dampening effect on accurate violence assessments and all aspects of violence prevention and intervention efforts. In America, coverage of mass school shootings and murders dominates the twenty-four-hour news cycle to the point that it is both traumatizing and desensitizing to viewers. At the same time, the mainstream media is relatively silent on gun-related homicides in black communities, especially within the context of structural causes.

The stunning shortage of nuanced discussions about the historical, social, and structural factors that give rise to the high burden of homicides in some black communities hinders public awareness of the violence in these neighborhoods. In addition, without hearing the voices of black youth, the public's understanding of what constitutes neighborhood violence is limited. For instance, black youth have identified excessive policing of their communities as a significant and ongoing form of structural violence. However, this broader framing of violence is rarely acknowledged in popular media discourse, although it has real implications for accurate violence aware-ness and assessments among black youth in low-income, highly segregated communities.

After the mass school shooting in Parkland, Florida, in February 2018, I received a media inquiry from a well-known West Coast news outlet. The reporter said, "I'm looking to write how the national conversation around gun violence and mass school shootings is largely leaving out black and brown kids, their perspectives, and the violence they experience on a regular basis." Although this one reporter wanted to tell this story, in general the mass media have neglected it. The glaring discrepancy is not lost on the scholars and community activists who have been sounding the alarm on this media coverage disparity for decades.

In the United States, from January to October 2018, 288 mass shootings occurred, including the one in Parkland, Florida, in which seventeen people were murdered and seventeen others were wounded. Mass school shoot-ings continue to occur almost every week in the United States.[3] Statistics show that most mass school shootings are typically committed by young white males and do not occur in spaces where the majority of victims are nonwhite.[4] These dynamics influence the volume of media coverage and the narratives scripted about the perpetrator, the causes, and possible solutions; for example, "Mental illness is to blame. He was isolated. He came from a troubled family and was bullied at school." These narratives might have some validity; however, they are in striking contrast to the dark and biased media narratives scripted about violence committed by young black males, which often use terms such as "super-predator," "gangbanger," "thug," and "inner-city shooter." These unrepresentative and prejudiced narratives limit opportunities for black youth and make their constrained outcomes seem natural and inevitable.[5] These narratives also direct resources away from these youth and their neighborhoods because they cause the public to view these youth as predatory and less deserving of resources. The lack of sus-tained, accurate media attention veils the struggles of black youth growing up in many of impoverished neighborhoods. The skewed media coverage of mass school shootings miseducates the public about the accurate picture of violence in America. Skewed narratives also drive funding to schools in lopsided percentages, with funding not allocated proportionally to the neighborhoods that are hardest hit by neighborhood and gun violence.

Less than 1 percent of all homicides occur within schools.[6] Between the time of the mass shooting at Columbine High School in 1999 and 2016, approximately 141 people were killed in a mass murder or attempted mass murder at a school.[7] In 2015 alone, a staggering 15,696 homicides took place, with black males bearing the highest burden.[8] This trend shows that the majority of murders occur in neighborhoods, not in school settings. After Columbine and leading up to 2015, the U.S. Department of Justice spent almost $870 million on school officers alone.[9] In 2014, schools and universities spent an additional estimated $768 million on security measures. In 2016, these figures climbed to a total of $907 million. In 2016, overall school security markets were estimated at $4.9 billion.[10] Too seldom are significant resources dedicated toward educational success, economic empowerment, and job creation in low-resourced communities, which are the social drivers that can help to reduce neighborhood homicide rates. The media message on American violence must shift to reflect a more complex and accurate profile of violence, especially in black and poor America.

During the 2018 March for Our Lives demonstration in Washington, DC, more than one million people advocated for tighter gun control laws. Media coverage highlighted several white high school students from Parkland, Florida, who expressed utter surprise to learn after the school murders, that dozens of their black and Latino classmates had numerous siblings and other family members who had been murdered by gun violence. Neighborhood segregation still exists across many American cities. In addition, structural, socioeconomic, and racial advantage protects privileged groups from experiencing the daily threats of gun violence suffered by America's truly disadvantaged.

The American media has the power to influence people's perception of gun violence and not flatten complex issues into simple narratives. However, few elements in the mainstream media have a sustained interest in or appetite for the topic. When taking media calls on violence in America, I make a point of always thanking reporters for their work on this topic and encouraging them to keep sustained attention on it. Typically, a handful of major daily stories work their way through America's twenty-four-hour news system to the exclusion of all others. In addition, the rapid, tunnel-vision of American news culture, coupled with the competition for ratings and advertising dollars, does not promote sustained coverage of gun and neighborhood violence in America. I am struck by how in-depth and nuanced British news reports on social issues are, compared with news reports in the United States. However, British newscasts are not subject to media ratings that affect advertising dollars or to the resulting American news philosophy of "if the story bleeds, it leads."

In contrast to the low level of general public knowledge of neighborhood violence in the United States, much of which is never reported, there are arguably higher levels of such awareness among teachers, community workers, and advocates in low-resourced neighborhoods. In a conversation with three young black male high school teachers working in a low-income Chicago South Side community, I asked, "How do teachers know when youth are exposed to violence in their neighborhoods?" They mentioned two techniques: peace circles and letters students write to themselves. In this context, the peace circle consists of a small number of students typically sitting in a circle of chairs without tables. Students hold a "talking stick" as they take turns speaking about neighborhood violence and sharing what happened, what they did, and potential solutions for coping with or reducing the number of such instances. The teachers also indicated that students are invited to write letters to themselves about neighborhood violence. School administrators collect these letters, and social workers follow up on a case-by-case basis. However, these and other mechanisms for detecting neighborhood violence are not common in schools or other settings where youth need them the most.

A common assumption is that neighborhood violence in economically disadvantaged communities also affects parents, who would be aware of the level of violence being experienced by their children. However, this is not always the case, as many youth do not disclose violent incidents to peers, family members, or teachers. Mary (whom we met in chapter 5) did not report the homicides and suicide she witnessed when a mentally ill mother flung her three children and herself off a fourteen-story building. She had blocked it out as a way of coping. Daniel, another young person

I spoke with, did not report to anyone that he had seen a teenage boy shot and thrown into the trunk of a car until our interview four years later. He was scared that reporting the shooting might result in serious injury to his family or himself, reciting the popular phrase "snitches get stiches." And Bernard did not report that he had seen one of his fellow gang members shoot a boy.

Research has shown that even among low-income black families residing in public housing, parents tended to underestimate and misclassify their children's exposure to neighborhood violence and distress symptoms.[11] Furthermore, when parents underestimated rates of violence exposure, their children reported higher violence participation, lower self-esteem, and less problem-solving capacity, accompanied by a higher degree of behavioral and mental distress. These findings suggest that parents' early and accurate detection of violence exposure can help reduce mental anguish and possibly violence participation among youth.

A necessary step to improving detection, assessment, and intervention for youth exposed to neighborhood violence is to promote public health campaigns to increase awareness of the severity of neighborhood violence across America—especially the role of guns, given that many instances of neighborhood violence involve their use. Currently, few broad-based campaigns are supporting such efforts. Broadly framing gun and neighborhood violence as significant threats to educational, mental health, and public health outcomes has the potential to increase national awareness of the appalling prevalence of these types of violence.

Recently, I presented to a group of mental health providers, showing them graphs illustrating that the United States has the highest rate of homicides and gun-related deaths among high-income countries (e.g., England, France, Germany, Italy). For example, our country's homicide rate is thirty-two times higher than that of France. Several attendees were unaware of this fact, as are many Americans, including those who plan and provide public health services. This lack of awareness hampers the development of effective violence assessments, programming, and policy. Public service announcements targeting youth, parents, and adolescent service providers could make more people aware of the early indicators of neighborhood violence exposure, thereby providing necessary cues for seeking assistance and reducing the stigma associated with reporting exposure to violence.[12]

Broadening public awareness of neighborhood violence and its after-effects could assist parents, caregivers, teachers, and community workers to recognize early signs of violence exposure and help youth access treatment or important social support services. Community workers and social service providers are the backbone of the U.S. mental health system. Schools of social work and other allied professions can provide strong leadership in training practitioners and service providers, especially those who work in educational, medical, child welfare, juvenile justice, and community agencies, to recognize the harmful effects associated with violence exposure.

The Me Too movement has begun to transform our society's view of sexual harassment and abuse, especially in the workplace. A similar public campaign drawing attention to neighborhood violence, backed by balanced, substantive, and sustained media attention and supported across public and private sectors, has the potential to be equally transformative. Such a collaborative effort could greatly increase public awareness of the broader impact of neighborhood violence and its many ramifications.

Improving Violence Assessment and Intervention

Improving assessment and intervention for people exposed to neighborhood violence is another major challenge. As discussed in previous chapters, research shows that youth exposed to neighborhood violence are at increased risk of a broad number of mental health and behavioral problems.[13] Some agencies and schools in low-resourced neighborhoods make efforts to routinely screen youth for exposure to neighborhood violence or at least provide outlets for them to discuss these traumas. However, the routine application of such approaches to assess and help youth exposed to neighborhood violence has been limited.

In training and planning meetings with colleagues, I have often advocated the importance of assessing youth for neighborhood violence exposure, especially in communities in which violence rates are widely known to be higher. In Chicago, as in many other major American cities, the vast majority of neighborhood and gun violence is clustered in specific communities, which are typically low income, with underperforming schools and higher rates of unemployment relative to other city zip codes. While service providers in many of these neighborhoods acknowledge the reality of violence, the content of their agencies' assessment forms guides what they actually assess, treat, and are reimbursed for treating. Although the questionnaires typically address childhood sexual abuse and family violence, most major assessment forms do not include questions related to neighborhood violence exposure. Consequently, the influence of neighborhood violence exposure on youth mental health problems, school difficulties, peer associations, or sexual risk behaviors might be often underestimated.

In a study of youth clients and their therapists in a residential treatment center, researchers found a lack of agreement between the therapists' and clients' reports of neighborhood and family violence exposures. Therapists believed that youth experienced higher rates of family violence and lower levels of neighborhood violence, whereas clients actually reported higher rates of neighborhood violence and lower rates of family violence.[14] These findings might signal that clinical training programs need to better emphasize the commonness of neighborhood violence exposure, especially in low-resourced, high-stress neighborhoods. As one service provider from that study stated, "I never asked the question [regarding neighborhood violence experiences]. . . . It's not part of my assessments. I don't see any relevance to it, but with family members, of course [it's relevant]. . . . Some of the questions, it seemed to me, what the hell, it's [neighborhood violence is] just not important."[15] In my current scholarship and work with community partners, the biggest concern is not whether neighborhood violence exposure is significant among residents in low-resourced communities but how to measure it accurately.

Another challenge related to assessing neighborhood violence is how best to do so with common assessment tools that are applicable across multiple disciplines, such as social work, psychology, and psychiatry. These tools need to incorporate cultural, ecological, and family considerations.[16] The National Institutes of Health[17] has identified several standardized measures for assessing neighborhood violence exposure:

- Survey of Exposure to Community Violence (SECV), self-report version[18]
- My Exposure to Violence (My ETV), parent/caregiver report version[19]
- Children's Report of Exposure to Violence (CREV)[20]
- Screen for Adolescent Violence Exposure (SAVE)[21]
- Conflict Tactics Scale (CTS)[22]

These assessment instruments, although widely used in research, have not been sufficiently adopted in practice. One challenge to incorporating these measures into broad, diverse practice settings is how best to assess for exposure to neighborhood violence as both victim and aggressor. Researchers and service providers at times make artificial distinctions between victims of violence and those who may participate in violence. Sometimes these experiences overlap, and the complex reasons youth may engage in violence sometimes blur the lines, making limited terms such as *victim* or *perpetrator* inadequate. A similar tension exists in assessing and labeling domestic violence. I have shown in previous narratives how some youth use violence as a form of self-defense in response to neighborhood threats or violence. Thus, researchers and service providers need to be educated and trained to accurately assess the full range of violence experiences without making judgments or oversimplifying complex relational and neighborhood dynamics.

I am most familiar with training programs in social work, and from this perspective I notice that although many social work schools frequently focus on family neglect, abuse, and violence, much more attention needs to be paid to neighborhood violence, including its commonness, negative aftereffects, and assessment, as well as intervention techniques. Training social workers and other mental health service providers to systematically use standardized neighborhood violence measures when assessing youth in low-resourced communities could significantly improve neighborhood violence assessment and intervention efforts.[23]

Increasing the Provision of Evidence-Based Programs Addressing Violence

Evidence-based programs are those that have been shown in rigorous research to produce positive results. Several challenges, as well as opportunities, exist for developing and promoting effective programs to reduce neighborhood violence rates and the impact on youth, families, and communities. The customary academic approach to designing and deploying interventions has been to focus on evidence-based interventions: programs that move from university research development and testing into communities. In practice, the lag time between the development of an intervention program and its adoption in community settings can range from five to ten years, depending on the focus of the intervention. Many interventions designed in the academy are never adopted by the communities for which they are intended, often because of the prohibitive cost of replicating these programs. Other programs languish because they fail to meet real-world practical standards or are not sustainable in communities and agencies that are poorly resourced.

Seldom recognized in university settings are practice-evidence programs, the flip side of evidence-based programs. Practice-evidence programs are effective approaches developed by communities on the basis of their know-how and knowledge of local community needs. Many of these programs have the potential to be refined and evaluated in conjunction with university partners. One example from Chicago is Mothers Against Senseless Killings, discussed in more detail in chapter 9. This program capitalizes on grassroots efforts by mothers involving monitoring and reconnecting with children in need of nurturing. Seeing and treating youth who are involved in gun violence as children with guns, not as thugs or criminals, crafts a new narrative for them that comes from within their community and not from law enforcement.[24] The development of more effective neighborhood violence prevention programs requires university–community partnerships that recognize communities as having not just needs but expertise that can inform academic knowledge development. This paradigm calls for a shift away from colonial notions of knowledge development toward a revised

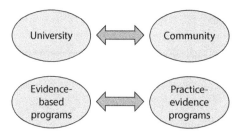

Figure 8.2

Advancing university and community collaborations to address neighborhood violence

model that recognizes and views community and university expertise as being equal and not ranked (figure 8.2).

Other challenges related to developing effective neighborhood violence prevention programs are how to evaluate whether these programs are effective and which criteria and whose standards to use. In university settings, randomized controlled trials have long been considered the highest standard for measuring program effectiveness. Randomized controlled trials, first used in medicine, involve eliminating the possibility that significant results could be attributed to chance by randomly assigning one group to the program being tested and another group to the standard service (or no services). An overreliance on such trials for establishing program effectiveness can obscure the significance of programs that are developed in community settings. Overly privileging the principles of evidence used in randomized controlled trials can also diminish the equal value of evidence provided by community workers, clinicians, families, and youth regarding program utility.

In the following section, I discuss some evidence-based and practice-evidence programs for reducing neighborhood violence and its common aftereffects. Some have been validated using the standards of randomized controlled trials, whereas the effectiveness of others has been established based on clinical and client observations and reports. These program approaches represent the commonly used methods for addressing the most common mental health distress symptoms associated with exposure to neighborhood violence. Neither the evidence-based nor the practice-evidence programs singularly address the broad range of possible negative aftereffects often associated with exposures to neighborhood violence (i.e., mental health disturbances, educational difficulties, problematic peer relationships, illicit drug use, risky sexual behaviors). An argument can be made that adequately addressing mental health disturbances may reduce the occurrence of school difficulties, poor peer relationships, drug use, and unsafe sex, but the existing evidence is insufficient to either validate or refute this claim. Additionally, the blunt reality is that many black youth are not experiencing violence as a singular event but as a continuous state based on structural inequality, poverty, and racial and social stratification within the United States, and it is impossible for any single program to address all these complex factors. Nevertheless, in chapter 9, I highlight some innovative programs that are attempting to expand and address the broader definition of continuous trauma.

Trauma-Focused Cognitive Behavioral Therapy

Trauma-focused cognitive behavioral therapy (TF-CBT) is the most widely evaluated and randomized controlled trial–supported approach for treating exposure to neighborhood violence or similar traumas. These programs share standard features, including educating clients regarding trauma and common reactions to such exposures, training them in mental approaches to reframe why a trauma occurred, helping them to develop effective behavioral approaches to support healthy responses to trauma, and helping them confront their fears of recurring violence by using self-talk or other visualization techniques.[25] Some of these treatments include parent involvement in either individual sessions or joint youth–parent sessions along with individual sessions for each.[26] Some TF-CBT programs were developed to be conducted in group formats in schools to target PTSD, anxiety, and depression symptoms among youth exposed to neighborhood violence.[27]

Only two TF-CBT interventions specifically focus on exposure to violence outside the home.[28] These programs have components similar to those included in other TF-CBT interventions, such as educating clients about trauma symptoms, managing distress symptoms, and developing safety plans to reduce the possibility of being exposed to violence again. These programs specifically target reducing mental distress (e.g., PTSD, aggression, anxiety, depression).

More recently, in recognition of the fact that people in some impoverished neighborhoods experience continuous trauma, TF-CBT approaches have been increasingly applied in these settings. Typically, such programs comprise four elements: (1) prioritizing safety by acknowledging safety concerns and identifying safe and unsafe situations; (2) enhancing engagement by mobilizing supportive community members; (3) helping individuals make distinctions between distress reminders and real dangers; and (4) advocating for additional services, either by the practitioner or by the client. Although the effectiveness of this approach has not yet been assessed with randomized controlled trials, the approach incorporates all of the clinical elements that I have found useful when working with people who have been traumatized by neighborhood violence.

Practice-Evidence Programs

Practice-evidence programs often involve approaches that have been judged to be effective based on service provider or clinician data and/or observations. They are also deemed effective based on data or self-reports collected from multiple clients.

Psychoeducation entails providing information that may help youth and their caregivers understand the experience of neighborhood violence. This approach may involve teaching individuals about symptoms associated with such exposures, normalizing their reactions, and teaching them how to increase safety or minimize future risk.[29] Education is rarely a standalone approach to treating exposure to neighborhood violence but is an essential component of other approaches (e.g., TF-CBT, mental first aid). Professionals and trained volunteers can provide this education. Normalizing reactions such as fear, anxiety, and other emotions related to exposure to neighborhood violence is a powerful way to support clients who are traumatized by violence. In my clinical experience, it sends a powerful signal that they are not alone, that their reactions to the violent incidents are what makes them human, and that their feelings in response to such stressors do not represent character faults or personal weaknesses.

Crisis intervention is emergency mental health care aimed at helping individuals in serious situations to regain some level of improved functioning and minimizing the possibility of mental and behavioral harm associated with neighborhood trauma or violence.[30] Crisis intervention entails providing an immediate opportunity for individuals to express their feelings related to the traumatic event and receive emotional support. This opportunity can be provided in an individual or group format, in person or via the internet or phone. It may be limited to one to three sessions and is typically provided by trained professionals or volunteers who provide an emotional holding environment for individuals to process or stabilize their reactions to trauma before being referred for ongoing treatment.

Psychological first aid also represents a short-term approach to reducing the potential negative effects of exposure to neighborhood violence. In 1988, Pynoos and Nader first described psychological first aid as a trauma-specific response to a deadly shooting on school grounds, and this intervention model has been continually expanded and revised for application in multiple settings.[31] It includes discussing or clarifying the traumatic event, providing participants with an opportunity to express their feelings, normalizing their emotional and behavioral responses, teaching problem-solving approaches to manage difficult beliefs and behaviors, screening for distress symptoms, and making follow-up referrals if necessary. This approach typically involves two or three sessions and may be provided by trained professionals or volunteers.[32]

Mental health first aid is a relatively new approach that can be applied to providing immediate, short-term support to victims of neighborhood violence exposures. Although similar to psychological first aid, the mental health first aid approach is typically delivered by laypeople, not trained mental health care providers. This approach trains laypeople to identify, understand, and respond to signs of mental distress and substance misuse in order to connect individuals in crisis to appropriate professional, peer, social, and self-help care. It is typically limited to one session and is aimed at stabilizing a person in crisis until a professional can get to the scene or the individual is transferred to a professional setting.[33]

Traumatic bereavement programs are based on modified grief counseling approaches and have been provided to youth who have witnessed homicides or lost friends or family members to neighborhood homicides.[34] Grief counseling is focused on helping youth express reactions to their loss, reducing the negative mental and behavioral symptoms by discussing and beginning to accept their loss, recalling positive experiences of the deceased individual, and adjusting to and establishing a new normal after the loss.[35]

Locating Mental Health Services in Other Vital Youth Systems

Black youth and their families residing in highly segregated and impoverished neighborhoods are at greater risk of neighborhood violence exposure. Reaching these youth and families will likely require outreach and the provision of trauma-related services that extend beyond the walls of conventional mental health settings.[36] As noted, not all youth exposed to violence will need mental health care. However, prevalence estimates of PTSD among city youth who have experienced exposure to violence range from 24 percent to 34.5 percent,[37] suggesting that a considerable proportion of youth exposed to neighborhood violence experience significant mental trauma. Second, in comparison to their white counterparts, black adolescents are less likely to seek formal mental health services.[38] In segments of black communities, a popular catchphrase is "Black people don't seek mental health services; they go to church." This perspective points to a cultural stigma associated not only with reporting mental distress but also with seeking mental health services. Factors such as high cost, provider bias, and a lack of cultural familiarity with minority populations' mental health needs further compound the limitations related to the access and use of formal mental health services.

The surgeon general's report on mental health shows that parents from ethnic-minority backgrounds are more likely to consult family and community members for help for their children than are parents from nonminority backgrounds.[39] Also described in another report by the surgeon general are striking disparities for minorities in mental health services and the underlying knowledge base. Racial and ethnic minorities have less access to mental health service than do whites. They are less likely to receive needed care. When they receive care, it is more likely to be poor in quality. . . . A major finding . . . is that racial and ethnic minorities bear a higher burden from unmet mental health needs and thus suffer a more significant loss of their overall health and productivity.[40]

To help address the disparities in access to and use of mental health services, service providers must be culturally attuned and use flexible approaches to engage and treat black youth and their families. Interventions must consider and incorporate culturally significant forms of support and healing that are aligned with race, culture, family, and community norms.[41] I received excellent clinical training at the University of Michigan, but when I graduated, I saw clearly how many aspects of my treatment approaches were based on white middle-class norms. Several years ago, I sat with Wayne, a black fifteen-year-old, and his mother in my office. His mother reported that Wayne had not been sleeping and was having difficulty concentrating in school after he had witnessed a drive-by shooting in his neighborhood. Halfway into the session, she said, "His teacher said I should have him talk to a professional . . . but what I really think he needs is to go to church more, receive prayer, and that would heal his mind." I replied, "It seems your church and faith are really important parts of your supports, and that other professionals are also there. . . . How about inviting the pastor to attend next week's session so that together we can see how best to support you and Wayne as a team?" The following week, after she had signed the necessary consent forms, the pastor, Wayne, his mother, and I were sitting together in my office. Having the pastor there put Wayne's mother at ease. It also provided a unique opportunity for us to collectively validate the acceptability of mental health counseling and indigenous forms of helping, healing, and support such as faith traditions.

Additionally, moving mental health services and programs outside the walls of traditional mental health settings may reduce barriers to seeking assistance. As asserted by the surgeon general, the co-location of mental health services in central systems, such as health care, education, child welfare, and juvenile justice, as well as in community locations such as churches, community centers, and barber and beauty shops and nail salons, may serve to increase access to services.[42]

Improving the Coordination of Services and Interagency Collaboration

Because of the high probability that consequences of violence exposure will be observed in numerous contexts serving youth, there is a significant need for adequate training and interagency collaboration to reduce the broad effects of violence exposure. As noted, increased technical assistance and training for detecting, assessing, and intervening to address neighborhood violence exposure should be provided to agencies that serve youth and their families and to professionals in the fields of child welfare, education, health care, substance abuse prevention, and family services.[43] Currently, the U.S. Departments of Education, Health and Human Services, and Justice have diverse philosophies of who the client is and who should be the target of intervention and treatment approaches. Improving the capacity, coordination, and evaluation of quality mental health care services across systems is a critical step in fostering active interagency collaboration,[44] and bridging service and treatment ideologies across networks is paramount.

One model for such interagency collaboration can be found in the local HIV/AIDS care consortia funded by the Ryan White HIV/AIDS Program to provide continuity of care and maximize resources to serve people living with and affected by HIV and AIDS. The groups include people living with and affected by HIV and AIDS and various agencies. In such interagency collaboration, program staff are encouraged to share technical expertise and systematically gather input from youth and families.[45] Systematic data collection across all programs to inform strategic planning, evaluate impact, and secure greater resources is a common feature of these partnerships. Although the application of such partnerships to address directly youth violence has limitations, the model still has utility for fostering formal, ongoing interagency collaboration to address a serious public health issue. The World Health Organization also suggests that local partnerships among social workers, police, employers, health care providers, government officials, and educators may provide opportunities to pilot and evaluate programs.[46] The goals may also be advanced by establishing formal partnerships among federal regulatory agencies, research institutions and universities, family service agencies, and professional associations.[47]

In Chicago and elsewhere, several umbrella organizations are funding community-based agencies that conduct important neighborhood violence prevention and intervention efforts. Recently, I had a conversation with the executive director of one such umbrella organization who noted several challenges associated with integrating systems and coordinating practice and policy despite the significant benefits that come with such collaborations. The executive director asked,

> How do we know whether our partner agencies are serving the youth who need our services the most; that is, youth who are exposed to the higher rates of neighborhood violence or those most inclined to engage in violence? Several program participants are receiving scattered services from multiple partner agencies, so it is possible that there are some youth who are being under- or over-served. How could we track and address this possible loophole? How do we know that the agencies are providing the right set of programs? What are some of the useful ways for measuring program effectiveness? How do we promote and coordinate interagency collaborations?

These are common and important questions to grapple with when advancing interagency collaborations.

One model for using data to bridge program silos can be found in the Integrated Database on Child and Family Programs in Illinois, spanning the years 1977 to 2014. This database links information from schools;

correctional facilities; and Medicaid, welfare benefits, child welfare, and unemployment programs and services. As in other places, a small number of families in Illinois typically use the bulk of the state's service resources. If more precise information were available to illuminate the circumstances of these families, their service history, and their neighborhood conditions, then the state could likely provide those families with better, more efficient services. Illinois and several other states are using administrative data across multiple service providers to obtain a more comprehensive picture of the service needs and gaps of high-need residents.[48]

Summary and Conclusion

Black youth in many impoverished neighborhoods across America experience appalling levels of gun homicides fueled by violent structural arrangements at the city, state, and federal system levels. Gun violence and neighborhood violence are serious medical and public health issues. However, America's response to gun violence and its related aftereffects is anemic and disjointed, shortcomings not helped by partial media coverage. The media has the capacity to educate and/or misinform the public on the reality of violence in America. It also has the ability, when working in tandem with advocacy groups, to help shift cultural norms and societal policy and practices. The Me Too movement to combat sexual harassment and violence, especially in the workplace, is one such example. Unfortunately, the predominant media discourse about neighborhood violence in America pivots around school and other mass shootings, which account for less than 2 percent of all homicides nationwide. Too little nuanced, sustained attention is given to the links among gun violence, race, poverty, and disadvantage in America. This limitation has a dampening effect on efforts to humanize and make the public aware of the problem of neighborhood and gun violence in impoverished black communities and can thus negatively affect all aspects of care, including assessment, treatment, and program funding.

Several recommendations may help improve the overall capacity and coordination of violence prevention and treatment programs for youth and families exposed to neighborhood and gun violence (see figure 8.1). Increasing public awareness of neighborhood violence and its effects may increase the number of people reporting violence exposure and enrolling in treatment programs. Awareness is also necessary for educating parents and service providers, who can lessen the negative mental and behavioral effects on youth exposed to violence. In impoverished communities, some schools and community agencies make efforts to assess youth for exposure to neighborhood violence. However, such efforts are limited at best. Formal assessment procedures need to incorporate nuanced items for detecting violence exposure and involvement that can identity youth in need of treatment. Although some widely used programs have been developed to support youth and families exposed to neighborhood violence, many more such programs are needed, especially those that target the broad range of mental and behavioral problems often associated with such exposure. In developing violence prevention and response programs, researchers and community members need to work collaboratively in the design, testing, and execution of these programs, recognizing each other's mutual expertise. In addition, mental health supports and services need to be provided and promoted, not only in agency settings, but also in churches, community centers, and in-home settings. Youth impacted by trauma may move throughout schools, mental health clinics, juvenile justice systems, child welfare settings, and public health clinics. It is important for these systems to overcome the challenges associated with interagency collaboration to capitalize on opportunities for improving the overall coordination of treatment and care for these youth, their families, and their communities.

9

MAKING A DIFFERENCE

Rebuilding the Village

Human progress is neither automatic nor inevitable. . . . Every step toward the goal of justice [in America] requires sacrifice, suffering, and struggle; the tireless exertions and passionate concern of dedicated individuals.
—MARTIN LUTHER KING JR.

The motivations that prompted me to write this book come full circle in this chapter. I wrote it because the complex stories of black youth and their families, constrained in the margins of America and exposed to high rates of neighborhood and gun violence, had to be told. I had read too many accounts in which neighborhoods overwhelmed by violence were represented in a top-down, pathologizing, colonial, and overly simplistic narrative. Much like First Lady Nancy Reagan's "Just Say No" antidrug campaign in the 1980s, which grossly oversimplified complex societal, historical, and economic issues, the existing narratives subdue the voices of these communities, and the causes of gun and neighborhood violence are often presented by law enforcement as individual problems requiring individual solutions. I wanted to shift the narratives from demonizing to humanizing and link these communities' stories and challenges to those of all Americans. I also wanted to provide conceptual models to help mental health care providers, teachers, juvenile justice system personnel, and public health workers view the actions of children and youth and their responses to violence through the lens of trauma and to consider how a traumatized youth with few resources might look and act.

In addition, after two decades of giving countless media interviews on neighborhood violence and its consequences, I became frustrated that the interviews were seldom geared toward solutions. Reporters and I sometimes engaged in complex conversations about neighborhood and gun violence and its enablers—poverty, joblessness, inadequate schools, structural oppression and racism, and the absence of sensible gun control measures—but most of these ideas were then presented as little more than a footnote in the published articles. One reporter readily agreed with me about the need for serious societal change to alter the social and economic factors that fuel neighborhood and gun violence. He then argued that those changes are too complex, cost too much, and would take many decades before any incremental adjustment could be seen. He also pointed out that some problems actually bring profits. He concluded, "Have we not been trying to solve the issue of poverty for centuries?" To the proponents of his view, I refer you to chapter 4 of this book; we have not yet tried to solve poverty equally for everyone.

On one occasion, I sensed that the large-scale societal solutions I was pitching were incongruent with the reporter's belief in the American dream, which expounds the myth of individuality and equal possibilities, suggesting that all successes and failures are self-made and that we can all pull ourselves up by our bootstraps regardless of adverse circumstances. The Hollywood and media depiction of this archetype promotes and oversimplifies narratives of American success stories. Many have pointed out the opposing viewpoint: Some people simply have no boots, let alone bootstraps with which to pull themselves up.

One of these reporters, a Chicago feature writer with whom I developed a close working relationship over the years, introduced me to the newspaper truism I mentioned in chapter 8, "if it bleeds, it leads," to demonstrate that negative news and narratives sell. Psychologists refer to this tendency as the negativity bias: the collective appetite for individuals to remember or seek out bad events. We are all conditioned on some level to gravitate toward negative, attention-grabbing news headlines. A major problem with the incomplete, damaging, and stigmatized stories in the news media about black youth and other disadvantaged populations and their misfortunes (all individually attributed) is that these stories justify the marginalization of these groups from full inclusion in America, rationalize the biased treatment they receive, and validate that their poor social outcomes are inevitable. Reporting on American presidents, politicians, celebrities, and movie stars is also subject to negative scripting to feed the human appetite and our negativity bias. However, such people have status, privilege, and significant financial means. From such a roost, all press is good press, and negative scripting typically is not detrimental. However, for impoverished black populations who already have constrained opportunities and few resources, such biased, skewed scripting is colossally damaging.

In my social work classes, students often struggle to decide whether they want to focus on working with individuals, families, and small groups or working in policy practice (i.e., system-level change). I often loosely evoke a well-known parable to highlight the equal importance of these two domains:

Two people were standing on a riverbank and saw a baby floating down the river in a basket. One person jumped in and pulled the baby to safety. Several minutes later, they both saw another baby floating down the river in a basket, and the same person repeated the rescue. After the twelfth such episode, the other person on the riverbank stated, "I am going to go upstream and see who is putting these babies into the river and stop them."

This story illustrates the importance of combining programs that fix a problem with efforts that prevent future problems. In this chapter, I discuss programs in Chicago that are meant to both prevent and fix the emotional, behavioral, and structural causes of neighborhood violence. In many cases, these programs repair some of the damage that comes from being exposed to neighborhood violence, prevent further damage from occurring, and to a lesser extent curtail some of the structural drivers of violence (e.g., school failure, unemployment). Many of these programs were not in existence when I began my research on neighborhood violence almost two decades ago, which speaks to the progress we have made in these communities.

The Chicago Citywide Violence Prevention Plan

Although some common factors are associated with violence involvement, each city has unique blueprints and challenges that create impoverished neighborhood niches in which interpersonal violence escalates. Consequently, violence prevention policies and community-based approaches must be localized. In Chicago, almost half of the city's homicide victims are youth between the ages of ten and twenty-five years.[1] Therefore, a focus on youth violence prevention is essential. The City of Chicago has developed a plan to prevent violence, intervene when it happens, and provide resources for individuals affected by violence.[2]

Fifty community leaders representing government, faith, community, media, university, and foundation partners developed this plan, which represents a modest start. Several of the city initiatives are duplicate programs or provide bandwidth to initiatives already being implemented by community stakeholders. Many of the measures are suppression driven, using traditional law enforcement approaches. None of its measures addresses the major structural drivers of violence or direct significant resources to the neighborhoods with high rates of poverty by establishing economic empowerment zones in areas with concentrated disadvantage. The effort is in many ways a bandage approach to the city's neighborhood violence problems, which are mostly concentrated in neighborhoods that have endured sustained disadvantage, with random spillover incidents extending into many of the city's more affluent neighborhoods.

City prevention efforts are provided in the form of CeaseFire, a violence prevention program operated by the Chicago Police Department that is modeled after the Boston "Operation Cease Fire" in four city districts. This initiative places a heavy emphasis on a singular message of deterrence to gang members from law enforcement, community and service providers: Stop the violence to avoid facing the full weight of the law. In some regards, this approach echoes the cursory "Just Say No" antidrug campaign of the 1980s. It does not adequately address the structural drivers of gang involvement or the real need to provide youth with healthy, viable alternatives to joining gangs to meet their safety, belonging, or economic needs.

The Youth Shooting Review is another intervention strategy identified by the city plan. This effort engages experts from government agencies and the nonprofit sector to investigate the causes of individual shootings. The intent is to generate information that could lead to a reduction in gang shootings. However, we already know from a host of systematic studies that to reduce youth involvement with violence and other antisocial behaviors, we need to provide youth with viable opportunities for advancement to adulthood, schools that perform well, viable jobs with living wages, and culturally responsive mentoring programs, all of which can help youth develop positive self-worth and a sense of hope for the future.[3]

The City of Chicago has identified several programs with an intervention focus. One Summer Chicago is intended to help high-need youth get jobs while school is out of session and especially targets youth who are under the care of the Department of Children and Family Services. Trauma-focused cognitive behavioral therapy (see chapter 8), often delivered in a group format, is intended to help youth understand the connection between emotion regulation and more appropriate responses to personal conflicts.

Six initiatives have been designed as response programs. The Safe Passage Program is operated by Chicago Public Schools in thirty-five high schools in high-need communities. Community watchers line designated routes to these schools to reassure students and parents that it is safe to attend school and to reduce the barriers to attending and concentrating at school.

The Gang School Safety Team is operated by the Chicago Police Department and aims to disrupt retaliation by youth and their families after a person has been the victim of violence; the program typically involves officers visiting the schools of those affected.

The SAFE Communities Program helps to build partnerships among neighbors to monitor their neighborhoods and reduce the amount of overall illegal activity such as drug sales and street violence. This effort is similar to that of neighborhood community watch groups.

The Chicago Department of Public Health's Office of Violence Prevention operates the Safe Start initiative, which aims to increase awareness among community members and social service providers of the effects of neighborhood violence.

The Jail Alternatives and Diversion program provides alternatives to incarceration. Instead of serving jail time, youth serving probation can report to a designated center to participate in programs to earn high school credits.

Finally, the Aftercare Services program aims to reduce recidivism by providing services to youth discharged from state-run youth correctional facilities. In principle, aftercare plans are expected to be individualized in order to address the unique mental health and/or substance abuse needs of youth.[4]

Figure 9.1

The Chicago Safe Passage Program aims to provide children and youth with violence-free routes to and from school.

Source: Dexter R. Voisin

To date, I am unaware of any official evaluations of the effectiveness of these citywide initiatives. As is typically the case with many such efforts, stakeholders have persistent concerns about whether the youth most in need are being captured or accessing these programs. Engaging in systematic follow-up with these youth is difficult because of the typically limited staffing of these programs and the sometimes highly mobile nature of these youth. Finally, these programs do not substantially address ongoing barriers to participation, such as transportation, lack of social support, or programs not being culturally responsive.

To address these problems, the city needs to employ innovative, multifaceted, more holistic approaches to address the structural drivers of neighborhood violence, such as income inequality, racism, school failure, inadequate housing and health care, disproportionate rates of incarceration, community hopelessness, and mistrust of law enforcement. Much of the public rhetoric emanating from city officials does little to address these larger issues. Therefore, I believe there is a real opportunity for Chicago officials to build more trusting relationships with neighborhoods of high need and directly target the structural drivers of neighborhood violence while addressing its symptoms and aftereffects.

Community Programs Working to Make a Difference

For decades, the resilience of impoverished black communities has been tried by racial inequality, schools that do not teach, the vanishing of sustainable jobs, and the dismantling of social services and the black family. In the remainder of this chapter, I highlight the incredible resilience of these communities, which exist in the margins of America and are attempting to rebuild their "villages." "It takes a village a raise a child" is a popular African proverb. It refers to the impact that both the nuclear family and the larger community can have on the development of a child. My own development was positively shaped by a host of neighbors, honorary aunts and uncles, and other adults in the community who disciplined, mentored, and monitored me and other neighborhood children and who cultivated our self-esteem. Parenting extended beyond the nuclear family and was taken up by community members. This mantra is now referenced with nostalgia and considered a myth by many. Many of the programs highlighted here are attempting to rebuild the pillars of the village by providing youth with mentorship, supporting educational completion and job attainment, fostering self-esteem, instilling discipline, and changing the self-narratives of these youth.

Many of the community programs highlighted in this chapter adopt a restorative justice approach. Such a method seeks to resolve infractions in ways that are agreeable to the parties involved yet recognizes that social inequalities exist and tries not to deepen such disparities. This approach is in direct contrast to the punishment ideology. One example of a restorative justice approach is having someone who damaged another person's property repair it without involving police or obtaining a criminal record, which can constrain social interaction, employment, political participation, and involvement in society.

The community programs discussed in this chapter are meant to illustrate efforts to reduce neighborhood violence and its common aftereffects; the list is not meant to be exhaustive. In actuality, most well-designed, culturally responsive programs that support positive youth development have the potential to curtail youth involvement in or exposure to neighborhood violence. However, I focus on programs specifically designed to prevent, interrupt, or treat the effects of neighborhood violence. Many of these programs and interventions use the arts, counseling, targeted case management, gang cessation efforts, and job skills development to address neighborhood trauma and its effects.

Mothers Against Senseless Killings

Mothers Against Senseless Killings (MASK) is a grassroots organization of mostly mothers who work year-round to help reduce gun violence in selected West Side and South Side neighborhoods where homicides rates are high. Founded in 2015 by Tamar Manasseh, the group seeks "to put eyes on the streets, interrupt violence and crime, and teach children to grow up as friends rather than enemies," according to their website. The primary mission of this multiracial coalition is to reduce neighborhood violence and to address food and housing insecurity, which are known structural drivers of neighborhood violence. During the hot summer months, shootings and murders tend to escalate across America. MASK members wear pink T-shirts, grill hot dogs, and give hugs to youth. One of their target areas is the intersection of 75th Street and Stewart Avenue in the Englewood community—one of the most violent neighborhoods and blocks in America. Since establishing a presence here, the organization reports that "there have been no murders, shootings, or even fistfights on that block." The group intervenes to prevent violence and retaliatory killings without police intervention by communicating directly with individuals within the community. Youth are valuable; they are not murderers or killers but young people in need of mothering and a mother, the group believes. According to Manasseh, "You cannot underestimate the power of the mother." Through their community engagement efforts, MASK is targeting many of the components that research shows help to reduce harmful youth behaviors and promote and rebuild healthy communities. Community adult monitoring of youth reduces a wide range of harmful youth behaviors (e.g., violence engagement, risky sex, drug use). It extends parenting from individual households into the neighborhood. It promotes the collective ability of a community to control its surroundings and thereby prevent problems or respond to them when they occur. More importantly, MASK is helping black youth to change negative social and group norms and to see themselves as valuable and deserving of a future without violence. This program has received some state funding but is primarily supported by donations.

Cure Violence

Cure Violence (formerly known as CeaseFire) was founded in 2000 by Gary Slutkin, an epidemiologist. In 2012 this program was contracted by the Chicago Police Department and awarded one million dollars to provide their services to two additional districts. That arrangement, however, dissolved after a brief pilot period.

According to its website, the organization aims to reduce the spread of gun violence by using public health strategies similar to those used to stop the spread of disease: by detecting and interrupting conflicts, identifying and treating individuals at the highest risk of violence, and changing social norms. Violence is treated as an epidemic and seen as being contagious (i.e., violence begets violence) through negative social norms around the acceptance of violence.

The Cure Violence model trains and dispatches paid outreach workers who have community credibility to prevent and disrupt violence in the streets before it becomes deadly. Some of the violence interrupters are former gang members. The model focuses on changing group and community norms by using and promoting nonviolent strategies for resolving conflicts. Interrupters embed themselves in affected neighborhoods and work to defuse tense situations by arranging and assisting with funerals, bringing food, talking with gang leaders, and engaging hospitalized victims of gun violence and their family members to prevent retaliatory violence. The Cure Violence program has been replicated in other American cities, including Camden (New Jersey), New Orleans, New York, and Philadelphia, and in a number of international cities. An evaluation of Chicago neighborhoods where the program has been implemented found a 41 percent to 73 percent reduction in shootings and a 100 percent reduction of retaliatory homicides in five of eight communities, according to the U.S. Department of Justice.[5] In Chicago, Cure Violence is funded by private, state, federal, and university donors.

Saint Sabina Outreach Services

Saint Sabina Outreach Services is operated by the Faith Community of St. Sabina and was founded by Reverend Michael Pfleger. The church and its auxiliary programs are located in Englewood, one of the most impoverished and highest-crime neighborhoods in both Chicago and the United States, where the unemployment rate is approximately 35 percent and the average yearly income is $10,599. Saint Sabina Outreach Services operates programs geared toward positive youth development and helping communities rebuild themselves, thus providing structural deterrents to violence involvement and exposure. The St. Sabina Academy is a Catholic elementary school running from prekindergarten through eighth grade. The St. Sabina Employment Resource Center offers a full range of services to help individuals find sustainable career opportunities. And the ARK of St. Sabina offers year-round mentoring, sports, and arts programs to help youth achieve their full potential.

Saint Sabina Outreach Services operates three programs designed to reduce gun violence among youth who belong to gangs. In 2012, the Peace Tournament was launched and supported by several high-profile National Basketball Association players who served as basketball coaches for rival gang members. The tournament marked the start of another program known as the Peace Maker program. Four former gang members serve as outreach workers to current gang members, providing them with alternatives to gang involvement and nonviolent means for resolving conflict and avoiding retaliation between gangs. Finally, the Strong Futures program connects justice system–involved, disconnected youth and young adults with full-time employment opportunities. The organization's website provides several testimonials from youth who obtained full-time employment through its programs.

Although the reasons are multifaceted, Englewood is now leading other Chicago neighborhoods by showing a 43 percent decrease in homicide rates from 2016 to 2017.[6] From a developmental perspective, programs like Saint Sabina are reducing neighborhood violence by developing healthy self-esteem, promoting hope for the future and positive alternatives to help youth achieve a sense of belonging, and generating income for youth in this low-resourced community.

I Grow Chicago

Also located in the Englewood neighborhood, I Grow Chicago aims to reduce neighborhood violence by addressing some of its structural drivers, such as poverty, unemployment, hunger, and hopelessness. According to the organization's philosophy of change, the organization "started in the streets, and is transforming the streets." The program operates out of the Peace House, once a boarded-up house marked for demolition. This house, often referred to by residents as "Grandma's House," is a space for community gathering and healing, providing approximately fifteen programs that address everyday needs such as helping clients obtain and pay for state identification cards and bus cards, providing guidance on what to wear to and providing free clothes for job interviews, and providing resume assistance. It is also home to a community garden where neighborhood residents grow their own food, as well as a number of other resources. Services for youth include after-school programs, summer camps, individualized tutoring, and a small basketball court, to name a few. The programs are important vehicles for removing common barriers associated with fully maturing and participating in society, such as covering small costs before a first paycheck is received. More importantly, the programs provide residents with a sense of safety, trust, and community that is often lacking in areas where neighborhood violence is high. Programs are infused with the message that participants are "loved, intelligent, and respected," a powerful counternarrative to the widespread negative portrayal and treatment of those living in impoverished circumstances.

Teaching community members yoga is a novel approach that I Grow Chicago uses to address the causes and sometimes damaging responses to neighborhood violence. Residents are trained as yoga instructors to be teachers and healers for their own community. Yoga teaches participants how to be in the moment, to focus on their breathing and its connection to their bodies, and to self-regulate. The hope is that these skills will translate into thinking before reacting to high-pressure or revenge situations, which can turn deadly. Before the start of the outdoor yoga class, a security guard protecting the class participants approaches nearby gang members, reassuring them that the class gathering is not a threat. The class teaches participants principles of cognitive behavior, enabling them to make connections between their thinking and subsequent behaviors. One yoga instructor, Tameka, shared in a newspaper interview an example of the program's success: During a yoga class, a shooting took place nearby, and one young man from the class ran toward the scene. When he arrived,

Figure 9.2

Yoga at I Grow Chicago: A yoga instructor walks her students through a pose called Shavasana. Yoga is used to teach community members how to self-regulate the impact of neighborhood stress.

Source: I Grow Chicago

Figure 9.3

Yoga at I Grow Chicago: In a sidewalk yoga class, an instructor teaches children how to self-regulate the impact of neighborhood stress.

Source: I Grow Chicago

his response to the incident was not automatic. Instead, he paused and returned to the I Grow Center to process and think through the incident, avoiding a potentially dangerous knee-jerk response.[7]

Taking a Closer Look

My research team and I had the opportunity to interview staff of some additional community-based programs that are working to make a difference. We posed the following questions:

- How did the program come about?
- How do key aspects of the program address the causes and consequences of neighborhood violence?
- Outside of funding, what are some of the challenges related to scaling and sustaining the program?
- What are some of this program's key performance indicators?
- What are some important lessons learned from program participants and frontline staff, and how are those lessons being incorporated into the program?
- How does the program's design or emphasis challenge, reframe, or endorse the narratives regarding youth residing in neighborhoods at risk of violence?
- What aspects of the program, if any, adopt a restorative justice approach?

Project FIRE

This program incorporates glassblowing as a therapeutic activity to address some of the mental and social disruptions caused by exposure to neighborhood violence. We interviewed Bradley Stolbach, a licensed pediatric clinical psychologist at the University of Chicago who is also the clinical director of the hospital-based violence intervention program Healing Hurt People–Chicago and a co-creator of Project FIRE. According to Stolbach, "The evolution and development of this project was organic." A colleague at the University of Chicago's Comer Children's Hospital shared with him the therapeutic nature of glassblowing and introduced him to Pearl Dick, a glass artist who later became the project's other co-creator. Together, Stolbach and Dick expanded the after-school glassblowing program that Dick had already been running and added mentorship and trauma education components for youth who had been affected by neighborhood violence. With funding from the University of Chicago Medicine Urban Health Initiative Faculty Fellowship, they developed a blueprint for a program on Chicago's South Side and launched Project FIRE as a pilot program in 2014.

Since the launch of the pilot, the program has served male youth aged fourteen to eighteen years who meet weekly in a small group format. Participants are referred to Project FIRE by Healing Hurt People–Chicago through the hospital where they received treatment after a violent injury. This program is modeled after the Sanctuary Model S.E.L.F. framework, so named for its emphasis on *s*afety, *e*motions, *l*oss and *l*etting go, and the *f*uture. According to Stolbach, "Everything in kids' lives often connects to one or all four of those things."

Noah, whose story was presented in chapter 5, is now a member of Project FIRE. He was shot in a gang-related incident and taken to a hospital emergency department. Noah recalled, "Being shot was my wake-up call; I have more than thirty pieces of bullet fragments in my body which I have to live with." During his recovery, a hospital social worker introduced him to the program. For him, the program was literally life-changing. It has introduced him to a group of youth who, as he describes, are "trying to do positive things with their lives."

Stolbach highlighted seven main components of the program:

1. *Mindfulness*: Youth exposed to neighborhood trauma and violence often experience distress symptoms, which might include hyperarousal, reoccurring thoughts, and bodily stress. Glassblowing is a whole-body experience that incorporates being mindful, being present in the moment, and sitting with the experience at hand. Its blend of danger and creativity

demands such a focus. It also allows participants to have fun and produce something unique.

2. *Safety*: A fixed feeling of safety eludes many youth who live in neighborhoods with high rates of gun violence. Stolbach remarked on the irony that molten glass at two thousand degrees Fahrenheit can be considered safe. However, as a psychotherapist, I see the healing power of this irony. The danger involved with glassblowing, unlike that in the neighborhoods of the program's participants, is something that can be controlled by these youth, and the process allows them to potentially transform and release fears that they must confront on regular basis.

3. *Economics and self-esteem*: In addition to teaching a unique art, Project FIRE provides participants with four hours of weekly employment at the project location. According to Stolbach, "It encourages them to develop a different narrative about themselves and changes how other people view them."

4. *A collaborative medium*: Research has shown that levels of neighborhood trust and cohesion are lower in communities that experience high rates of neighborhood violence. Stolbach shared that one "can't do this [art] alone. . . . Creating something beautiful is really powerful. . . . When you're working with people who you might otherwise be running away from or shooting, it changes a lot." He explained how conflicts in the neighborhood have been interrupted because of relationships that developed among participants in the program.

5. *Mentorship*: "We teach young people how to blow glass, and we also address [their] trauma," Stolbach said. Through mentorship provided by N'Kosi Barber, a member of the program staff, participants can learn what it means to have a career as an artist. Barber, who is black, says that "art and glassblowing saved [his] life." Being exposed to positive ethnic reflectors has been shown to help youth adopt positive social norms.

6. *Relationships*: Stolbach shared that he had been surprised "how quickly and strongly [the participants] got attached to each other." He continued, "Affiliation needs are huge at that age. This is another way [instead of a street organization] to meet those needs. Because it is positive and creative, not destructive, and it's about who they are, not who they're

with, it can be much more powerful." The program emphasizes organic relationship development and provides a support system that is "like a family," rather than exploiting a young person's need for affiliation, as street organizations do.

7. *Dedicated staff*: An important element, Stolbach emphasized, is Pearl Dick, Project FIRE's artist. "She's not someone who they would typically be connected with," he said. The intervention is not separable from her—she makes it what it is. I had an opportunity to observe Stolbach and Dick's interaction (who are both white) with several of the project participants at a community forum. The mutual care, connection, and regard the staff and participants showed toward each other were transparent. In my clinical work with youth over the years, I have found that positive change in youth depends less on what therapeutic mode is used (e.g., cognitive behavioral versus psychodynamic) and much more on the strength and bond of the therapeutic relationship. Youth need to know that someone believes in them without judgment.

Participation in Project FIRE is limited to those who have been directly affected by neighborhood violence (i.e., wounded or shot), and, because of legal and liability issues, the workshop can accept only youth aged fourteen to eighteen years. Space and scale are additional limitations hindering program expansion. The location can accommodate only fifteen participants at once; however, the small-group setting and the close relationships that participants are able to develop with each other and the staff are what makes the program successful, according to Stolbach. More youth could benefit from the program, but expanding it while keeping the small-group format would require finding more artists, as they are central to the method of delivery.

Measuring how programs are effective and by whose standards (e.g., those of participants, program administrators, and/or funders) is complex. Because prospective Project FIRE participants are referred to the program by Healing Hurt People–Chicago, the same key performance indicators (KPIs) used at Healing Hurt People–Chicago are used to measure Project FIRE's impact. The three main KPIs are reinjury, recidivism, and retaliation. Stolbach reported that for many of these indicators, participants are at 80 to 90 percent. Although some of the mental health KPIs also show improvements, these improvement are smaller, Stolbach explained, because the program does not involve individual therapy sessions. He mentioned that a less explicit but important result is that participants are not on the streets for the four hours they participate in the program each week, and he cited anecdotal evidence of individuals who had been hurt when they were supposed to be at the program. In Chicago and elsewhere across the country, violent crime data show spikes in rates of gun violence during certain times of day, during periods when the weather changes from colder to warmer, and during specific holiday periods. Therefore, especially for people at risk of neighborhood violence, being in safer spaces when violence is most likely to peak is paramount; however, the larger question of how to address structural inequalities to make communities safer must still be addressed.

In terms of the program itself, Stolbach noted the importance of safety in all its forms—physical, social, moral, emotional, and psychological—as well as relationships among participants. On a practical level, he said, the program cannot challenge or change participants' personal, behavioral, or peer norms if participants have real barriers getting to the program. Over the past decade, the field of behavioral health has increasingly recognized the need to address structural barriers that prevent people from accessing health care or adopting positive change. Stolbach and his colleagues are currently exploring optimal ways of supporting participants by reducing transportation barriers to program attendance. While Project FIRE budgets for public transportation, program participants can work with their targeted intervention specialists through Healing Hurt People–Chicago to come up with different transportation plans (e.g., the use of ride-sharing apps) when necessary. If a different method is chosen, the cost is deducted from the participant's pay, circumventing the need to pay before money is earned. Being flexible and addressing the antiquated adage that "if you build it, they will come" are key. Finally, Stolbach shared that program staff have learned from participants the importance of having "a space where you can be accepted for and express who you are." I have learned over the past two decades of conducting, studying, and teaching psychotherapy that behind individuals' many external veneers, the universal cry of the human heart must be seen, accepted, and valued and that people have the capacity to heal and change when validation, support, and access to real opportunities are present.

Project FIRE seeks to counteract the negative stereotypes often promoted about young black males residing in low-income neighborhoods. It challenges the deficit-based and limited narrative. Stolbach commented that when young black men are mentioned, "the picture of them blowing glass" is not what immediately comes to mind. I have often shared with my social work students the power of narratives to become self-producing. In terms of restorative justice, Stolbach believes the principles of the Healing Hurt People program align with a restorative justice approach because it provides black youth with a positive self-narrative and income-earning opportunities while acknowledging the risky contexts in which many of them reside. It also provides youth with nonviolent approaches and opportunities for addressing the real issues of gun violence and crime prevalent in some of their neighborhoods. However, Stolbach acknowledged that on occasion, program staff have seen a need for more tangible interventions, such as housing, and have used outside consultants to complement the program's efforts.

Project FIRE is connected with several other Chicago-based organizations doing similar work: Storycatchers Theatre, a musical theater program for incarcerated youth; YMCA Chicago's spoken-word Story Squad and Urban Warriors programs, which pair high-risk youth with combat veterans; and Free Write, an expressive arts and literacy program. Stolbach also mentioned two other programs he admires: Louder Than a Bomb, which provides an opportunity for young authors, and Passages, a wilderness therapy program. While he would love to collaborate more with these organizations, he said it could work only "if we had a different system where everyone is funded to collaborate." Instead, the competitive funding system encourages organizations to spend their time "trying to keep their funding and keep their funders happy," which does not foster or provide incentives for collaboration.

Figure 9.4

Youth participants of Project FIRE creating glass art

Source: Pearl Dick, Project FIRE

Bright Star Community Outreach

Bright Star Community Outreach (BSCO) is a community-based outreach program that takes a community health approach by providing trauma counseling modeled after The Urban Resilience Network (TURN) model. My colleagues and I interviewed its founder, Chris Harris, who is the pastor

Figure 9.5

A piece of glass art created by Project FIRE participants

Source: Pearl Dick, Project FIRE

of Chicago's Bright Star Church, and its chief operating officer, Rodney Carter, Bright Star Church's assistant pastor. Carter described TURN as a model he hoped would allow them not only to "achieve [their] mission as Bright Star" but also to expand the approach nationally. According to the BSCO website, the program's mission is to "empower residents to share in the responsibility of building community through resource development and collaborative partnerships."

BSCO was established in 2009 by Harris, a native of Chicago's Bronzeville community, after visiting the NATAL Israel Trauma and Resiliency Center in Tel Aviv for victims of terror and war. He saw a need for taking a "holistic and coordinated approach" in efforts to support and strengthen youth and families. One of the unique aspects of the BSCO program, Carter described, is that it uses community-sourced data to inform its work "instead of assuming" what the community needs. Based on this research, BSCO has developed a two-phase approach to its work. The first phase has five main scopes:

1. *Counseling*—to provide community-based trauma counseling for individuals with post-traumatic stress disorder.
2. *Mentorship*—to expand youths' points of reference.
3. *Parenting and family support*—to support families as a unit.
4. *Workforce development*—to improve access to employment, which, according to Carter, is "one of the best forms of violence prevention."
5. *Advocacy*—to empower youth and families to "fight for what they believe in."

In the second phase, the program focuses on these topics at a larger, community-based scale that allows program staff to determine the focus of their work. Community members have identified trauma-informed care, workforce development, education, and violence prevention as their current priorities.

The community's voice determines the focus of all of BSCO's work. As a community, they used asset mapping to explore areas for potential partnerships with existing organizations and, subsequently, where they could address gaps in programming. The process pointed to a clear need for programs focused on "youth as a whole." The program's school and families initiative aims to address that gap by building support systems for youth at risk of involvement in the justice system. This process involves group sessions with the youth, the family, and an educator for several weeks to explore ways to improve support both in and out of the classroom. The program is being expanded to include other youth for whom families and educators think it might be helpful. Another initiative Carter described was multisystemic therapy, which is built around a similar concept of developing support systems. Multisystemic therapy is targeted to youth between the ages of twelve and seventeen years who are "either justice-involved youth or at risk for being justice involved." The clinician's role is twofold: They provide cognitive behavioral therapy as well as case management to expand the youth's network of role models. Carter explained that "wherever we're not the resource, we don't mind being the referrer." They build relationships with other organizations to connect participants with the resources they need and recognize that community-led capacity-building is more effective than one organization trying to do it all. "Only community can build community," Carter said.

Some of the challenges BSCO faces are related to the process of getting community members to "embrace the system concept." They have to believe they can do better together, rather than trying to get by individually. BSCO's coalition-based model has attracted funders including Northwestern University, the University of Chicago, Cigna (a health insurance company), and the United Way. However, this support involves bridging a gap between the research and community worlds: "Getting partners to be receptive and getting researchers to understand things won't be successful if the community isn't involved," Carter explained. Building understanding about the need for mutual engagement has taken time, but community members have started to become more open to research as they see how it benefits them.

Evaluation occurs on individual and community levels. On the individual level, BSCO looks at suspensions of individual students through the TEAM (*t*ruancy, *e*ducation, *a*nd *m*entoring) program. When students are suspended or expelled, this program provides them with a place to go during school hours, where they can do homework and learn conflict resolution skills. One of the indicators of success is if students do not return to the program; Carter said that as of 2016, more than 80 percent of students "never came back again." On a community level, BSCO looks at trends across the Bronzeville community. They conduct youth surveys every two to three years and examine changes over time in terms of risk and protective factors. In these surveys, participants are asked about truancy, alcohol and drug use, and trauma. In 2015, they surveyed 1,800 youth across nineteen schools in Bronzeville. They had an 81 percent response rate and plan to compare the results with those of surveys conducted in 2018. Some of their main findings from these surveys were related to programming, through which people feel they can make a difference and build positive peer relationships.

Outside of the robust data from the surveys, BSCO has learned the importance of helping researchers and residents understand each other's work. Furthermore, they have learned how to build the community's trust, especially of those who come in to support the community. Harris explained, "Those who are not a part of the fabric of the community have to be introduced . . . by the community" to have an impact. Researchers not from Bronzeville have to "recognize, receive, and respect" the voices of community members to truly build a partnership.

BSCO is working to change the narratives of under-resourced urban communities, breaking down the notions that they do not want help and that they cannot help themselves. The program is building a narrative that "a determined community can make a tremendous impact with limited resources," according to Harris. The program is demonstrating the diversity of those who want to support urban communities while emphasizing the necessity of outsiders' putting away their assumptions and letting the community lead.

Harris emphasized BSCO's openness to collaborating with "anyone who is willing to collaborate with us," and he is energized about bridging the silos between organizations wanting to support their community. A pioneer in using faith and community liaisons to offer trauma counseling, BSCO wants to encourage other groups and communities to follow its lead. Through the development of partnerships with hospitals, community-based organizations, faith-based organizations, the United Way, and Cigna, BSCO is paving the way for organizations in nine other states that have pledged to implement the model. Harris hopes that if they "prove it out here first," the model will spread to other communities nationwide and will help people gain access to the resources they deserve.

The Crime Lab

The Crime Lab is a project of the University of Chicago Urban Labs program that aims to address five main aspects of urban life: crime, education, health, poverty, and energy and environment. Through partnerships with leaders across sectors including policy and philanthropy, the Crime Lab works to identify "opportunities to deepen [its] work," according to Roseanna Ander, the executive director of the Crime Lab.

Ander explained the impetus for creating the Crime Lab. In 2007, a University of Chicago doctoral student was shot after defending his dissertation. Conversations about how to prevent youth violence in Chicago were already occurring, particularly through a series of *Chicago Tribune* articles on changing the narratives about kids who were being shot. However, this incident spurred the University of Chicago to think about what more it could do to be helpful to Chicago. Jens Ludwig and Harold Pollack, professors of social service administration at the University of Chicago, decided they needed to collect and examine evidence to help policy-makers, funders, and practitioners "better improve efforts over time." The Crime Lab believes that the university should be "leveraging in-house expertise to do high-quality research to tackle real-world challenges rather than just theoretical issues," Ander explained. In 2008, with seed money from the university, they launched the Crime Lab to partner with frontline practitioners and produce better evidence about what works. An Education Lab was also developed to "work alongside the Crime Lab," to make explicit the connection between crime and the education system.

The Crime Lab focuses on violence as a "very multifaceted phenomenon," intending to "identify a portfolio of strategies that can address and reduce the likelihood that violence happens in the first place." The lab's researchers are learning about a variety of interventions and working with a number of stakeholders, including the Chicago Police Department. Through this partnership, they hope to address the "consequence of using more enforcement than necessary" and explore ways to reduce the number of arrests and the amount of violence.

Recognizing that violence is "not unique to urban areas," Ander explained that it "manifests differently" in those areas. This viewpoint informs the focus of the Crime Lab, which takes a specific "interest in populations that are paying the highest price for interpersonal violence." The researchers are exploring a range of strategies to prevent violence on a larger scale by working with stakeholders from the public sector to guide spending and budgeting so they can have a greater impact. Looking only at how the philanthropic sector spends its money on community-based programs, for example, takes focus away from how redirecting funds to a community approach might better meet the community's needs. Ander described the lab's interest in finding ways in which they can "see a path toward public-sector investment to help scale those strategies." Their goal is to identify the effective aspects of various programs so that the "broader field can learn from it."

Challenges include not just the absence of sufficient funding for programs but "the way funding decisions are made and the timeline of contracts" for nonprofit organizations. Because nonprofits often have year-to-year contracts, planning for sustainability and capacity-building can be difficult when they have to focus their energy on maintaining funding. "Too often, funding is not necessarily allocated based on need or impact but [on] the notion that every community should get the same resources," Ander shared. The Crime Lab's goal is to support frontline organizations in their efforts to become sustainable by helping them examine and communicate the impact of long-term investment in their organizations. They also hope to find better mechanisms for "understanding duplication of and gaps in services."

A key metric of the Crime Lab's work involves assessing the demand for its work and examining whether the public sector is applying the evidence being generated by investing in the strategies the lab recommends. For instance, Chicago Public Schools decided to direct Title 1 funding toward "more intensive support in math classrooms" as a result of evidence shown by the Crime Lab, Ander noted. Other programs that have generated long-term funding as a result of the Crime Lab's assessments include the city's

One Summer Chicago youth employment program, Youth Guidance's Becoming a Man program, and the Strategic Decision Support Centers launched by the Chicago Police Department. These centers use technology such as gunshot detectors, software that helps district leaders determine where to deploy officers, surveillance cameras, and mobile phones so that officers can receive real-time information.

Through the Crime Lab's work, its researchers have learned about the lack of value attributed to the work of community-based organizations, first responders, teachers, and other frontline practitioners. As a society, we do little to "support [their] capacity and well-being to do this work long-term," Ander noted. Our society values work in the private sector more, instead of asking what kind of support frontline practitioners need. Furthermore, Ander has learned that sometimes the idea of what it takes to do this work is "overly simplified." One example is found in mentorship programs, she said. According to studies by the Crime Lab, "not all programs that try to match young people with positive adults really have impact" because youth need more than just a positive role model. Instead, mentorship programs should look more closely at the adults in these roles and how their skills can meet the needs of the young people they are supporting.

Ander emphasized a concern for understanding the "broader context" of violence and those involved:

> We need to be careful about seeing individuals through one dimension. . . . Even for young people who may pick up a gun, if we only look at them through that act, we are missing the fact that every single one of them was themselves failed or a victim first, before they became a perpetrator.

She stresses the importance of recognizing how these circumstances drive rational decisions that outsiders may have difficulty understanding. While the Crime Lab mainly focuses on negative outcomes of violence and the broad impact it has throughout communities, she also hopes the lab's work can help people see the "incredible resilience and strength and capacity for doing really important work in these neighborhoods." She wants the

Crime Lab's work to shed light on the challenges that communities are facing while articulating what it means to grow up experiencing the complex trauma associated with neighborhood violence.

The Crime Lab has worked to evaluate a number of restorative justice programs. Some of the Chicago Public Schools' socioemotional learning programs are focused on restorative practices in different settings, and the lab is researching this approach. They are starting to see it as an "interesting complement to other, more formal approaches" to challenges in schools. They have supported an overhaul of discipline procedures within Chicago Public Schools to incorporate more restorative justice approaches and plan to continue evaluating the effectiveness of these programs. Some of the programs Ander highlighted are Choose to Change, a partnership between a youth advocate program and a children's home, and Quiet Time, a meditation program in Chicago Public Schools showing "encouraging results." She noted that a lot of work is being done using a trauma-informed lens, and she hopes the Crime Lab will help improve the long-term sustainability of these programs.

The Urban Youth Trauma Center

The Urban Youth Trauma Center at the University of Illinois at Chicago was developed to respond to neighborhood violence with a trauma-informed approach. This approach acknowledges how trauma symptoms may contribute to individuals' problems, in contrast to punitive approaches, which primarily attribute blame. The center is partnered with agencies in California, New York, Ohio, and Texas through the National Child Traumatic Stress Network. According to Jaleel Abdul-Adil, a co-director of the center and an associate professor of clinical psychology at the University of Illinois at Chicago, the "program is geared toward supporting communities of color that suffer from chronic violence exposures but are unserved or underserved." The program supports community-based agencies and nongovernmental organizations that provide violence prevention and interruption services by helping to culturally adapt, implement, and test service programs that have been recognized as effective. The Urban Youth Trauma

Center also forges relationships and encourages information-sharing among service providers so that they can learn from each other and better respond to overall community needs and service gaps.

The Urban Youth Trauma Center has created a trauma-based adaptation of the World Health Organization's best practices of violence prevention. Delivering the program content using age-appropriate and culturally relatable means is important. Abdul-Adil has used rap music and hip-hop culture to disseminate some program messages and engage youth. It is all about making a difference: "I'm not a hypothesis tester. I want to be a life changer, and that is why we use evidence-based practices," he said.

Abdul-Adil stated that the technical expertise they offer service providers takes into account many of the social and structural factors that drive neighborhood violence: early exposure to interpersonal violence, which normalizes the use and reproduction of violence; the absence of basic resources (e.g., employment, adequate food, job training), which links poverty to violence and crime; and under-resourced and failing schools, which create barriers to legitimate employment and lead to engagement in alternative and illegal economies. Reactive and brutal policing, he believes, undermines the community's trust and leads to disproportionate numbers of biased arrests and family fragmentation. He views the large presence of street gangs as a problem contributing to neighborhood violence but recognizes that they exist to fill the void created by the lack of positive opportunity, safety, and employment. He stated, "Gangs exist not because they are inherently part of the community but because [young people] are trying to survive."

The Urban Youth Trauma Center promotes the following to support organizations that provide comprehensive and integrative care to youth affected by trauma:

1. *Encouraging early detection and treatment*—to increase awareness of the needs of traumatized youth and their associated concerns.
2. *Disseminating trauma-informed programs*—to increase the technical capacity of community-based agencies to provide trauma programs that are effective for youth.

3. *Providing a coordinated and integrated system of trauma care*—to work with multiple service providers to share resources, lessons learned, and strategic plans.

Performance measures are based on fidelity to program principles and the level of youth attendance at participating programs. According to Abdul-Adil, two primary lessons stand out from the work: the importance of focusing on youths' resilience and including their voices. He said, "Even with some of the most challenging situations with youth and their families . . . they show strengths and are able to transcend very difficult challenges." Furthermore, he emphasized that youth "know a lot more than we sometimes credit them [for]. . . . It is important for them to give program feedback and on occasions deliver the programs." Involving youth in program delivery, he said, helps to build credibility and improve engagement among other young people.

Through its programs, the Urban Youth Trauma Center addresses historical trauma, the dynamics of oppression, and institutional and structural violence. For example, in programs addressing violence in low-resourced, high-stress communities, the communities are not blamed for the challenges they face. The center's work also incorporates an understanding of intergenerational trauma, the "transmission of maladaptive dynamics and how institutions have played a role in that." Abdul-Adil pointed to the collective responsibility to understand these dynamics and dismantle oppressive institutions: "We think everybody in society plays a role in forming a collective, protective web. There's nobody who can say, 'This does not pertain to me.'"

Summary and Conclusion

James Baldwin remarked that the black child in America grows up in the shadow of the stars and stripes.[8] However, despite entrenched structural inequalities and the accompanying violence, many disadvantaged black communities are forging ahead and finding ways to redefine their narratives and futures, as well as their place in an America that is both beautiful and violent. Let us not fear, for we are not without answers. America is built on the ideal of working toward a more just society. Some decades have seen the nation move closer to this ideal.

The programs discussed in this chapter are attempting to make positive differences in the lives of black youth residing in neighborhoods beset by guns and violence. These programs support families and re-create the village concept, which supports positive youth development by extending child-rearing functions to community members outside the home. They recognize that many youth involved in violence are not gangbangers needing incarceration but children needing parenting, guidance, and opportunities. Fathers are absent from the home, and families are fragmented in part because of the high burden of incarceration that black men bear in disproportionate numbers in a handful of Chicago's South and West Side neighborhoods. These programs recognize that young black men need positive male mentoring and opportunities to see healthy reflections of themselves to counter the negative media coverage and biased historical narratives that often portray them as deficient or dangerous. In so doing, the programs help youth to reframe their narratives as positive and focused on hope and a future. As our research has shown among youth on Chicago's South Side, having a positive sense of the future is associated with a significant reduction in delinquent acts, drug use, and risky sex and better rates of mental health and school involvement. According to the concept of reciprocal change, creating a positive change for youth in one domain can have beneficial effects in other areas. For instance, providing increased community monitoring of youth that is driven by care and support rather than punishment might prevent initial or retaliatory violence, as MASK has shown. Supportive monitoring also promotes the development of positive self-esteem, which is related to better academic engagement and lower rates of problem behaviors such as delinquent acts and illicit drug use, factors that can bring black youth to the attention of correctional systems and fuel the cycle of incarceration, poverty, family and community disruption, and neighborhood violence. Many of these programs recognize that education, employment, and positive peer networks are important structural and social factors to reduce violence involvement among youth.

More community providers and residents are being trained to recognize the early signs of trauma to help youth access services earlier and to reduce or avoid the common misstep of responding to trauma symptoms with punitive measures, thereby avoiding compounding trauma with added trauma. Interagency collaborations allow programs to share data and learn from each other in conjunction with university partnerships that provide information, training, and evaluation. These programs are helping to fill the gap in the availability of trauma-informed programs that are culturally and practically relevant for youth residing in low-resourced neighborhoods. However, most of these programs are engaging in trauma responses—or pulling the babies from the river, to return to the parable recounted earlier in this chapter.

Policies and larger macro-level interventions focused on prevention are needed to decrease the factors that have paved the road to concentrated poverty and neighborhood violence in some black communities. These goals require sensible gun control legislation and federal policies ensuring universal background checks and limiting access to guns for those with mental illness. More importantly, against the backdrop of entrenched racialized capitalism, in which poverty is punished and the social ailments of marginalized Americans become economic drivers that fuel the livelihood of others, a shift from pseudo-treatment (i.e., punishment) to prevention is required. The U.S. government spends billions more dollars on treatment than prevention, whether for crime, sexually transmitted infections, or obesity. This spending paradigm needs to be retooled to shift high-paying jobs from punishment to prevention by supporting and providing necessary resources for low-income neighborhoods and then demonstrating the economic benefits for society that can result from such spending shifts, as capitalism is sustained by profits.

Some Closing Thoughts

The need for personal safety is universal. As my interviewee Noah stated, "Violence is a big distraction from people really knowing who they are and figuring out what they can actually become." On a larger societal level, his quote speaks truth to power. If people live with the fear that their lives can be easily snuffed out by a wandering bullet, if first grade students are terrified that they will be murdered in the classroom, if parishioners are alarmed that they could be executed while praying, then it is difficult, if not impossible, for Americans to imagine and strive for what we and our nation can fully become.

In 1998, I was working on my dissertation study of the relationship between high rates of neighborhood violence and elevated rates of drug use and unsafe sex among black youth in New York City. I sat down with a group of eleven black high school youth living in pre-gentrified Harlem to get their input on the questions I was drafting to measure neighborhood violence. The meeting ended with one of the youth, Jeff, saying to me, "I know you are black and all, but there is no way you can really understand what our lives are like. . . . My brother and several of my friends' brothers were killed before they got to thirty. . . . You made it past thirty." I have never forgotten what he said.

Twenty years later, in 2018, I interviewed Kenneth, a twenty-one-year-old black male from Chicago's South Side Woodlawn community. He had been shot twice, at the ages of fourteen and nineteen years old. I recounted what Jeff had shared with me two decades earlier and asked him what he thought about some young black youth believing they would not live past age thirty years. He replied, "Nah, I don't believe most brothers think that way. That is something the media pushes on us, then black men throw their lives away believing that." That was his truth, and I am sure there would be wide variation and complexity if other black youth responded to this question. In Kenneth's case, I wondered whether his involvement with Project FIRE and being exposed to opportunities he referred to as "outside his bubble" had offered him a different image and future for himself to counteract the media's narrative.

I am writing these final sentences on July 4, 2018, the day celebrating America's independence. We are once more at a crossroads, facing the opportunity to (re)define our nation and reconcile the present with our past. As we celebrate our independence, hundreds of refugees are fleeing violence and flocking daily to our borders, risking their lives and possible separation from their children to seek safety and a better life. President Ronald Reagan referred to this country as "a shining city upon a hill whose beacon light guides freedom-loving people everywhere." Against this

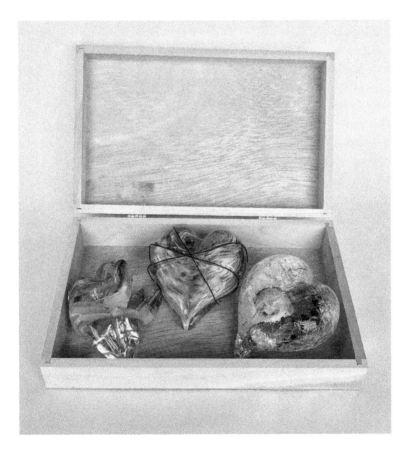

Figure 9.6

Works of art created by Project FIRE participants

Source: Pearl Dick, Project FIRE

backdrop, I recall the words of James Baldwin, who wrote about the black child in America growing up "in the shadow of the stars and stripes," and those of President Bill Clinton, who referred to the "people and communities who have not been touched by America's prosperity." To this, I would add "but who have been touched and scarred by America's violence." Yet, despite our country's entrenched structural inequalities, Jeff, Noah, Jesse, David, Mary, and the other youth quoted in this book, along with countless other black youth, families, and communities, are forging ahead, finding ways to redefine their narratives and find their place in America the violent and beautiful.

NOTES

1. The Beginning

1. Nancy Scheper-Hughes and Philippe Bourgois, eds., *Violence in War and Peace: An Anthology* (Malden, MA: Blackwell, 2004), 1.
2. Scheper-Hughes and Bourgois, *Violence in War and Peace*, 1.
3. Etienne G. Krug, James A. Mercy, Linda L. Dahlberg, and Anthony B. Zwi, "The World Report on Violence and Health," *Lancet* 360, no. 9339 (2002): 1083–88, quote at 1084.
4. Paul Farmer, "On Suffering and Structural Violence: A View from Below," *Race/Ethnicity: Multidisciplinary Global Contexts* 3, no. 1 (2009): 12–13.
5. Farmer, "On Suffering," 19.
6. Scheper-Hughes and Bourgois, *Violence in War and Peace*, 1.
7. Sudhir Venkatesh, *Floating City: A Rogue Sociologist Lost and Found in New York's Underground Economy* (New York: Penguin, 2013), 73.
8. Linda Alcoff, "The Problem of Speaking for Others," *Cultural Critique* 20 (Winter 1991–1992): 5–32; Linda Alcoff, "The Problem of Speaking for Others," in *Voice in Qualitative Inquiry: Challenging Conventional, Interpretive, and Critical Conceptions in Qualitative Research*, ed. Alecia Y. Jackson and Lisa A. Mazzei (New York: Routledge, 2009), 129–48.
9. Krug et al., "World Report on Violence and Health," 6.
10. Quoted in John Wagner and Mark Berman, "Trump Threatens to 'Send in the Feds' to Address Chicago 'Carnage,'" *Washington Post*, January 25, 2017, www.washingtonpost.com /news/post-politics/wp/2017/01/24/trump-threatens-to-send-in-the-feds-to-address -chicago-carnage/?utm_term=.e84689ca542a.
11. Kim Janssen, "Ta-Nehisi Coates: 'Chicago' Is 'Code for Black People,'" *Chicago Tribune*, October 18, 2017, www.chicagotribune.com/news/chicagoinc/ct-met-ta-nehisi-coates-1018 -chicago-inc-20171017-story.html.

2. The Tale of Two Americas

1. James Baldwin, "The Negro Child—His Self-Image," *Saturday Review*, December 21, 1963, 42–44, published as "A Talk to Teachers," in *Child Development and Learning*, ed. William C. Johnson (New York: MSS Information, 1973), 7–12.
2. Baldwin, "A Talk to Teachers," 8.
3. Baldwin, "A Talk to Teachers," 9.
4. Baldwin, "A Talk to Teachers," 11.
5. Chad Stone, Danilo Trisi, Arloc Sherman, and Roderick Taylor, "A Guide to Statistics on Historical Trends in Income Equality," Center on Budget and Policy Priorities, updated August 29, 2018, www.cbpp.org/research/poverty-and-inequality/a-guide-to-statistics-on -historical-trends-in-income-inequality.
6. Dedrick Asante-Mohammed, Chuck Collins, Josh Hoxie, and Emanuel Nieves, "The Road to Zero Wealth: How the Racial and Wealth Divide Is Hollowing Out America's Middle Class," Institute for Policy Studies, September 2017, www.ips-dc.org/wp-content /uploads/2017/09/The-Road-to-Zero-Wealth_FINAL.pdf.
7. Asante-Mohammed et al., "The Road to Zero Wealth," 5.
8. Jamelle Bouie, "The Wealth Gap Between Whites and Blacks Is Widening," *Slate*, September 17, 2017, www.slate.com/articles/news_and_politics/politics/2017/09/the_wealth _gap_between_whites_and_blacks_is_widening.html.
9. Bouie, "The Wealth Gap."
10. Nurith Aizenman, "Gun Violence: How the U.S. Compares with Other Countries," *Goats and Soda* (blog), *NPR*, October 6, 2017, www.npr.org/sections/goatsandsoda/2017/10 /06/555861898/gun-violence-how-the-u-s-compares-to-other-countries.
11. Organisation for Economic Cooperation and Development (OECD), *Education at a Glance 2014: OECD Indicators* (Paris: OECD Publishing, 2014), http://dx.doi.org/10.1787 /eag-2014-en.
12. Aizenman, "Gun Violence."
13. "Child Poverty," National Center for Children in Poverty, accessed February 9, 2018, www .nccp.org/topics/childpoverty.html.
14. Michelle Ye Hee Lee, "Does the United States Really Have 5 Percent of the World's Population and One Quarter of the World's Prisoners?" *Washington Post*, April 30, 2015, www.washingtonpost.com/news/fact-checker/wp/2015/04/30/does-the-united-states -really-have-five-percent-of-worlds-population-and-one-quarter-of-the-worlds -prisoners/?utm_term=.8a9c742b25f1.
15. Lee, "Does the United States?"
16. Gilda Sedgh, Lawrence B. Finer, Akinrinola Bankole, Michelle A. Eilers, and Susheela Singh, "Adolescent Pregnancy, Birth, and Abortion Rates Across Countries: Levels and Recent Trends," *Journal of Adolescent Health* 56, no. 2 (2015): 223–30.
17. Erin Grinshteyn and David Hemenway, "Violent Death Rates: The U.S. Compared with Other High-Income OECD Countries, 2010," *American Journal of Medicine* 129, no. 3 (2016): 266–73.

18. Erin Dooley, "Here's Why the Federal Government Can't Study Gun Violence," *ABC News*, October 6, 2017, http://abcnews.go.com/US/federal-government-study-gun-violence/story?id=50300379.

19. "Uniform Crime Report: Crime in the United States, 2016," U.S. Department of Justice, Fall 2017, https://ucr.fbi.gov/crime-in-the-u.s/2016/crime-in-the-u.s.-2016/topic-pages/murder.pdf, 1.

20. "The Counted: People Killed by Police in the United States," *Guardian*, accessed February 17, 2018, www.theguardian.com/us-news/series/counted-us-police-killings.

21. "The Counted: About the Project," *Guardian*, accessed October 9, 2018, www.theguardian.com/us-news/ng-interactive/2015/jun/01/about-the-counted.

22. "The Counted: About the Project."

23. "The Counted: About the Project."

24. Jasmine Gonzalez, "U.S. Has Highest Rates of Gun Violence Among Developed Countries," *New Trier News*, December 15, 2017, https://newtriernews.org/examiner/2017/12/15/u-s-has-highest-rates-of-gun-violence-among-developed-countries/.

25. Philip J. Cook and Jens Ludwig, *Gun Violence: The Real Costs* (Oxford: Oxford University Press, 2000).

26. Katherine Kaufer Christoffel, "Firearm Injuries: Epidemic Then, Endemic Now," *American Journal of Public Health* 97, no. 4 (2007): 626–29.

27. Grinshteyn and Hemenway, "Violent Death Rates."

28. Grinshteyn and Hemenway, "Violent Death Rates."

29. Erin Richardson and David Hemenway, "Homicide, Suicide, and Unintentional Firearm Fatality: Comparing the United States with Other High-Income Countries, 2003," *Journal of Trauma and Acute Care Surgery* 70, no. 1 (2011): 238–43.

30. "Gun Violence in America," Everytown, last modified February 1, 2019, https://everytownresearch.org/gun-violence-america/.

31. Grinshteyn and Hemenway, "Violent Death Rates."

32. "Gun Violence in America," Everytown, last modified February 1, 2019, https://everytownresearch.org/gun-violence-america/.

33. "Background Checks Matter," Everytown for Gun Safety, accessed April 20, 2018, https://everytownresearch.org/wp-content/uploads/2018/04/Background-Check_one-pager_040418.pdf.

34. Lois Beckett, "How the Gun Control Debate Ignores Black Lives," *ProPublica*, November 24, 2015, www.propublica.org/article/how-the-gun-control-debate-ignores-black-lives.

35. Katherine A. Fowler, Shane P. D. Jack, Bridget H. Lyons, Carter J. Betz, and Emiko Petrosky, "Surveillance for Violent Deaths—National Violent Death Reporting System, 18 States, 2014," *Morbidity and Mortality Weekly Report* 67, no. SS-2 (2018): 1–36, https://www.cdc.gov/mmwr/volumes/67/ss/ss6702a1.htm.

36. Grinshteyn and Hemenway, "Violent Death Rates."

37. Perri Klass, "A Pediatrician's View on Gun Violence and Children," *New York Times*, July 18, 2016, https://well.blogs.nytimes.com/2016/07/18/a-pediatricians-view-on-gun-violence-and-children/.

38. Klass, "A Pediatrician's View."

39. "Gun Violence in America," Everytown for Gun Safety, accessed October 10, 2018, https://everytownresearch.org/gun-violence-america/.

40. "Gun Violence by the Numbers," Everytown for Gun Safety, accessed April 20, 2018, https://everytownresearch.org/gun-violence-by-the-numbers/.

41. Charles Mock, Susan Pilcher, and Ronald Maier, "Comparison of the Costs of Acute Treatment for Gunshot and Stab Wounds: Further Evidence of the Need for Firearms Control," *Journal of Trauma* 36, no. 4 (1994): 516–21. The authors found that mean and median charges were higher for gunshot wounds ($14,541; $7,541) than for stab wounds ($6,446; $4,249).

42. Ted R. Miller, Children's Safety Network Economics and Data Analysis Resource Center, Pacific Institute for Research and Evaluation, December 2012, http://www.pire.org/documents/GSWcost2010.pdf.

43. Laurence Ralph, *Renegade Dreams: Living Through Injury in Gangland Chicago* (Chicago: University of Chicago Press, 2014).

44. Lois Beckett, "Domestic Violence and Guns: The Hidden American Crisis Ending Women's Lives," *Guardian*, April 11, 2017, www.theguardian.com/us-news/2017/apr/11/domestic-violence-shooting-deaths-women-husbands-boyfriends.

45. Patricia Tjaden and Nancy Thoennes, *Full Report of the Prevalence, Incidence, and Consequences of Intimate Partner Violence Against Women: Findings from the National Violence Against Women Survey* (Washington, DC: U.S. Department of Justice, 2000).

46. "Gun Violence by the Numbers."

47. April Fulton, "In Texas and Beyond, Mass Shootings Have Roots in Domestic Violence," *NPR*, November 7, 2017, www.npr.org/sections/health-shots/2017/11/07/562387350/in-texas-and-beyond-mass-shootings-have-roots-in-domestic-violence.

48. Kirsten Powers, "Angela Corey's Overzealous Prosecution of Marissa Alexander," *Daily Beast*, July 19, 2013, www.thedailybeast.com/angela-coreys-overzealous-prosecution-of-marissa-alexander.

49. "Background Checks Matter."

50. Kerry Shaw, "10 Essential Facts About Guns and Suicide," *The Trace*, September 6, 2016, www.thetrace.org/2016/09/10-facts-guns-suicide-prevention-month/.

51. Melonie Heron, "Deaths: Leading Causes for 2012," *National Vital Statistics Reports* 64, no. 10 (Hyattsville, MD: National Center for Health Statistics, 2015).

52. Beckett, "How the Gun Control Debate Ignores Black Lives."

53. Grinshteyn and Hemenway, "Violent Death Rates."

54. "Gun Violence by the Numbers."

55. "Gun Violence by the Numbers."

56. John Sullivan, Reis Thebault, Julie Tate, and Jennifer Jenkins, "Number of Fatal Shootings by Police Is Nearly Identical to Last Year," *Washington Post*, July 1, 2017, www.washingtonpost.com/investigations/number-of-fatal-shootings-by-police-is-nearly-identical-to-last-year/2017/07/01/98726cc6-5b5f-11e7-9fc6-c7ef4bc58d13_story.html?utm_term=.1e54b180f460.

57. Madison Park, "Police Shootings: Trials, Convictions Are Rare for Officers," *CNN*, March 27, 2018, www.cnn.com/2017/05/18/us/police-involved-shooting-cases/index.html.

58. Olivia B. Waxman, "How the U.S. Got Its Police Force," *Time*, updated May 18, 2017, http://time.com/4779112/police-history-origins/.

59. Isabel Wilkerson, "Mike Brown's Shooting and Jim Crow Lynchings Have Too Much in Common. It's Time for America to Own Up," *Guardian*, August 25, 2014, www.theguardian .com/commentisfree/2014/aug/25/mike-brown-shooting-jim-crow-lynchings-in -common.

60. Noah Berlatsky, "When Chicago Tortured: The Second City Is Still Grappling with a Long History of Police Brutality," *Atlantic*, December 17, 2014, www.theatlantic.com /national/archive/2014/12/chicago-police-torture-jon-burge/383839/.

61. Terrence McCoy, "Ferguson Shows How a Police Force Can Turn Into a Plundering 'Collection Agency,'" *Washington Post*, March 5, 2015, www.washingtonpost.com/news /morning-mix/wp/2015/03/05/ferguson-shows-how-a-police-force-can-turn-into-a -plundering-collection-agency/?utm_term=.685f69eb93a9.

62. Charles Goodwin, "Professional Vision," *American Anthropologist* 96, no. 3 (1994): 606–33, https://anthrosource.onlinelibrary.wiley.com/doi/abs/10.1525/aa.1994.96.3.02a00100.

63. Holly Yan, Khushbu Shah, and Emanuella Grinberg, "Ex-officer Michael Slager Pleads Guilty in Shooting Death of Walter Scott," *CNN*, May 2, 2017, www.cnn.com/2017/05/02 /us/michael-slager-federal-plea/index.html.

64. Yan, Shah, and Grinberg, "Ex-officer Michael Slager Pleads Guilty."

65. Yan, Shah, and Grinberg, "Ex-officer Michael Slager Pleads Guilty."

66. Sam Morris, "Mass Shootings in the U.S.: There Have Been 1,624 in 1,870 Days," *Guardian*, February 15, 2018, www.theguardian.com/us-news/ng-interactive/2017/oct/02/america- mass-shootings-gun-violence.

67. Morris, "Mass Shootings."

68. Lois Beckett, Rich Harris, Nadja Popovich, Jan Diehm, and Mona Chalabi, "America's Gun Problem Is So Much Bigger Than Mass Shootings," *Guardian*, June 21, 2016, www .theguardian.com/us-news/2016/jun/21/gun-control-debate-mass-shootings-gun-violence.

69. Jennifer Mascia, "15 Statistics That Tell the Story of Gun Violence in 2015," *The Trace*, December 23, 2015, www.thetrace.org/2015/12/gun-violence-stats-2015/.

70. Beckett et al., "America's Gun Problem."

71. Joel Miller, "Gun Violence and Mental Illness: Myths and Evidence-Based Facts," American Mental Health Counselors Association, October 3, 2017, www.amhca.org/blogs/joel -miller/2017/10/03/gun-violence-and-mental-illnessmyths-and-evidence-based-facts.

72. Beckett et al., "America's Gun Problem."

73. Beckett et al., "America's Gun Problem."

74. Beckett, "How the Gun Control Debate Ignores Black Lives."

75. Beckett, "How the Gun Control Debate Ignores Black Lives."

76. Philip J. Cook, Richard J. Harris, Jens Ludwig, and Harold A. Pollack, "Some Sources of Crime Guns in Chicago: Dirty Dealers, Straw Purchasers, and Traffickers," *Journal of Criminal Law and Criminology* 104, no. 4 (2015): 717–59.

77. Beckett et al., "America's Gun Problem."

78. Beckett et al., "America's Gun Problem."

79. Beckett et al., "America's Gun Problem."

80. "Why Is Chicago a Murder Capital? Clues from a Bloody Month," *Fox News*, September 29, 2016, www.foxnews.com/us/2016/09/29/why-is-chicago-murder-capital-clues-from-bloody -month.html; "FBI: Chicago Officially America's Murder Capital," *Fox News*, September 19, 2013, www.foxnews.com/us/2013/09/19/fbi-chicago-officially-america-murder-capital .html; "Murder Cases in Chicago Set to Hit the Highest Level in 20 Years with as Many as 90 Shootings a Week," *Weekly Challenger* (Tampa Bay, FL), August 29, 2016, http:// theweeklychallenger.com/murder-cases-set-to-hit-highest-level-in-20-years-90-shootings -a-week/.

81. Quoted in John Wagner and Mark Berman, "Trump Threatens to 'Send in the Feds' to Address Chicago 'Carnage,'" *Washington Post*, January 25, 2017, www.washingtonpost .com/news/post-politics/wp/2017/01/24/trump-threatens-to-send-in-the-feds-to -address-chicago-carnage/?utm_term=.e84689ca542a.

82. Beckett et al., "America's Gun Problem."

83. William J. Wilson, "The Other Side of Black Lives Matter," Brookings, December 14, 2015, www.brookings.edu/blog/social-mobility-memos/2015/12/14/the-other-side-of-black -lives-matter/.

84. Doreen Massey, "Geographies of Responsibility," *Geografiska Annaler: Series B, Human Geography* 86, no. 1 (2004): 5–18.

85. Kellee White and Luisa N. Borrell, "Racial/Ethnic Residential Segregation: Framing the Context of Health Risk and Health Disparities," *Health & Place* 17, no. 2 (2011): 438–48.

86. Anthony A. Braga, Andrew V. Papachristos, and David M. Hureau, "The Concentration and Stability of Gun Violence at Micro Places in Boston, 1980–2008," *Journal of Quantitative Criminology* 26, no. 1 (2010): 33–53.

87. Steven W. Perry, "A BJS Statistical Profile, 1992–2002: American Indians and Crime," U.S. Department of Justice, Office of Justice Programs, Bureau of Justice Statistics, 2004, www.bjs.gov/content/pub/pdf/aic02.pdf.

88. Perry, "A BJS Statistical Profile."

89. Garfield Hylton, "But What About Black-on-Black Crime?" *Abernathy*, accessed April 20, 2018, https://abernathymagazine.com/but-what-about-black-on-black-crime/.

90. Hylton, "But What About Black-on-Black Crime?"

91. Heather C. West, "Prison Inmates at Midyear 2009—Statistical Tables," U.S. Department of Justice, Bureau of Justice Statistics, June 2010, NCJ 230113, www.bjs.gov/content/pub /pdf/pim09st.pdf.

92. Mark T. Berg, "Accounting for Racial Disparities in the Nature of Violent Victimization," *Journal of Quantitative Criminology* 30, no. 4 (2014): 629–50.

93. Berg, "Accounting for Racial Disparities."

94. Natalie Y. Moore, *The South Side: A Portrait of Chicago and American Segregation* (New York: St. Martin's, 2016).

95. Ford Fessenden and Haeyoun Park, "Chicago's Murder Problem," *New York Times*, May 27, 2016, www.nytimes.com/interactive/2016/05/18/us/chicago-murder-problem.html.

96. Kenneth T. Jackson, "Federal Subsidy and the Suburban Dream" and "The Cost of Good Intentions," chapters 11 and 12 in *Crabgrass Frontier: The Suburbanization of the United States* (New York: Oxford University Press, 1985), 190–230.

97. Jeff Crump, Kathe Newman, Eric S. Belsky, Phil Ashton, David H. Kaplan, Daniel J. Hammel, and Elvin Wyly, "Cities Destroyed (Again) for Cash: Forum on the U.S. Foreclosure Crisis," *Urban Geography* 29, no. 8 (2008): 745–84; Elvin Wyly, Markus Moos, Daniel Hammel, and Emanuel Kabahizi, "Cartographies of Race and Class: Mapping the Class Monopoly Rents of American Subprime Mortgage Capital," *International Journal of Urban and Regional Research* 33, no. 2 (2009): 332–54.

98. Joel Rast, "Manufacturing Industrial Decline: The Politics of Economic Change in Chicago, 1955–1998," *Journal of Urban Affairs* 23, no. 2 (2001): 175–90; William Julius Wilson, "When Work Disappears," *Political Science Quarterly* 111, no. 4 (1996–1997): 567–95.

99. Michelle Alexander, *The New Jim Crow: Mass Incarceration in the Age of Colorblindness* (New York: New Press, 2012), 12–13.

100. Ta-Nehisi Coates, "The Case for Reparations," *Atlantic*, June 2014, www.theatlantic.com/magazine/archive/2014/06/the-case-for-reparations/361631/.

101. Robert J. Sampson, *Great American City: Chicago and the Enduring Neighborhood Effect* (Chicago: University of Chicago Press, 2012), 77.

102. Wilson, "The Other Side of Black Lives Matter."

103. Fessenden and Park, "Chicago's Murder Problem."

104. Fessenden and Park, "Chicago's Murder Problem."

105. Max Kapustin, Jens Ludwig, Marc Punkay, Kimberley Smith, Lauren Speigel, and David Welgus, "Gun Violence in Chicago, 2016," University of Chicago Crime Lab, January 2017, https://urbanlabs.uchicago.edu/attachments/store/2435a5d4658e2ca19f4f225b810ceod bdb9231cbdb8d702e784087469ee3/UchicagoCrimeLab+Gun+Violence+in+Chicago +2016.pdf.

106. Jeff Asher, "Murder Rates Don't Tell Us Everything About Gun Violence," *FiveThirtyEight*, October 30, 2015, https://fivethirtyeight.com/features/murder-rates-don't -tell-us-everything-about-gun-violence/.

107. Linda Qiu, "Fact-Checking a Comparison of Gun Deaths and Terrorism Deaths," *PolitiFact*, October 5, 2015, www.politifact.com/truth-o-meter/statements/2015/oct/05 /viral-image/fact-checking-comparison-gun-deaths-and-terrorism-/.

108. Ruth Igielnik and Anna Brown, "Key Takeaways on Americans' Views of Guns and Gun Ownership," Pew Research Center, June 22, 2017, www.pewresearch.org/fact-tank/2017/06/22 /key-takeaways-on-americans-views-of-guns-and-gun-ownership/.

109. Christopher Ingraham, "There Are Now More Guns Than People in the United States," *Washington Post*, October 5, 2015, www.washingtonpost.com/news/wonk/wp/2015/10/05 /guns-in-the-united-states-one-for-every-man-woman-and-child-and-then -some/?utm_term=.823e72f48c9d.

110. Mascia, "15 Statistics."

111. Patrick Blanchfield, "The Gun Control We Deserve," *N+1*, April 21, 2016, https:// nplusonemag.com/online-only/online-only/the-gun-control-we-deserve/.

112. Adam Winkler, *Gunfight: The Battle Over the Right to Bear Arms in America* (New York: Norton, 2011).

113. Blanchfield, "The Gun Control We Deserve."

114. Winkler, *Gunfight*, 19.

115. Winkler, *Gunfight*, ix–x.

116. Winkler, *Gunfight*, x.

117. Blanchfield, "The Gun Control We Deserve"; Winkler, *Gunfight*, 12.

118. Winkler, *Gunfight*.

119. Blanchfield, "The Gun Control We Deserve"; Winkler, *Gunfight*, 8.

120. Blanchfield, "The Gun Control We Deserve."

121. David A. Graham, "The Second Amendment's Second-Class Citizens," *Atlantic*, July 7, 2016, www.theatlantic.com/politics/archive/2016/07/alton-sterling-philando-castile-2nd -amendment-guns/490301/.

122. Cook et al., "Some Sources."

123. Cook et al., "Some Sources"; Philip J. Cook, Jens Ludwig, Sudhir Venkatesh, and Anthony A. Braga, "Underground Gun Markets," *The Economic Journal* 117, no. 524 (2007): F588–F618.

124. Cook et al., "Some Sources"; Cook et al., "Underground Gun Markets."

125. Cook et al., "Some Sources"; Martin Weil, Clarence Williams, and Julie Zauzmer, "Federal Judge Declares DC Ban on Carrying Handguns in Public Unconstitutional," *Washington Post*, July 27, 2014, www.washingtonpost.com/local/crime/federal-judge -overturns-dc-handgun-ban/2014/07/26/906bc366-1534-11e4-98ee-daea85133bc9_story .html?utm_term=.8b73e973c456.

126. Winkler, *Gunfight*, 14.

127. Winkler, *Gunfight*, 7–8.

128. "Not Your Grandparents' NRA: Howe Leadership of the NRA Puts Americans at Risk," Everytown for Gun Safety, April 2014, https://everytownresearch.org/documents/2015/04 /not-your-grandparents-nra.pdf.

129. "Not Your Grandparents' NRA."

130. Lauren Gambino, "NRA Contributions: How Much Money Is Spent on Lawmakers?" *Guardian*, February 16, 2018, www.theguardian.com/us-news/2018/feb/16/florida-school -shooting-focus-shifts-to-nra-gun-lobby-cash-to-lawmakers.

131. Cook et al., "Some Sources."

132. Anthony A. Braga, Garen J. Wintemute, Glenn L. Pierce, Philip J. Cook, and Greg Ridge-way, "Interpreting the Empirical Evidence on Illegal Gun Market Dynamics," *Journal of Urban Health* 89, no. 5 (2012): 779–93.

133. Braga et al., "Interpreting the Empirical Evidence."

134. Braga et al., "Interpreting the Empirical Evidence," 791.

135. Braga et al., "Interpreting the Empirical Evidence."

136. Braga et al., "Interpreting the Empirical Evidence," 785–86.

137. "Background Checks Matter."

138. "Background Checks Matter."

139. Melissa Jeltsen, "Study Finds States with Background Checks Have Fewer Mass Shootings," *HuffPost*, November 12, 2015, www.huffingtonpost.ca/entry/background-checks -mass-shootings_us_5644aab1e4b045bf3dedebfd?ec_carp=4969236368890860349.

140. "Latest Gun Violence Research: States with Background Checks Have Fewer Domestic Violence Homicides, Fewer Police Killed by Guns," Everytown for Gun Safety, January 16, 2015, https://everytown.org/press/latest-gun-violence-research-states-with-background -checks-have-fewer-domestic-violence-homicides-fewer-police-killed-by-guns/.

141. "Latest Gun Violence Research."

142. "Point, Click, Fire: An Investigation of Illegal Online Gun Sales," City of New York, December 2011, https://everytownresearch.org/documents/2015/04/point-click-fire.pdf.

143. "Point, Click, Fire."

144. "Point, Click, Fire."

145. "Gun Show Undercover: Report on Illegal Sales at Gun Shows," City of New York, October 2009, https://everytownresearch.org/documents/2015/04/gun-show-undercover.pdf.

146. "Gun Show Undercover."

147. "Gun Show Undercover," 5.

148. "Gun Show Undercover," 6–7.

149. Jonathan Masters, "Gun Control Around the World: A Primer—Lessons from Canada to Japan," *Atlantic*, January 12, 2016, www.theatlantic.com/international/archive/2016/01 /worldwide-gun-control-policy/423711/.

150. Michael Shurkin, "A Brief History of the Assault Rifle," *Atlantic*, June 30, 2016, www .theatlantic.com/technology/archive/2016/06/a-brief-history-of-the-assault-rifle /489428/.

151. Masters, "Gun Control Around the World."

152. Masters, "Gun Control Around the World."

153. Adam Weinstein and the Mother Jones News Team, "The Trayvon Martin Killing, Explained," *Mother Jones*, March 18, 2012, www.motherjones.com/politics/2012/03/what -happened-trayvon-martin-explained/.

154. Jennifer D. Carlson, "States, Subjects and Sovereign Power: Lessons from Global Gun Cultures," *Theoretical Criminology* 18, no. 3 (2014): 335–53; Weinstein and Mother Jones News Team, "The Trayvon Martin Killing."

155. For example, Carlson, "States, Subjects"; CNN Wire Staff, "Timeline of Events in Trayvon Martin Case," *CNN*, April 23, 2012, www.cnn.com/2012/04/23/justice/florida -zimmerman-timeline/; Ryan Bort, "A Timeline of George Zimmerman's Bizarre Life After Killing Trayvon Martin," *CNN*, May 12, 2016, www.newsweek.com/george-zimmerman -timeline-trayvon-martin-459300.

156. Carlson, "States, Subjects."

157. Yara Mekawi and Konrad Bresin, "Is the Evidence from Racial Bias Shooting Task Studies a Smoking Gun? Results from a Meta-analysis," *Journal of Experimental Social Psychology* 61 (2015): 120–30.

158. Christopher S. Koper, Daniel J. Woods, and Bruce E. Kubu, "Gun Violence Prevention Practices Among Local Police in the United States," *Policing: An International Journal of Police Strategies and Management* 36, no. 3 (2013), 577–603.

159. Koper, Woods, and Kubu, "Gun Violence Prevention Practices."

160. Keon L. Gilbert and Rashawn Ray, "Why Police Kill Black Males with Impunity: Applying Public Health Critical Race Praxis (PHCRP) to Address the Determinants of Policing Behaviors and 'Justifiable' Homicides in the USA," *Journal of Urban Health* 93, suppl. 1 (2016): 122–40.

161. "Targeted Fines and Fees Against Communities of Color: Civil Rights and Constitutional Implications," U.S. Commission on Civil Rights, September 2017, www.usccr.gov /pubs/2017/Statutory_Enforcement_Report2017.pdf.

162. Koper, Woods, and Kubu, "Gun Violence Prevention Practices," 578.

163. "A Weekend in Chicago," *New York Times*, June 4, 2016, www.nytimes.com/interactive /2016/06/04/us/chicago-shootings.html.

164. Alexander, *The New Jim Crow*; Sheila B. Murphy and Marsha Rosenbaum, "Two Women Who Used Cocaine Too Much: Class, Race, Gender, Crack, and Coke," in *Crack in America: Demon Drugs and Social Justice*, ed. Craig Reinarman and Harry G. Levine (Berkeley: University of California Press, 1997), 98–112; Dorothy E. Roberts, *Killing the Black Body: Race, Reproduction, and the Meaning of Liberty* (New York: Vintage, 1999), 17–21.

165. Harriet Jones, "Opioids and Heroin: From Drug War to Public Health Crisis," *WNPR*, October 7, 2016, http://wnpr.org/post/opioids-and-heroin-drug-war-public-health -crisis.

3. Not All Violence Is the Same: Race- and Place-Based Violence

1. Centers for Disease Control and Prevention (CDC), Web-Bbased Injury Statistics Query and Reporting System (WISQARS), National Center for Injury Prevention and Control, Office of Statistics and Programming, 2010.

2. C. Wright Mills, *The Sociological Imagination* (Oxford: Oxford University Press, 2000).

3. Jessica Chasmar, "Rahm Emanuel Blames Chicago Violence on 'Shortage of Values,'" *Washington Times*, August 6, 2018, www.washingtontimes.com/news/2018/aug/6/rahm -emanuel-blames-chicago-violence-shortage-valu/.

4. Patrick Wolfe, "Settler Colonialism and the Elimination of the Native," *Journal of Genocide Research* 8, no. 4 (2006): 387–409.

5. Sudhir Venkatesh, *Floating City: A Rogue Sociologist Lost and Found in New York's Underground Economy* (New York: Penguin, 2013), 95.

6. Bente Appel Esbensen and Bibbi Thomé, "Being Next of Kin to an Elderly Person with Cancer," *Scandinavian Journal of Caring Sciences* 24, no. 4 (2010): 648–54.

7. Howard N. Snyder and Melissa Sickmund, *Juvenile Offenders and Victims: 2006 National Report* (Washington, DC: U.S. Department of Justice, Office of Justice Programs, Office of Juvenile Justice and Delinquency Prevention, 2006).

8. CDC, National Center for Injury Prevention and Control, Office of Statistics and Programming, Web-based Injury Statistics Query and Reporting System, 2010.

9. Laura Kann et al., "Youth Risk Behavior Surveillance—United States, 2013," *Morbidity and Mortality Weekly Report* 63, no. 4 (2014): 1–168.

10. Snyder and Sickmund, *Juvenile Offenders and Victims*, 21.

11. "Teen Homicide, Suicide and Firearm Deaths," Child Trends, August 23, 2016, www .childtrends.org/indicators/teen-homicide-suicide-and-firearm-deaths/.

12. Robert J. Sampson, Jeffrey D. Morenoff, and Thomas Gannon-Rowley, "Assessing 'Neighborhood Effects': Social Processes and New Directions in Research," *Annual Review of Sociology* 28, no. 1 (2002): 443–78.

13. Elizabeth S. Anderson, "What Is the Point of Equality?" *Ethics* 109, no. 2 (1999): 287–337; Arielle R. Baskin-Sommers, Deborah R. Baskin, Ira B. Sommers, and Joseph P. Newman, "The Intersectionality of Sex, Race, and Psychopathology in Predicting Violent Crimes," *Criminal Justice and Behavior* 40, no. 10 (2013): 1068–91; Jonathan Crane, "The Epidemic Theory of Ghettos and Neighborhood Effects on Dropping Out and Teenage Childbearing," *American Journal of Sociology* 96, no. 5 (1991): 1226–59; Tama Leventhal and Jeanne Brooks-Gunn, "The Neighborhoods They Live In: The Effects of Neighborhood Residence on Child and Adolescent Outcomes," *Psychological Bulletin* 126, no. 2 (2000): 309; Laurence Steinberg, "Impact of Puberty on Family Relations: Effects of Pubertal Status and Pubertal Timing," *Developmental Psychology* 23, no. 3 (1987): 451; William Julius Wilson, *The Truly Disadvantaged: The Inner City, the Underclass, and Public Policy* (Chicago: University of Chicago Press, 2012).

14. Leventhal and Brooks-Gunn, "The Neighborhoods They Live In."

15. Fredrick Butcher, Joseph D. Galanek, Jeff M. Kretschmar, and Daniel J. Flannery, "The Impact of Neighborhood Disorganization on Neighborhood Exposure to Violence, Trauma Symptoms, and Social Relationships Among At-Risk Youth," *Social Science & Medicine* 146 (2015): 300–306.

16. Eugene Aisenberg and Todd Herrenkohl, "Community Violence in Context: Risk and Resilience in Children and Families," *Journal of Interpersonal Violence* 23, no. 3 (2008): 296–315; Mary Beth Selner-O'Hagan, Daniel J. Kindlon, Stephen L. Buka, Stephen W. Raudenbush, and Felton J. Earls, "Assessing Exposure to Violence in Urban Youth," *Journal of Child Psychology and Psychiatry* 39, no. 2 (1998): 215–24.

17. Selner-O'Hagan et al., "Assessing Exposure"; Albert D. Farrell and Steven E. Bruce, "Impact of Exposure to Community Violence on Violent Behavior and Emotional Distress Among Urban Adolescents," *Journal of Clinical Child Psychology* 26, no. 1 (1997): 2–14.

18. Gregory Smithsimon, "Are African American Families More Vulnerable in a Largely White Neighborhood?" *Guardian*, February 21, 2018, www.theguardian.com/books/2018 /feb/21/racial-segregation-in-america-causes.

19. Kelly M. Bower, Roland J. Thorpe Jr., Charles Rohde, and Darrell J. Gaskin, "The Intersection of Neighborhood Racial Segregation, Poverty, and Urbanicity and Its Impact on Food Store Availability in the United States," *Preventive Medicine* 58 (2014): 33–39.

20. Melissa Sickmund, "Census of Juveniles in Residential Placement Databook," U.S. Department of Justice, Office of Justice Programs, Office of Juvenile Justice and Delinquency Prevention Fact Sheet, June 2000, www.ncjrs.gov/pdffiles1/ojjdp/fs200008.pdf.

21. Stephen L. Buka, Theresa L. Stichick, Isolde Birdthistle, and Felton J. Earls, "Youth Exposure to Violence: Prevalence, Risks, and Consequences," *American Journal of Orthopsychiatry* 71, no. 3 (2001): 298.

22. Andrea D. Gurmankin, Daniel Polsky, and Kevin G. Volpp, "Accounting for Apparent 'Reverse' Racial Disparities in Department of Veterans Affairs (VA)–Based Medical Care: Influence of Out-of-VA Care," *American Journal of Public Health* 94, no. 12 (2004): 2076–78.

23. Sandro Galea and Roger D. Vaughan, "The Invisible Forces That Create the Health of Populations: A Public Health of Consequence, April 2018," *American Journal of Public Health* 108, no. 4 (2018): 445–46.

24. Paul Farmer, "On Suffering and Structural Violence: A View from Below," *Race/Ethnicity: Multidisciplinary Global Contexts* 3, no. 1 (2009): 13.

25. Audre Lorde, "The Master's Tools Will Never Dismantle the Master's House," in *Feminist Postcolonial Theory: A Reader*, ed. Reina Lewis and Sara Mills (New York: Routledge, 2003), 25.

26. Lorde, "The Master's Tools," 25.

27. Lorde, "The Master's Tools," 25.

28. Patricia Hill Collins, *Black Feminist Thought: Knowledge, Consciousness, and the Politics of Empowerment* (New York: Routledge, 2000), 6.

29. bell hooks, *Outlaw Culture: Resisting Representations* (New York: Routledge, 1994); bell hooks, *Teaching to Transgress: Education as the Practice of Freedom* (New York: Routledge, 2014).

30. Kimberle Crenshaw, "Mapping the Margins: Intersectionality, Identity Politics, and Violence Against Women of Color," *Stanford Law Review* 43, no. 6 (1991): 1242.

31. Crenshaw, "Mapping the Margins," 1242.

32. Crenshaw, "Mapping the Margins," 1244; describing Kimberle Crenshaw: Kimberle Crenshaw, "Demarginalizing the Intersection of Race and Sex: A Black Feminist Critique of Antidiscrimination Doctrine, Feminist Theory and Antiracist Politics," *University of Chicago Legal Forum* 1989, article 8, https://chicagounbound.uchicago.edu/uclf/vol1989/iss1/8.

33. Crenshaw, "Mapping the Margins," 1244.

34. Etienne G. Krug, Linda L. Dahlberg, James A. Mercy, Anthony B. Zwi, and Rafael Lozano, eds., *World Report on Violence and Health* (Geneva, Switzerland: World Health Organization, 2002), 8.

35. Charles M. Payne, *I've Got the Light of Freedom: The Organizing Tradition and the Mississippi Freedom Struggle* (Berkeley: University of California Press, 2007), xx.

36. Payne, *I've Got the Light of Freedom*, xviii.

37. Aimé Césaire, *Discourse on Colonialism*, quoted in Frantz Fanon, *Black Skin, White Masks* (London: Pluto, 2008), 1.

38. Goff, quoted in American Psychological Association, "Black Boys Viewed as Older, Less Innocent Than Whites, Research Finds," March 6, 2014, www.apa.org/news/press /releases/2014/03/black-boys-older.aspx; Phillip Atiba Goff, Matthew Christian Jackson, Brooke Allison Lewis Di Leone, Carmen Marie Culotta, and Natalie Ann DiTomasso, "The Essence of Innocence: Consequences of Dehumanizing Black Children," *Personality and Social Psychology* 106, no. 4 (2014): 526–45.

39. Aneeta Rattan, Cynthia S. Levine, Carol S. Dweck, and Jennifer L. Eberhardt, "Race and the Fragility of the Legal Distinction Between Juveniles and Adults," *PloS One* 7, no. 5 (2012): e36680.

40. Philip Bump, "People—Including Cops—See Black Kids as Less Innocent and Less Young Than White Kids," *Atlantic*, March 10, 2014, www.theatlantic.com/politics/archive /2014/03/people-including-cops-view-black-kids-less-innocent-and-less-young-white -kids/359026/.

41. Alice O'Connor, *Poverty Knowledge: Social Science, Social Policy, and the Poor in Twentieth-Century U.S. History* (Princeton, NJ: Princeton University Press, 2009).

42. O'Connor, *Poverty Knowledge*, 22.

43. Farmer, "On Suffering," 11; Max Liboiron, "The Perils of Ruin Porn: Slow Violence and the Ethics of Representation Discard Studies," *Discard Studies* (blog), March 23, 2015, https://discardstudies.com/2015/03/23/the-perils-of-ruin-porn-slow-violence-and-the -ethics-of-representation/.

44. Rob Nixon, *Slow Violence and the Environmentalism of the Poor* (Cambridge, MA: Harvard University Press, 2011), 2.

45. Karen Halttunen, "Humanitarianism and the Pornography of Pain in Anglo-American Culture," *The American Historical Review* 100, no. 2 (1995): 303–34.

46. Dexter R. Voisin, Jason D. P. Bird, Melissa Hardestry, and Cheng Shi Shiu, "African American Adolescents Living and Coping with Community Violence on Chicago's Southside," *Journal of Interpersonal Violence* 26, no. 12 (2011): 2483–98.

47. Olivia B. Waxman, "How the U.S. Got Its Police Force," *Time*, updated May 18, 2017, http://time.com/4779112/police-history-origins/.

4. The Road to Concentrated Poverty and Neighborhood Violence

1. Eduardo Bonilla-Silva, "Rethinking Racism: Toward a Structural Interpretation," *American Sociological Review* 62, no. 3 (1997): 465–80.

2. Dean Kalahar, "The Decline of the African American Family," *American Thinker* (blog), March 29, 2014, www.americanthinker.com/articles/2014/03/the_decline_of_the_african american_family.html.

3. "Historical National Population Estimates: July 1, 1900, to July 1, 1999," U.S. Census Bureau, revised June 28, 2000, www.census.gov/population/estimates/nation/popclockest .txt; "1860 Census: Population of the United States," U.S. Census Bureau, last revised January 16, 2018, www.census.gov/library/publications/1864/dec/1860a.html.

4. Stewart E. Tolnay, "The African American 'Great Migration' and Beyond," *Annual Review of Sociology* 29 (2003): 209–32; Isabel Wilkerson, "Part I: In the Land of the Forefathers," in *The Warmth of Other Suns: The Epic Story of America's Great Migration* (New York: Random House, 2010), 1–16; "The Great Migration, 1910 to 1970," U.S. Census Bureau, September 13, 2012, www.census.gov/dataviz/visualizations/020/.

5. Wilkerson, "Part I: In the Land of the Forefathers."

6. Wilkerson, "Part I: In the Land of the Forefathers."

7. Eric Foner, *A Short History of Reconstruction, 1863–1877* (New York: Harper & Row, 1990); Eduardo Mendieta, introduction to *Abolition Democracy: Beyond Prison, Torture and Empire*, by Angela Davis (New York: Seven Stories, 2005), 7–18.

8. Mendieta, introduction.

9. Foner, *A Short History*; Tolnay, "The African American 'Great Migration' and Beyond."

10. Foner, *A Short History*, 79.

11. Foner, *A Short History*, 46.

12. Mendieta, introduction.

13. Foner, *A Short History*; Tolnay, "The African American 'Great Migration' and Beyond."

14. Michelle Alexander, *The New Jim Crow: Mass Incarceration in the Age of Colorblindness* (New York: New Press, 2012); Mendieta, introduction.

15. Alexander, *The New Jim Crow*.

16. Alexander, *The New Jim Crow*; Mendieta, introduction.

17. Foner, *A Short History*.

18. Jerrold M. Packard, "Slavery Transformed Into Peonage, 1865–1896," in *American Nightmare: The History of Jim Crow* (New York: St. Martin's Griffin, 2003), 39–79.

19. Packard, "Slavery Transformed"; Andrew L. Shapiro, "Challenging Criminal Disenfranchisement Under the Voting Rights Act: A New Strategy," *Yale Law Journal* 103, no. 2 (1993): 537–66; Tolnay, "The African American 'Great Migration' and Beyond."

20. Packard, "Slavery Transformed."

21. Alexander, *The New Jim Crow*; Mendieta, introduction; Marc Mauer, "Voting Behind Bars: An Argument for Voting by Prisoners," *Harvard Law Journal* 54, no. 3 (2011): 549–66.

22. James Kilgore, "Racism and Mass Incarceration in the U.S. Heartland: Historical Roots of the New Jim Crow," People Demanding Action, November 29, 2015, http://peoplede mandingaction.org/component/k2/item/446-racism-and-mass-incarceration-in-the-us -heartland-historical-roots-of-the-new-jim-crow.

23. Foner, *A Short History*.

24. Alexander, *The New Jim Crow*; Henry Louis Gates Jr., "Making a Way Out of No Way (1897–1940)," episode 4 of *The African Americans: Many Rivers to Cross*, directed by Phil Bertelsen, written and presented by Henry Louis Gates Jr. (Los Angeles: Kunhardt McGee Productions and Inkwell Films, 2013).

25. Alexander, *The New Jim Crow*; Foner, *A Short History*; Stewart E. Tolnay and E. M. Beck, "Racial Violence and Black Migration in the South, 1910 to 1930," *American Sociological Review* 57, no. 1 (1992): 103–16.

26. Tolnay and Beck, "Racial Violence."

27. Mendieta, introduction; Packard, "Slavery Transformed."

28. Harold L. Wilensky and Charles N. Lebeaux, *Industrial Society and Social Welfare* (New York: Free Press, 1965).

29. "Table 4. Population: 1790 to 1990," U.S. Census Bureau, March 9, 1999, https://www.census.gov/population/www/censusdata/files/table-4.pdf; "Table 18. Nativity of the Population by Urban–Rural Residence and Size of Place: 1870 to 1940 and 1960 to 1990," U.S. Census Bureau, March 9, 1999, www.census.gov/population/www/documentation/twps0029/tab18.html.

30. Michael Ratcliffe, "A Century of Delineating a Changing Landscape: The Census Bureau's Urban and Rural Classification, 1910 to 2010," U.S. Census Bureau Geography Division, n.d., www2.census.gov/geo/pdfs/reference/ua/Century_of_Defining_Urban.pdf; "Table 18. Nativity of the Population."

31. Wilensky and Lebeaux, *Industrial Society*.

32. James Leiby, *A History of Social Welfare and Social Work in the United States* (New York: Columbia University Press, 1978).

33. Leiby, *A History of Social Welfare*.

34. Ashley S. Timmer and Jeffrey G. Williams, "Immigration Policy Prior to the 1930s: Labor Markets, Policy Interactions, and Globalization Backlash," *Population and Development Review* 24, no. 4 (1998): 739–71; Leiby, *A History of Social Welfare*.

35. Timmer and Williams, "Immigration Policy"; Tolnay, "The African American 'Great Migration' and Beyond."

36. Tolnay, "The African American 'Great Migration' and Beyond."

37. Wilkerson, "Part I: In the Land of the Forefathers."

38. Tolnay, "The African American 'Great Migration' and Beyond."

39. Campbell Gibson and Kay Jung, "Historical Census Statistics on Population Totals by Race, 1790 to 1990, and by Hispanic Origin, 1970 to 1990, for Large Cities and Other Urban Places in the United States," U.S. Census Bureau Population Division Working Paper No. 76, U.S. Census Bureau, February 2005, www.census.gov/population/www/documentation/twps0076/twps0076.pdf.

40. Tolnay, "The African American 'Great Migration' and Beyond"; Stanley Lieberson, *Piece of the Pie: Blacks and White Immigrants Since 1880* (Berkeley: University of California Press, 1980); Douglas S. Massey and Nancy A. Denton, *American Apartheid: Segregation and the Making of the Underclass* (Cambridge, MA: Harvard University Press, 1993).

41. Gordon W. Allport, *The Nature of Prejudice* (Oxford: Addison-Wesley, 1954); Herbert Blumer, "Race Prejudice as a Sense of Group Position," *Pacific Sociological Review* 1, no. 1 (1958): 3–7; Robert A. LeVine and Donald T. Campbell, *Ethnocentrism: Theories of Conflict, Ethnic Attitudes, and Group Behavior* (New York: John Wiley, 1972); Marylee C. Taylor, "How White Attitudes Vary with the Racial Composition of Local Populations: Numbers Count," *American Sociological Review* 63, no. 4 (1998): 512–35.

42. Allport, *The Nature of Prejudice*.

43. Lieberson, *Piece of the Pie*; Tolnay, "The African American 'Great Migration' and Beyond."

44. Robert L. Boyd, "The Great Migration to the North and the 'Black Metropolis' of the Early Twentieth Century: A Reevaluation of the Role of Black Community Size," *The Social Science Journal* 51, no. 1 (2014): 6–11.

45. Tolnay, "The African American 'Great Migration' and Beyond."

46. Boyd, "The Great Migration to the North."

47. Tolnay, "The African American 'Great Migration' and Beyond."

48. Tolnay, "The African American 'Great Migration' and Beyond."

49. Boyd, "The Great Migration to the North"; Tolnay, "The African American 'Great Migration' and Beyond."

50. Tolnay, "The African American 'Great Migration' and Beyond."

51. Cathy J. Cohen, *The Boundaries of Blackness: AIDS and the Breakdown of Black Politics* (Chicago: University of Chicago Press, 1999).

52. Lieberson, *Piece of the Pie.*

53. Kevin Fox Gotham, "Urban Space, Restrictive Covenants and the Origins of Racial Residential Segregation in a U.S. City, 1900–50," *International Journal of Urban and Regional Research* 24, no. 3 (2000): 616–33; Tolnay, "The African American 'Great Migration' and Beyond."

54. Gotham, "Urban Space."

55. Lieberson, *Piece of the Pie.*

56. Gotham, "Urban Space"; Lieberson, *Piece of the Pie.*

57. Gotham, "Urban Space."

58. Gotham, "Urban Space"; Charles L. Nier III, "Perpetuation of Segregation: Toward a New Historical and Legal Interpretation of Redlining Under the Fair Housing Act," *John Marshall Law Review* 32, no. 3 (1999): 617–66.

59. Gibson and Jung, "Historical Census Statistics."

60. William H. Frey, "Central City White Flight: Racial and Nonracial Causes," *American Sociological Review* 44 (1979): 425–88.

61. Frey, "Central City White Flight."

62. Gotham, "Urban Space"; Desmond King, *Separate and Unequal: Black Americans and the U.S. Federal Government* (Oxford: Oxford University Press, 1995).

63. Gibson and Jung, "Historical Census Statistics."

64. Frey, "Central City White Flight."

65. Pamela S. Karlan, "Ballots and Bullets: The Exceptional History of the Right to Vote," *University of Cincinnati Law Review* 71 (2002–2003): 1345–72.

66. Boyd, "The Great Migration to the North."

67. Massey and Denton, *American Apartheid*; William Julius Wilson, *When Work Disappears: The World of the New Urban Poor* (New York: Vintage, 1996).

68. Massey and Denton, *American Apartheid.*

69. Tolnay, "The African American 'Great Migration' and Beyond."

70. Nancy Leong, "Racial Capitalism," *Harvard Law Review*, June 20, 2013, https://harvardlawreview.org/2013/06/racial-capitalism/.

71. Leong, "Racial Capitalism."

72. Charles M. Payne, *I've Got the Light of Freedom: The Organizing Tradition and the Mississippi Freedom Struggle* (Berkeley: University of California Press, 2007).

73. Lucy Madison, "Condi Rice: U.S. Will Never Be 'Race Blind,'" *CBS: Face the Nation*, November 27, 2011, www.cbsnews.com/news/condi-rice-us-will-never-be-race-blind/.

74. Child Welfare Information Gateway, *Racial Disproportionality and Disparity in Child Welfare* (Washington, DC: U.S. Department of Health and Human Services, Children's Bureau, 2016).

75. "A New Majority: Low Income Students in the South's Public Schools," Southern Education Foundation, 2013, www.southerneducation.org/getattachment/c2b340ba-c31b-43b8-9d23-333a7f9b090c/A-New-Majority-Low-Income-Students-in-the-South-s.aspx.

76. Carlos R Soltero, "San Antonio ISD v. Rodriguez (1973) and the Search for Equality in School Funding," in *Latinos and American Law: Landmark Supreme Court Cases* (Austin: University of Texas Press, 2006), 77–94.

77. Sean F. Reardon, "The Widening Academic Achievement Gap Between the Rich and the Poor: New Evidence and Possible Explanations," in *Whither Opportunity? Rising Inequality, Schools, and Children's Life Chances*, ed. Greg J. Duncan and Richard Murnane (New York: Russell Sage Foundation; Chicago: Spencer Foundation, 2011), 91–116.

78. "Investigation Shows Inequality in School Funding Is a Legacy of Racial Injustice," Equal Justice Initiative, May 16, 2016, https://eji.org/news/investigation-shows-inequality-school-funding-legacy-racial-injustice.

79. "Investigation Shows Inequality in School Funding."

80. Tom LoBianco, "Report: Aide Says Nixon's War on Drugs Targeted Blacks, Hippies," *CNN*, updated March 24, 2016, www.cnn.com/2016/03/23/politics/john-ehrlichman-richard-nixon-drug-war-blacks-hippie/index.html.

81. Alexander, *The New Jim Crow*.

82. Alexander, *The New Jim Crow*; "Legal Scholar: Jim Crow Still Exists in America," *NPR*, January 16, 2012, www.npr.org/2012/01/16/145175694/legal-scholar-jim-crow-still-exists-in-america.

83. Christopher Ingraham, "White People Are More Likely to Deal Drugs, but Black People Are More Likely to Get Arrested for It," *Washington Post*, September 30, 2014, www.washingtonpost.com/news/wonk/wp/2014/09/30/white-people-are-more-likely-to-deal-drugs-but-black-people-are-more-likely-to-get-arrested-for-it/?utm_term=.bca2df44bb77.

84. Joseph L. Gastwirth and Tapan K. Nayak, "Statistical Aspects of Cases Concerning Racial Discrimination in Drug Sentencing: Stephens v. State and U.S. v. Armstrong," *Journal of Criminal Law and Criminology* 87, no. 2 (1997): 583; "Drugs and Racial Discrimination" (editorial), *New York Times*, January 12, 2006, www.nytimes.com/2006/01/12/opinion/drugs-and-racial-discrimination.html.

85. Pew Charitable Trusts, *Collateral Costs: Incarceration's Effect on Economic Mobility* (Washington, DC: Pew Charitable Trusts, 2010).

86. Aaron Smith, "The U.S. Legal Marijuana Industry Is Booming," *CNN Money*, January 31, 2018, http://money.cnn.com/2018/01/31/news/marijuana-state-of-the-union/index.html.

87. Peter Wagner and Wendy Sawyer, "Mass Incarceration: The Whole Pie 2018," Prison Policy Initiative, March 14, 2018, www.prisonpolicy.org/reports/pie2018.html.

88. Tom Kertscher, "U.S. Incarcerates More People Than China or Russia, State Supreme Court Candidate Joe Donald Says," *PolitiFact*, December 9, 2015, www.politifact.com/wisconsin /statements/2015/dec/09/joe-donald/us-incarcerates-more-people-china-or-russia-state-/.

89. Wagner and Sawyer, "Mass Incarceration."

90. Alexander, *The New Jim Crow*.

91. Diana B. Elliott, Kristy Krivickas, Matthew W. Brault, and Rose M. Kreider, "Historical Marriage Trends from 1890–2010: A Focus on Race Differences," (SEHSD Working Paper No. 2012–12, presented at the annual meeting of the Population Association of America, San Francisco, CA, May 2012); Becky Pettit and Bruce Western, "Mass Imprisonment and the Life Course: Race and Class Inequality in U.S. Incarceration," *American Sociological Review* 69, no. 2 (2004): 151–69.

92. Stephan Thernstrom and Abigail Thernstrom. *America in Black and White: One Nation, Indivisible* (New York: Simon & Schuster, 1999), 237.

93. Robert J. Sampson, "Urban Black Violence: The Effect of Male Joblessness and Family Disruption," *American Journal of Sociology* 93, no. 2 (1987): 348–82.

94. Alexia Elajalde-Ruiz, "Report Says Youth Unemployment Chronic, Concentrated and Deeply Rooted," *Chicago Tribune*, January 28, 2017, www.chicagotribune.com/business /ct-youth-unemployment-data-0129-biz-20170127-story.html.

95. Angela Davis, *Abolition Democracy: Beyond Prison, Torture and Empire* (New York: Seven Stories, 2005).

96. Davis, *Abolition Democracy*.

97. Anthony C. Thompson, "Navigating the Hidden Obstacles to Ex-offender Reentry," *Boston College Law Review* 45, no. 2 (2004): 255–306.

98. Matthew R. Durose, Alexia D. Cooper, and Howard N. Snyder, *Recidivism of Prisoners Released in 30 States in 2005: Patterns from 2005 to 2010* (Washington, DC: U.S. Department of Justice, Office of Justice Programs, Bureau of Justice Statistics, 2014).

99. Todd R. Clear, Natasha A. Frost, Michael Carr, Geert Dhondt, Anthony Braga, and Garrett A. R. Warfield, *Predicting Crime Through Incarceration: The Impact of Rates of Prison Cycling on Rates of Crime in Communities* (Washington, DC: National Criminal Justice Reference Service, 2014).

100. Clear et al., *Predicting Crime*.

101. Jeffrey D. Morenoff, Robert J. Sampson, and Stephen W. Raudenbush, "Neighborhood Inequality, Collective Efficacy, and the Spatial Dynamics of Urban Violence," *Criminology* 39, no. 3 (2001): 517–58.

102. Salim Muwakkil, "Black Chicago Divided," *In These Times*, July 20, 2011, http://inthese times.com/article/11604/black_chicago_divided/.

103. Robert J. Sampson and Charles Loeffler, "Punishment's Place: The Local Concentration of Mass Incarceration," *Daedalus* 139, no. 3 (2010): 20–31.

104. Muwakkil, "Black Chicago Divided."

105. Sampson and Loeffler, "Punishment's Place."

106. Carl Takei, "From Mass Incarceration to Mass Control, and Back Again: How Bipartisan Criminal Justice Reform May Lead to a For-Profit Nightmare," *University of Pennsylvania Journal of Law and Social Change* 20 (2017): 125.

107. Alexander, *The New Jim Crow.*

108. J. Hirby, "What Is the Average Cost to House Inmates in Prison," The Law Dictionary, accessed September 19, 2018, https://thelawdictionary.org/article/what-is-the-average-cost -to-house-inmates-in-prison/.

109. Eric Schlosser, "The Prison-Industrial Complex," *Atlantic*, December 1998, www.theatlantic .com/magazine/archive/1998/12/the-prison-industrial-complex/304669/.

110. Michael Myser, "The Hard Sell," *CNN Money*, March 15, 2007, http://money.cnn.com /magazines/business2/business2_archive/2006/12/01/8394995/index.htm.

111. Myser, "The Hard Sell."

112. Ben Iddings, "The Big Disconnect: Will Anyone Answer the Call to Lower Excessive Prisoner Telephone Calls?" *North Carolina Journal of Law & Technology* 8, no. 1 (2006): 159–203.

113. Wilfred Chan, "Columbia Becomes First U.S. University to Divest from Prisons," *CNN*, updated June 24, 2015, https://www.cnn.com/2015/06/23/us/columbia-university-prison -divest/index.html.

114. Alexander, *The New Jim Crow.*

115. Iddings, "The Big Disconnect."

116. Hirby, "What Is the Average Cost."

117. Schlosser, "The Prison-Industrial Complex."

118. Schlosser, "The Prison-Industrial Complex."

119. Schlosser, "The Prison-Industrial Complex."

120. Schlosser, "The Prison-Industrial Complex."

121. Adam Gelb and Jacob Denney, "National Prison Rate Continues to Decline Amid Sentencing, Re-entry Reforms," Pew Charitable Trusts, January 16, 2018, www.pewtrusts .org/en/research-and-analysis/articles/2018/01/16/national-prison-rate-continues-to -decline-amid-sentencing-re-entry-reforms.

122. M. L. Nestel, "Handcuffing of 2 Black Men in Starbucks in Philadelphia Called 'Reprehensible Outcome' by CEO," *ABC News*, April 15, 2018, https://abcnews.go.com/News /black-men-walked-starbucks-cuffs-trespassing/story?id=54470047.

123. Schlosser, "The Prison-Industrial Complex."

124. Christina Caron, "A Black Yale Student Was Napping, and a White Student Called the Police," *New York Times*, May 9, 2018, www.nytimes.com/2018/05/09/nyregion/yale-black -student-nap.html.

125. "The War on Marijuana in Black and White," American Civil Liberties Union, June 2013, www.aclu.org/files/assets/aclu-thewaronmarijuana-rel2.pdf.

126. "The War on Marijuana."

127. Stephanie L. Rivaux, Joyce James, Kim Wittenstrom, Donald J. Baumann, Janess Sheets, Judith Henry, and Victoria Jeffries, "Race, Poverty, and Risk: Understanding the Decision to Provide Services and Remove Children," in *Challenging Racial Disproportionality*

in Child Welfare: Research, Policy, and Practice, ed. D. K. Green, K. Belanger, R. G. McRoy, and L. Bullard (Washington, DC: CWLA, 2011), 91–100.

128. Rivaux et al., "Race, Poverty, and Risk."

129. Alan J. Dettlaff, Stephanie L. Rivaux, Donald J. Baumann, John D. Fluke, Joan R. Rycraft, and Joyce James. "Disentangling Substantiation: The Influence of Race, Income, and Risk on the Substantiation Decision in Child Welfare," *Children and Youth Services Review* 33, no. 9 (2011): 1630–37; Stephanie L. Rivaux, Joyce James, Kim Wittenstrom, Donald Baumann, Janess Sheets, Judith Henry, and Victoria Jeffries, "The Intersection of Race, Poverty, and Risk: Understanding the Decision to Provide Services to Clients and to Remove Children," *Child Welfare* 87, no. 2 (2008): 151–68.

130. "Race Matters: Unequal Opportunity Within the Child Welfare System," Annie E. Casey Foundation, accessed October 17, 2018, www.aecf.org/m/resourcedoc/aecf -RACEMATTERSchildwelfare-2006.pdf.

131. Dorothy Roberts, *Shattered Bonds: The Color of Child Welfare* (New York: Basic Books, 2002).

132. Roberts, *Shattered Bonds*.

133. Roberts, *Shattered Bonds*.

134. Jon M. Hussey, Jen Jen Chang, and Jonathan B. Kotch, "Child Maltreatment in the United States: Prevalence, Risk Factors, and Adolescent Health Consequences," *Pediatrics* 118, no. 3 (2006): 933–42.

135. Robert J. Sampson, *Great American City: Chicago and the Enduring Neighborhood Effect* (Chicago: University of Chicago Press, 2012).

136. Clifford R. Shaw and Henry D. McKay, *Juvenile Delinquency and Urban Areas* (Chicago: University of Chicago Press, 1942).

137. Morenoff, Sampson, and Raudenbush, "Neighborhood Inequality."

138. Robert J. Sampson, Jeffrey D. Morenoff, and Thomas Gannon-Rowley, "Assessing 'Neighborhood Effects': Social Processes and New Directions in Research," *Annual Review of Sociology* 28, no. 1 (2002): 443–78.

139. Patrick Sharkey, *Stuck in Place: Urban Neighborhoods and the End of Progress Toward Racial Equality* (Chicago: University of Chicago Press, 2013).

140. Ruth D. Peterson and Lauren J. Krivo, *Divergent Social Worlds: Neighborhood Crime and the Racial–Spatial Divide* (New York: Russell Sage Foundation, 2010), 104.

141. Peterson and Krivo, *Divergent Social Worlds*, 91.

142. Sampson, *Great American City*.

143. "Healthy Chicago 2.0," City of Chicago, 2016. Courtesy of Nik Prachand.

144. "Race and Ethnicity in Englewood, Chicago, Illinois," Statistical Atlas, accessed October 17, 2018, https://statisticalatlas.com/neighborhood/Illinois/Chicago/Englewood/Race-and -Ethnicity.

145. "Race and Ethnicity in Rogers Park, Chicago, Illinois," Statistical Atlas, accessed October 17, 2018, https://statisticalatlas.com/neighborhood/Illinois/Chicago/Rogers-Park/Race-and -Ethnicity.

146. Poem courtesy of David Flynn.

5. The Scars of Violence

Portions of this chapter were previously published in Dexter R. Voisin, Esther J. Jenkins, and Lois Takahashi, "Toward a Conceptual Model Linking Community Violence and HIV-Related Risk Behaviors Among Adolescents: Directions for Research," *Journal of Adolescent Health* 49, no. 3 (2011): 230–36, and Dexter R. Voisin, Anna Hotton, and Torsten Neilands, "Exposure to Community Violence and Sexual Behaviors Among African American Youth: Testing Multiple Pathways," *Behavioral Medicine* 44, no. 1 (2018): 19–27.

The chapter epigraph is from Bessel A. van der Kolk, *The Body Keeps the Score: Brain, Mind, and Body in the Healing of Trauma* (New York: Penguin, 2014).

1. Van der Kolk, *The Body Keeps the Score*.
2. Dexter R. Voisin, Esther J. Jenkins, and Lois Takahashi, "Toward a Conceptual Model Linking Community Violence and HIV-Related Risk Behaviors Among Adolescents: Directions for Research," *Journal of Adolescent Health* 49, no. 3 (2011): 230–36.
3. Voisin, Jenkins, and Takahashi, "Toward a Conceptual Model."
4. Barbara Rector Hill, "Englewood, 1912–1950: In Celebration of Chicago's Sesquicentennial," 1988; Dominic A. Pacyga and Ellen Skerrett, "Chicago, City of Neighborhoods: Histories and Tours," 1986; Gerald E. Sullivan, ed. "The Story of Englewood, 1835–1923," 1924.
5. Chau Tu, "An Economic Breakdown of Chicago's Englewood Neighborhood," *Marketplace*, February 11, 2013, www.marketplace.org/2013/02/11/wealth-poverty/guns-and-dollars/economic-breakdown-chicagos-englewood-neighborhood.
6. "Mental Health and African Americans," U.S. Department of Health and Human Services, Office of Minority Health, last modified September 15, 2017, http://minorityhealth.hhs.gov/omh/browse.aspx?lvl=4&lvlid=24.
7. "Mental Health and African Americans."
8. Gayla Margolin and Elana B. Gordis, "The Effects of Family and Community Violence on Children," *Annual Review of Psychology* 51 (2000): 445–79.
9. Sandro Galea and Roger D. Vaughan, "The Invisible Forces That Create the Health of Populations: A Public Health of Consequence, April 2018," *American Journal of Public Health* 108, no. 4 (2018), 445–46.
10. Margolin and Gordis, "The Effects of Family and Community Violence."
11. "Continuous Traumatic Stress," American Psychological Association, May 2013, www.apa.org/pubs/journals/special/6041905.aspx.
12. Stephen L. Buka, Theresa L. Stichick, Isolde Birdthistle, and Felton J. Earls, "Youth Exposure to Violence: Prevalence, Risks, and Consequences," *American Journal of Orthopsychiatry* 71, no. 3 (2001): 298–310; Margolin and Gordis, "The Effects of Family and Community Violence."
13. Margaret Rosario, Suzanne Salzinger, Richard S. Feldman, and Daisy S. Ng-Mak, "Intervening Processes Between Youths' Exposure to Community Violence and Internalizing Symptoms Over Time: The Roles of Social Support and Coping," *American Journal of Community Psychology* 41, nos. 1–2 (2008): 43–62.

14. Michael R. McCart, Daniel W. Smith, Benjamin E. Saunders, Dean G. Kilpatrick, Heidi Resnick, and Kenneth J. Ruggiero, "Do Urban Adolescents Become Desensitized to Community Violence? Data from a National Survey," *American Journal of Orthopsychiatry* 77, no. 3 (2007): 434–42.

15. Margolin and Gordis, "The Effects of Family and Community Violence."

16. Deborah Gorman-Smith and Patrick Tolan, "The Role of Exposure to Community Violence and Developmental Problems Among Inner-City Youth," *Development and Psychopathology* 10, no. 1 (1998): 101–16.

17. Gorman-Smith and Tolan, "The Role of Exposure."

18. Margolin and Gordis, "The Effects of Family and Community Violence."

19. Patrick J. Fowler, Carolyn J. Tompsett, Jordan M. Braciszewski, Angela J. Jacques-Tiura, and Boris B. Baltes, "Community Violence: A Meta-analysis on the Effect of Exposure and Mental Health Outcomes of Children and Adolescents," *Development and Psychopathology* 21, no. 1 (2009): 227–59.

20. Robert J. Sampson, "Neighborhood Inequality, Violence, and the Social Infrastructure of the American City," in *Research on Schools, Neighborhoods, and Communities: Toward Civic Responsibility*, ed. William F. Tate IV (Lanham, MD: Rowman & Littlefield, 2012), 11–28.

21. Kristin Mmari, Beth Marshall, Trevor Hsu, Ji Won Shon, and Amenze Eguavoen, "A Mixed Methods Study to Examine the Influence of the Neighborhood Social Context on Adolescent Health Service Utilization," *BMC Health Services Research* 16 (2016): 433.

22. Katherine Quinn, Dexter R. Voisin, Alida Bouris, and John Schneider, "Psychological Distress, Drug Use, Sexual Risks and Medication Adherence Among Young HIV-Positive Black Men Who Have Sex with Men: Exposure to Community Violence Matters," *AIDS Care* 28, no. 7 (2016): 866–72.

23. Centers for Disease Control and Prevention, "Neighborhood Safety and the Prevalence of Physical Inactivity—Selected States, 1996," *Morbidity and Mortality Weekly Report* 48, no. 7 (1999): 143–46; Ross C. Brownson, Elizabeth A. Baker, Robyn A. Housemann, Laura K. Brennan, and Stephen J. Bacak, "Environmental and Policy Determinants of Physical Activity in the United States," *American Journal of Public Health* 91, no. 12 (2001): 1995–2003.

24. Penny Gordon-Larsen, Robert G. McMurray, and Barry M. Popkin, "Determinants of Adolescent Physical Activity and Inactivity Patterns," *Pediatrics* 105, no. 6 (2000): E83.

25. JoAnn Kuo, Carolyn C. Voorhees, Jennifer A. Haythornthwaite, and Deborah Rohm Young, "Associations Between Family Support, Family Intimacy, and Neighborhood Violence and Physical Activity in Urban Adolescent Girls," *American Journal of Public Health* 97, no. 1 (2007): 101–103.

26. Dexter R. Voisin, Torsten B. Neilands, and Shannon Hunnicutt, "Mechanisms Linking Violence Exposure and School Engagement Among African American Adolescents: Examining the Roles of Psychological Problem Behaviors and Gender," *American Journal of Orthopsychiatry* 81, no. 1 (2011): 61–71; Christopher C. Henrich, Mary Schwab-Stone, Kostas Fanti, Stephanie M. Jones, and Vladislav Ruchkin, "The Association of Community Violence Exposure with Middle-School Achievement: A Prospective Study," *Journal of Applied Developmental Psychology* 25, no. 3 (2004): 327–48; Jo Ann M. Farver, Lucia X.

Natera, and Dominick L. Frosch, "Effects of Community Violence on Inner-City Preschoolers and Their Families," *Journal of Applied Developmental Psychology* 20, no. 1 (1999): 143–58; David Schwartz and Andrea Hopmeyer Gorman, "Community Violence Exposure and Children's Academic Functioning," *Journal of Educational Psychology* 95, no. 1 (2003): 163–73.

27. Daisy S. Ng-Mak, Suzanne Salzinger, Richard S. Feldman, and C. Ann Stueve, "Pathologic Adaptation to Community Violence Among Inner-City Youth," *American Journal of Orthopsychiatry* 74, no. 2 (2004): 196.

28. Natasha K. Bowen and Gary L. Bowen, "Effects of Crime and Violence in Neighborhoods and Schools on the School Behavior and Performance of Adolescents," *Journal of Adolescent Research* 14, no. 3 (1999): 319–42.

29. Henrich et al., "The Association of Community Violence Exposure."

30. Voisin, Neilands, and Hunnicutt, "Mechanisms Linking Violence Exposure."

31. Jennifer A. Heissel, Patrick T. Sharkey, Gerard Torrats-Espinosa, Kathryn Grant, and Emma K. Adam, "Violence and Vigilance: The Acute Effects of Community Violent Crime on Sleep and Cortisol," *Child Development* 89, no. 4 (2018): e323–e331.

32. Dexter R. Voisin, Torsten B. Neilands, Laura F. Salazar, Richard Crosby, and Ralph J. DiClemente, "Pathways to Drug and Sexual Risk Behaviors Among Detained Adolescents," *Social Work Research* 32, no. 3 (2008): 147–57.

33. Voisin, Jenkins, and Takahashi, "Toward a Conceptual Model."

34. Dexter R. Voisin, Sadiq Patel, Jun Sung Hong, Lois Takahashi, and Noni Gaylord-Harden, "Behavioral Health Correlates of Exposure to Community Violence Among African-American Adolescents in Chicago," *Children and Youth Services Review* 69 (2016): 97–105.

35. Chicago Crime Commission, *The Gang Book* (Chicago: Chicago Crime Commission, 2018).

36. Chicago Crime Commission, *The Gang Book*.

37. Frederic M. Thrasher, *The Gang: A Study of 1,313 Gangs in Chicago*, 2nd ed. (Chicago: University of Chicago Press, 2013).

38. Substance Abuse and Mental Health Services Administration (SAMHSA), *Results from the 2013 National Survey on Drug Use and Health: Summary of National Findings*, NSDUH Series H-48, HHS Publication No. (SMA) 14–4863 (Rockville, MD: Substance Abuse and Mental Health Services Administration, 2014), www.samhsa.gov/data/sites/default/files /NSDUHresultsPDFWHTML2013/Web/NSDUHresults2013.pdf.

39. Nina Mulia, Yu Ye, Thomas K. Greenfield, and Sarah E. Zemore, "Disparities in Alcohol-Related Problems Among White, Black, and Hispanic Americans," *Alcoholism: Clinical and Experimental Research* 33, no. 4 (2009): 654–62.

40. SAMHSA, *Results from the 2013 National Survey*.

41. SAMHSA, *Results from the 2013 National Survey*.

42. Dean G. Kilpatrick, Ron Acierno, Benjamin Saunders, Heidi S. Resnick, Connie L. Best, and Paula P. Schnurr, "Risk Factors for Adolescent Substance Abuse and Dependence: Data from a National Sample," *Journal of Consulting and Clinical Psychology* 68, no. 1 (2000): 19–30.

43. Dexter R. Voisin, Laura F. Salazar, Richard Crosby, Ralph J. DiClemente, William L. Yarber, and Michelle Staples-Horne, "Witnessing Community Violence and Health-Risk Behaviors Among Detained Adolescents," *American Journal of Orthopsychiatry* 77, no. 4 (2007): 506–13.

44. Centers for Disease Control and Prevention (CDC), "Reproductive Health: Teen Pregnancy," last updated May 9, 2017, www.cdc.gov/teenpregnancy/about/index.htm.

45. CDC, "Sexually Transmitted Disease Surveillance Report, 2010," accessed October 30, 2013, www.cdc.gov/std/stats10/default.htm.

46. "Teen Births," 2016, Child Trends Databank, www.childtrends.org/indicators/teen-births.

47. "Teen Births."

48. CDC, "Reproductive Health: Teen Pregnancy."

49. Judith A. Levine, Harold Pollack, and Maureen E. Comfort, "Academic and Behavioral Outcomes Among the Children of Young Mothers," *Journal of Marriage and Family* 63, no. 2 (2001): 355–69.

50. Mignon R. Moore and P. Lindsay Chase-Lansdale, "Sexual Intercourse and Pregnancy Among African American Girls in High Poverty Neighborhoods: The Role of Family and Perceived Community Environment," *Journal of Marriage and Family* 63, no. 4 (2001): 1146–57.

51. Voisin, Jenkins, and Takahashi, "Toward a Conceptual Model."

52. Dexter R. Voisin, "Victims of Community Violence and HIV Sexual Risk Behaviors Among African American Adolescent Males," *Journal of HIV/AIDS Prevention & Education for Adolescents & Children* 5, nos. 3–4 (2003): 87–110.

53. Dexter R. Voisin, "The Relationship Between Violence Exposure and HIV Sexual Risk Behaviors: Does Gender Matter?" *American Journal of Orthopsychiatry* 75, no. 4 (2005): 497–506.

54. Voisin et al., "Witnessing Community Violence."

55. Abbey B. Berenson, Constance M. Wiemann, and Sharon McCombs, "Exposure to Violence and Associated Health-Risk Behaviors Among Adolescent Girls," *Archives of Pediatrics & Adolescent Medicine* 155, no. 11 (2001): 1238–42.

56. Berenson, Wiemann, and McCombs, "Exposure to Violence."

57. Arlene Rubin Stiffman, Peter Dore, Renee M. Cunningham, and Felton Earls, "Person and Environment in HIV Risk Behavior Change Between Adolescence and Young Adulthood," *Health Education Quarterly* 22, no. 2 (1995): 211–26.

58. Dexter R. Voisin and Torsten B. Neilands, "Low School Engagement and Sexual Behaviors Among African American Youth: Examining the Influences of Gender, Peer Norms, and Gang Involvement," *Children and Youth Services Review* 32, no. 1 (2010): 51–57.

59. Dexter R. Voisin, Kevin Tan, Anjanette Chan Tack, Devon Wade, and Ralph DiClemente, "Examining Parental Monitoring as a Pathway from Community Violence Exposure to Drug Use, Risky Sex, and Recidivism Among Detained Youth," *Journal of Social Service Research* 38, no. 5 (2012): 699–711.

60. "Trauma," American Psychological Association, accessed March 14, 2018, www.apa.org /topics/trauma/.

61. Ibram X. Kendi, "Post-Traumatic Slave Syndrome Is a Racist Idea," *Black Perspectives*, June 21, 2016, www.aaihs.org/post-traumatic-slave-syndrome-is-a-racist-idea/.

62. Kendi, "Post-Traumatic Slave Syndrome."

63. Paula Braveman and Laura Gottlieb, "The Social Determinants of Health: It's Time to Consider the Causes of the Causes," *Public Health Reports* 129, no. 1, suppl. 2 (2014): 19–31.

64. Braveman and Gottlieb, "The Social Determinants of Health."

65. Braveman and Gottlieb, "The Social Determinants of Health."

66. Braveman and Gottlieb, "The Social Determinants of Health."

67. Richard G. Wilkinson and Kate E. Pickett, "Income Inequality and Population Health: A Review and Explanation of the Evidence," *Social Science & Medicine* 62, no. 7 (2006): 1768–84.

68. National Scientific Council on the Developing Child, "Early Experiences Can Alter Gene Expression and Affect Long-Term Development," Working Paper 10, Harvard University, Center on the Developing Child, 2010, http://developingchild.harvard.edu/wp-content/uploads/2010/05/Early-Experiences-Can-Alter-Gene-Expression-and-Affect-Long-Term-Development.pdf.

69. National Scientific Council on the Developing Child, "Early Experiences."

70. Vincent J. Felitti, Robert F. Anda, Dale Nordenberg, David F. Williamson, Alison M. Spitz, Valerie Edwards, Mary P. Koss, and James S. Marks, "Relationship of Childhood Abuse and Household Dysfunction to Many of the Leading Causes of Death in Adults: The Adverse Childhood Experiences (ACE) Study," *American Journal of Preventive Medicine* 14, no. 4 (1998): 245–58.

71. "Social Determinants of Health," HealthyPeople.gov, accessed October 18, 2018, www.healthypeople.gov/2020/topics-objectives/topic/social-determinants-of-health.

72. Braveman and Gottlieb, "The Social Determinants of Health."

73. Robert Wood Johnson Foundation, "Breaking Through on the Social Determinants of Health and Health Disparities," Issue Brief 7, December 2009, www.commissiononhealth.org/PDF/0d5f4bd9-2209-48a2-a6f3-6742c9a7cde9/Issue%20Brief%207%20Dec%2009%20-%20Message%20Translation.pdf.

74. Charles H. Zeanah, Anna T. Smyke, Sebastian F. Koga, Elizabeth Carlson, and the Bucharest Early Intervention Project Core Group, "Attachment in Institutionalized and Community Children in Romania," *Child Development* 76, no. 5 (2005): 1015–28.

75. Charles H. Zeanah and Anna T. Smyke, "Building Attachment Relationships Following Maltreatment and Severe Deprivation," in *Enhancing Early Attachments: Theory, Research, Intervention, and Policy*, ed. Lisa J. Berlin, Yair Ziv, Lisa Amaya-Jackson, and Mark T. Greenberg (New York: Guilford, 2005), 195–216.

76. Zeanah and Smyke, "Building Attachment Relationships."

77. Voisin, Jenkins, and Takahashi, "Toward a Conceptual Model."

78. On psychological distress, Voisin, Hotton, and Neilands, "Exposure to Community Violence," and Kathleen E. Albus, Mark D. Weist, and Alina M. Perez-Smith, "Associations Between Youth Risk Behavior and Exposure to Violence: Implications for the Provision of Mental Health Services in Urban Schools," *Behavior Modification* 28, no. 4 (2004): 548–64. On mediation by peer influence, Dexter R. Voisin, Laura F. Salazar,

Richard Crosby, Ralph J. DiClemente, William L. Yarber, and Michelle Staples-Horne, "Teacher Connectedness and Health-Related Outcomes Among Detained Adolescents," *Journal of Adolescent Health* 37, no. 4 (2005): 337.e17–337.e23.

79. Margolin and Gordis, "The Effects of Family and Community Violence."

80. Margolin and Gordis, "The Effects of Family and Community Violence."

81. CDC, National Center for Injury Prevention and Control, Office of Statistics and Programming, Web-Based Injury Statistics Query and Reporting System, 2010.

82. Dexter R. Voisin, Anna Hotton, and Torsten Neilands, "Exposure to Community Violence and Sexual Behaviors Among African American Youth: Testing Multiple Pathways," *Behavioral Medicine* 44, no. 1 (2018): 19–27.

83. Richard A. Crosby, Ralph J. DiClemente, Gina M. Wingood, Laura F. Salazar, Eve Rose, and Jessica M. Sales, "The Protective Value of School Enrolment Against Sexually Transmitted Disease: A Study of High-Risk African American Adolescent Females," *Sexually Transmitted Infections* 83, no. 3 (2007): 223–27; Voisin et al., "Teacher Connectedness and Health-Related Outcomes."

84. Voisin, Hotton, and Neilands, "Exposure to Community Violence."

6. When Violence and Sex Are Entangled

Portions of this chapter were previously published in Dexter Voisin, Lois Takahashi, Kathryn Berringer, Sean Burr, and Jessica Kuhnen, "'Sex Is Violence': African-American Parents' Perceptions of the Link Between Exposure to Community Violence and Youth Sexual Behaviours," *Child & Family Social Work* 21, no. 4 (2016): 464–72.

1. "Woodlawn," Encyclopedia of Chicago, Chicago Historical Society, 2005, www.encyclopedia.chicagohistory.org/pages/1378.html.

2. "Woodlawn, Chicago, IL, Demographics," AreaVibes, accessed October 17, 2018, www.areavibes.com/chicago-il/woodlawn/demographics/; "Woodlawn, Chicago, IL, Employment," AreaVibes, accessed October 17, 2018, www.areavibes.com/chicago-il/woodlawn/employment/.

3. U.S. Department of Justice and Federal Bureau of Investigation, "2008 Crime in the United States," Uniform Crime Reporting, September 2009, https://ucr.fbi.gov/crime-in-the-u.s/2008.

4. Gayla Margolin and Elana B. Gordis, "The Effects of Family and Community Violence on Children," *Annual Review of Psychology* 51 (2000): 445–79.

5. Dexter R. Voisin, Esther J. Jenkins, and Lois Takahashi, "Toward a Conceptual Model Linking Community Violence and HIV-Related Risk Behaviors Among Adolescents: Directions for Research," *Journal of Adolescent Health* 49, no. 3 (2011): 230–36.

6. Dexter R. Voisin, Kevin Tan, Anjanette Chan Tack, Devon Wade, and Ralph DiClemente, "Examining Parental Monitoring as a Pathway from Community Violence Exposure to Drug Use, Risky Sex, and Recidivism Among Detained Youth," *Journal of Social Service Research* 38, no. 5 (2012): 699–711; Dexter R. Voisin, Torsten B. Neilands, Laura F. Salazar,

Richard Crosby, and Ralph J. DiClemente, "Pathways to Drug and Sexual Risk Behaviors Among Detained Adolescents," *Social Work Research* 32, no. 3 (2008): 147–57.

7. Dexter R. Voisin, Anna L. Hotton, and Torsten B. Neilands, "Testing Pathways Linking Exposure to Community Violence and Sexual Behaviors Among African American Youth," *Journal of Youth and Adolescence* 43, no. 9 (2014): 1513–26.

8. Voisin, Hotton, and Neilands, "Testing Pathways."

9. Sonya S. Brady and Geri R. Donenberg, "Mechanisms Linking Violence Exposure to Health Risk Behavior in Adolescence: Motivation to Cope and Sensation Seeking," *Journal of the American Academy of Child and Adolescent Psychiatry* 45, no. 6 (2006): 673–80.

10. Mindy Thompson Fullilove, Véronique Héon, Walkiria Jimenez, Caroline Parsons, Lesley L. Green, and Robert E. Fullilove, "Injury and Anomie: Effects of Violence on an Inner-City Community," *American Journal of Public Health* 88, no. 6 (1998): 924–27.

11. Dexter Voisin, Lois Takahashi, Kathryn Berringer, Sean Burr, and Jessica Kuhnen, "'Sex Is Violence': African-American Parents' Perceptions of the Link between Exposure to Community Violence and Youth Sexual Behaviours," *Child & Family Social Work* 21, no. 4 (2016): 464–72.

12. Philip J. Cook, Richard J. Harris, Jens Ludwig, and Harold A. Pollack, "Some Sources of Crime Guns in Chicago: Dirty Dealers, Straw Purchasers, and Traffickers," *Journal of Criminal Law and Criminology* 104, no. 4 (2015): 717–59.

13. Richard Spano, Alexander T. Vazsonyi, and John Bolland, "Does Parenting Mediate the Effects of Exposure to Violence on Violent Behavior? An Ecological–Transactional Model of Community Violence," *Journal of Adolescence* 32, no. 5 (2009): 1321–41.

14. "America's Families and Living Arrangements: 2017," U.S. Census Bureau, accessed April 12, 2018, www.census.gov/data/tables/2017/demo/families/cps-2017.html.

15. Juanita J. Cuffee, Denise D. Hallfors, and Martha W. Waller, "Racial and Gender Differences in Adolescent Sexual Attitudes and Longitudinal Associations with Coital Debut," *Journal of Adolescent Health* 41, no. 1 (2007): 19–26.

16. Ralph J. DiClemente, Gina M. Wingood, Eve S. Rose, Jessica M. Sales, Delia L. Lang, Angela M. Caliendo, James W. Hardin, and Richard A. Crosby, "Efficacy of Sexually Transmitted Disease/Human Immunodeficiency Virus Sexual Risk–Reduction Intervention for African American Adolescent Females Seeking Sexual Health Services," *Archives of Pediatrics & Adolescent Medicine* 163, no. 12 (2009): 1112–21.

17. "BAM—Becoming A Man," Youth Guidance, 2018, www.youth-guidance.org/bam/.

18. Voisin et al., "Pathways to Drug and Sexual Risk Behaviors."

7. Living and Parenting in the Presence of Everyday Dangers

Portions of this chapter were originally published in Dexter Voisin, Kathryn Berringer, Lois Takahashi, Sean Burr, and Jessica Kuhnen, "No Safe Havens: Protective Parenting Strategies for Black Youth Living in Violent Communities," *Violence and Victims* 31, no. 3 (2016): 523–36.

7. Living and Parenting in the Presence of Everyday Dangers

1. Gillian Mohney, "More Than 60 Shot, 9 Dead in Chicago's Bloody Holiday Weekend," *ABC 7 Eyewitness News*, July 7, 2014, http://abc7chicago.com/news/more-than-60-shot-9-dead-in-chicagos-bloody-holiday-weekend/161442/.

2. Deanese Williams-Harris, Megan Crepeau, and Elvia Malagon, "Homicides in Chicago Outpacing Last Year After Deadliest Day So Far in 2017," *Chicago Tribune*, February 23, 2017, www.chicagotribune.com/news/local/breaking/ct-man-61-found-shot-dead-in-garage-in-south-lawndale-20170222-story.html.

3. Richard S. Lazarus and Susan Folkman, *Stress, Appraisal, and Coping* (New York: Springer, 1984).

4. Steven L. Berman, William M. Kurtines, Wendy K. Silverman, and Lourdes T. Serafini, "The Impact of Exposure to Community Violence on Urban Youth," *American Journal of Orthopsychiatry* 66, no. 3 (1996): 329–36; Margaret Rosario, Suzanne Salzinger, Richard S. Feldman, and Daisy S. Ng-Mak, "Community Violence Exposure and Delinquent Behaviors Among Youth: The Moderating Role of Coping," *Journal of Community Psychology* 31, no. 5 (2003): 489–512.

5. Rosario et al., "Community Violence Exposure."

6. Berman, et al., "The Impact of Exposure."

7. Terry A. Wolfer, "Coping with Chronic Community Violence: The Variety and Implications of Women's Efforts," *Violence & Victims* 15 (2000): 283–302.

8. Ta-Nehisi Coates, "The Case for Reparations," *Atlantic*, June 2014, www.theatlantic.com/magazine/archive/2014/06/the-case-for-reparations/361631/.

9. Dexter R. Voisin, Jason D. P. Bird, Melissa Hardestry, and Cheng Shi Shiu, "African American Adolescents Living and Coping with Community Violence on Chicago's Southside," *Journal of Interpersonal Violence* 26, no. 12 (2011): 2483–98.

10. "Children's Exposure to Violence," Child Trends, 2016, www.childtrends.org/?indicators=childrens-exposure-to-violence.

11. Lazarus and Folkman, *Stress, Appraisal, and Coping*; Rosario et al., "Community Violence Exposure"; Wolfer, "Coping."

12. Anjanette M. Chan Tack and Mario L. Small, "Making Friends in Violent Neighborhoods: Strategies Among Elementary School Children," *Sociological Science* 4, no. 10 (2017): 224–48.

13. Chan Tack and Small, "Making Friends."

14. Centers for Disease Control and Prevention (CDC), National Center for Injury Prevention and Control, Office of Statistics and Programming, and Web-Based Injury Statistics Query and Reporting System, 2008, www.cdc.gov/ncipc/wisqars/.

15. Jean Bottcher, "Gender as Social Control: A Qualitative Study of Incarcerated Youths and Their Siblings in Greater Sacramento," *Justice Quarterly* 12, no. 1 (1995): 33–57.

16. CDC et al., 2008.

17. Murray B. Stein, John R. Walker, Andrea L. Hazen, and David R. Forde, "Full and Partial Posttraumatic Stress Disorder: Findings from a Community Survey," *American Journal of Psychiatry* 154, no. 8 (1997): 1114–19.

18. José Martín, "Policing Is a Dirty Job, But Nobody's Gotta Do It: 6 Ideas for a Cop-Free World," *Rolling Stone*, December 16, 2014, www.rollingstone.com/politics/news/policing -is-a-dirty-job-but-nobodys-gotta-do-it-6-ideas-for-a-cop-free-world-20141216.

19. Rosario et al., "Community Violence Exposure"; Wolfer, "Coping."

20. Karyn Horowitz, Mary McKay, and Randall Marshall, "Community Violence and Urban Families: Experiences, Effects, and Directions for Intervention," *American Journal of Orthopsychiatry* 75, no. 3 (2005): 356–68.

21. Neil B. Guterman, "The Role of Research in Defining a 'Practiceable' Problem for Social Work: The Parallax of Community and Family Violence Exposure Among Children and Youths," *Social Work Education* 21, no. 3 (2002): 313–22.

22. Dexter Voisin, "The Effects of Family and Community Violence Exposure Among Youth: Recommendations for Practice and Policy," *Journal of Social Work Education* 43, no. 1 (2007): 51–66.

23. Bradley D. Stein, Lisa H. Jaycox, Sheryl H. Kataoka, Marleen Wong, Wenli Tu, Marc N. Elliott, and Arlene Fink, "A Mental Health Intervention for Schoolchildren Exposed to Violence," *Journal of the American Medical Association* 290, no. 5 (2003): 603–11.

24. David Finkelhor and Richard Ormrod, "Homicides of Children and Youth," *Juvenile Justice Bulletin* (Washington, DC: U.S. Department of Justice, 2001).

25. William Ruger and Jason Sorens, "Freedom in the 50 States," Cato Institute, accessed April 5, 2018, www.freedominthe50states.org/education.

26. Finkelhor and Richard Ormrod, "Homicides of Children and Youth."

27. Amanda N. Burnside, Noni K. Gaylord-Harden, Suzanna So, and Dexter R. Voisin, "A Latent Profile Analysis of Exposure to Community Violence and Peer Delinquency in African American Adolescents," *Children and Youth Services Review* 91 (2018): 196–203.

28. Sarah A. Stoddard, Marc A. Zimmerman, and José A. Bauermeister, "Thinking About the Future as a Way to Succeed in the Present: A Longitudinal Study of Future Orientation and Violent Behaviors Among African American Youth," *American Journal of Community Psychology* 48, nos. 3–4 (2011): 238–46.

29. On self-esteem, Dong Ha Kim, Sarah M. Bassett, Lois Takahashi, and Dexter R. Voisin, "What Does Self-Esteem Have to Do with Behavioral Health Among Low-Income African American Youth?" *Journal of Youth Studies* 21, no. 8 (2018): 999–1010. On future orientation, Suzanna So, Dexter R. Voisin, Amanda Burnside, and Noni K.Gaylord-Harden, "Future Orientation and Health Related Factors Among African American Adolescents," *Children and Youth Services Review* 61 (2016): 15–21.

30. M. Brent Donnellan, Kali H. Trzesniewski, Richard W. Robins, Terrie E. Moffitt, and Avshalom Caspi, "Low Self-Esteem Is Related to Aggression, Antisocial Behavior, and Delinquency," *Psychological Science* 16, no. 4 (2005): 328–35.

31. Dexter Voisin, Kathryn Berringer, Lois Takahashi, Sean Burr, and Jessica Kuhnen, "No Safe Havens: Protective Parenting Strategies for Black Youth Living in Violent Communities," *Violence and Victims* 31, no. 3 (2016): 523–36.

32. Phillip L. Marotta and Dexter R. Voisin, "Pathways to Delinquency and Substance Use Among African American Youth: Does Future Orientation Mediate the Effects of Peer Norms and Parental Monitoring?" *Journal of Health Psychology*, published ahead of print, November 6, 2017, https://doi.org/10.1177/1359105317736912.

33. Horowitz, McKay, and Marshall, "Community Violence."

34. Sarah R. Lindstrom Johnson, Nadine M. Finigan, Catherine P. Bradshaw, Denise L. Haynie, and Tina L. Cheng, "Examining the Link Between Neighborhood Context and Parental Messages to Their Adolescent Children About Violence," *Journal of Adolescent Health* 49, no. 1 (2011): 58–63.

35. Voisin et al., "No Safe Havens."

36. Michel Martin and Ivory Toldson, "Are There Really More Black Men in Prison Than College?" *NPR*, April 23, 2013, www.npr.org/2013/04/23/178601467/are-there-really-more -black-men-in-prison-than-college; Ivory A. Toldson, "More Black Men in Jail Than in College? Wrong," *The Root*, February 28, 2013, www.theroot.com/more-black-men-in -jail-than-in-college-wrong-1790895415.

37. Horowitz, McKay, and Marshall, "Community Violence."

38. Horowitz, McKay, and Marshall, "Community Violence."

8. Joining the Broken Pieces: Practice and Policy Solutions and Systems Integration

Portions of this chapter were originally published in Dexter Voisin, "The Effects of Family and Community Violence Exposure Among Youth: Recommendations for Practice and Policy," *Journal of Social Work Education* 43, no. 1 (2007): 51–66, and Dexter R. Voisin and Kathryn R. Berringer, "Interventions Targeting Exposure to Community Violence Sequelae Among Youth: A Commentary," *Clinical Social Work Journal* 43, no. 1 (2015): 98–108.

1. U.S. Public Health Service, *Report of the Surgeon General's Conference on Children's Mental Health: A National Action Agenda* (Washington, DC: U.S. Department of Health and Human Services, 2000).

2. Office of Juvenile Justice and Delinquency Prevention, *Child Victims Act Model Courts Project Status Report 1999*, Technical Assistance Bulletin 4, no. 1 (Reno, NV: National Council of Juvenile and Family Court Judges, 2000).

3. "Mass Shootings in 2018," Gun Violence Archive, accessed October 16, 2018, www.gun violencearchive.org/reports/mass-shooting.

4. "Mass Shootings in 2018."

5. Leigh Donaldson, "When the Media Misrepresents Black Men, the Effects Are Felt in Real Life," *Guardian*, August 12, 2015, www.theguardian.com/commentisfree/2015/aug/12 /media-misrepresents-black-men-effects-felt-real-world.

6. Lois Beckett, Rich Harris, Nadja Popovich, Jan Diehm, and Mona Chalabi, "America's Gun Problem Is So Much Bigger Than Mass Shootings," *Guardian*, June 21, 2016, www .theguardian.com/us-news/2016/jun/21/gun-control-debate-mass-shootings-gun-violence.

7. Lauren Pearle, "School Shootings Since Columbine: By the Numbers," *ABC News*, February 12, 2016, https://abcnews.go.com/US/school-shootings-columbine-numbers /story?id=36833245.

8. Matthew Cella and Alan Neuhauser, "Race and Homicide in America, by the Numbers," *U.S. News & World Report*, September 29, 2016, www.usnews.com/news/articles /2016-09-29/race-and-homicide-in-america-by-the-numbers.

9. Julia Glum, "On Columbine Shooting Anniversary, School Security Industry Continues Expanding Despite Challenges," *International Business Times*, April 20, 2016, www.ibtimes .com/columbine-shooting-anniversary-school-security-industry-continues-expanding -despite-2356057.

10. Sasha Abramsky, "The School-Security Industry Is Cashing in Big on Public Fears of Mass Shootings," *Nation*, August 9, 2016, www.thenation.com/article/the-school-security -industry-is-cashing-in-big-on-public-fears-of-mass-shootings/.

11. Donna E. Howard, Sheila I. Cross, Xiaoming Li, and Weihua Huang, "Parent–Youth Concordance Regarding Violence Exposure: Relationship to Youth Psychosocial Functioning," *Journal of Adolescent Health* 25, no. 6 (1999): 396–406.

12. U.S. Public Health Service, *Report of the Surgeon General's Conference*.

13. Gayla Margolin and Elana B. Gordis, "The Effects of Family and Community Violence on Children," *Annual Review of Psychology* 51 (2000): 445–79.

14. Neil B. Guterman and Mark Cameron, "Young Clients' Exposure to Community Violence: How Much Do Their Therapists Know?" *American Journal of Orthopsychiatry* 69, no. 3 (1999): 382–91.

15. Neil B. Guterman, "The Role of Research in Defining a 'Practiceable' Problem for Social Work: The Parallax of Community and Family Violence Exposure Among Children and Youths," *Social Work Education* 21, no. 3 (2002): 313–22, quote at 317.

16. U.S. Public Health Service, *Report of the Surgeon General's Conference*.

17. National Institutes of Health, "Demographic and Social Measures: VIII. Exposure to Violence," accessed March 19, 2005, http://trans.nih.gov/CEHP/HBPdemo-violence .htm.

18. John E. Richters and William Saltzman, *Survey of Exposure to Community Violence: Self-Report Version* (Rockville, MD: National Institute of Mental Health, 1990).

19. Mary Beth Selner-O'Hagan, Daniel J. Kindlon, Stephen L. Buka, Stephen W. Raudenbush, and Felton J. Earls, "Assessing Exposure to Violence in Urban Youth," *Journal of Child Psychology and Psychiatry* 39, no. 2 (1998): 215–24.

20. Michele R. Cooley-Quille, Samuel M. Turner, and Deborah C. Beidel, "Emotional Impact of Children's Exposure to Community Violence: A Preliminary Study," *Journal of the American Academy of Child and Adolescent Psychiatry* 34, no. 10 (1995): 1362–68.

21. Teresa L. Hastings and Mary Lou Kelley, "Development and Validation of the Screen for Adolescent Violence Exposure (SAVE)," *Journal of Abnormal Child Psychology* 25, no. 6 (1997): 511–20.

22. Murray A. Straus and Richard J. Gelles, eds., *Physical Violence in American Families: Risk Factors and Adaptations to Violence in 8,145 Families* (New Brunswick, NJ: Transaction, 1990).

23. U.S. Public Health Service, *Report of the Surgeon General's Conference*.

24. Sam Cholke, "'Army of Moms' Starts Patrolling Southside After Shooting," *DNAinfo*, June 30, 2015, www.dnainfo.com/chicago/20150630/englewood/army-of-moms-starts -patrolling-englewood-after-shooting/.

25. Judith A. Cohen, Lucy Berliner, and Anthony P. Mannarino, "Psychosocial and Pharmacological Interventions for Child Crime Victims," *Journal of Traumatic Stress* 16, no. 2 (2003): 175–86.

26. On individual sessions, Judith A. Cohen, Esther Deblinger, Anthony P. Mannarino, and Robert A. Steer, "A Multisite, Randomized Controlled Trial for Children With Sexual Abuse–Related PTSD Symptoms," *Journal of the American Academy of Child and Adolescent Psychiatry* 43 (2004): 393–402; Judith A. Cohen and Anthony P. Mannarino, "A Treatment Outcome Study for Sexually Abused Preschool Children: Outcome During a One-Year Follow-Up," *Journal of the American Academy of Child and Adolescent Psychiatry* 36, no. 9 (1997): 1228–35; Esther Deblinger, Julie Lippmann, and Robert Steer, "Sexually Abused Children Suffering Posttraumatic Stress Symptoms: Initial Treatment Outcome Findings," *Child Maltreatment* 1, no. 4 (1996): 310–21; and David J. Kolko, "Individual Cognitive Behavioral Treatment and Family Therapy for Physically Abused Children and Their Offending Parents: A Comparison of Clinical Outcomes," *Child Maltreatment* 1, no. 4 (1996): 322–42. On joint and individual sessions, Cohen et al., "A Multisite, Randomized Controlled Trial" and Deblinger, Lippmann, and Steer, "Sexually Abused Children."

27. Sheryl H. Kataoka, Bradley D. Stein, Lisa H. Jaycox, Marleen Wong, Pia Escudero, Wenli Tu, Catalina Zaragoza, and Arlene Fink, "A School-Based Mental Health Program for Traumatized Latino Immigrant Children," *Journal of the American Academy of Child and Adolescent Psychiatry* 42, no. 3 (2003): 311–18; Bradley D. Stein, Lisa H. Jaycox, Sheryl H. Kataoka, Marleen Wong, Wenli Tu, Marc N. Elliott, and Arlene Fink, "A Mental Health Intervention for Schoolchildren Exposed to Violence," *Journal of the American Medical Association* 290, no. 5 (2003): 603–11.

28. Kataoka et al., "A School-Based Mental Health Program"; William R. Saltzman, Robert S. Pynoos, Christopher M. Layne, Alan M. Steinberg, and Eugene Aisenberg, "Trauma- and Grief-Focused Intervention for Adolescents Exposed to Community Violence: Results of a School-Based Screening and Group Treatment Protocol," *Group Dynamics: Theory, Research, and Practice* 5, no. 4 (2001): 291; Stein et al., "A Mental Health Intervention."

29. John S. March, Lisa Amaya-Jackson, Mary Cathryn Murray, and Ann Schulte, "Cognitive-Behavioral Psychotherapy for Children and Adolescents with Posttraumatic Stress Disorder After a Single-Incident Stressor," *Journal of the American Academy of Child and Adolescent Psychiatry* 37, no. 6 (1998): 585–93.

30. Lisa R. Jackson-Cherry and Bradley T. Erford, *Crisis Intervention and Prevention* (Upper Saddle River, NJ: Pearson Education, 2010).

31. Robert S. Pynoos and Kathi Nader, "Psychological First Aid and Treatment Approach to Children Exposed to Community Violence: Research Implications," *Journal of Traumatic Stress* 1, no. 4 (1988): 445–73; M. Brymer, C. Layne, A. Jacobs, R. Pynoos, J. Ruzek, A. Steinberg, E. Vernberg, and P. Watson, *Psychological First Aid: Field Operations Guide*, 2nd ed.

(Los Angeles: National Child Traumatic Stress Network, 2006), 5–6, www.nctsn.org/sites /default/files/resources//pfa_field_operations_guide.pdf.

32. Cohen, Berliner, and Mannarino, "Psychosocial and Pharmacological Interventions."

33. "Mental Health First Aid," National Council for Behavioral Health, 2014, www.mental healthfirstaid.org/cs/.

34. J. William Worden, "Tasks and Mediators of Mourning: A Guideline for the Mental Health Practitioner," *In Session: Psychotherapy in Practice* 2, no. 4 (1996): 73–80; Susan C. Smith, *The Forgotten Mourners: Guidelines for Working with Bereaved Children* (London: Jessica Kingsley, 1999).

35. Cohen, Berliner, and Mannarino, "Psychosocial and Pharmacological Interventions."

36. U.S. Public Health Service, *Report of the Surgeon General's Conference.*

37. Judith A. Cohen and Work Group on Quality Issues, "Practice Parameters for the Assessment and Treatment of Children and Adolescents with Posttraumatic Stress Disorder," *Journal of the American Academy of Child & Adolescent Psychiatry* 37, no. 10, suppl. (1998): 4S–26S.

38. Neil B. Guterman, Hyeouk C. Hahm, and Mark Cameron, "Adolescent Victimization and Subsequent Use of Mental Health Counseling Services," *Journal of Adolescent Health* 30, no. 5 (2002): 336–45.

39. U.S. Department of Health and Human Services, *Mental Health: A Report of the Surgeon General* (Rockville, MD: U.S. Department of Health and Human Services, Substance Abuse and Mental Health Services Administration, Center for Mental Health Services, National Institutes of Health, National Institute of Mental Health, 1999).

40. U.S. Department of Health and Human Services, *Mental Health: Culture, Race, and Ethnicity: A Supplement to Mental Health—A Report of the Surgeon General* (Rockville, MD: U.S. Department of Health and Human Services, Substance Abuse and Mental Health Services Administration, Center for Mental Health Services, 2001), 3.

41. Michael A. De Arellano, Angela E. Waldrop, Esther Deblinger, Judith A. Cohen, Carla Kmett Danielson, and Anthony R. Mannarino, "Community Outreach Program for Child Victims of Traumatic Events: A Community-Based Project for Underserved Populations," *Behavior Modification* 29, no. 1 (2005): 130–55.

42. U.S. Public Health Service, *Report of the Surgeon General's Conference.*

43. U.S. Public Health Service, *Report of the Surgeon General's Conference.*

44. U.S. Public Health Service, *Report of the Surgeon General's Conference.*

45. U.S. Public Health Service, *Report of the Surgeon General's Conference.*

46. Etienne G. Krug, Linda L. Dahlberg, James A. Mercy, Anthony B. Zwi, and Rafael Lozano, eds., *World Report on Violence and Health* (Geneva, Switzerland: World Health Organization, 2002), 1–3.

47. U.S. Public Health Service, *Report of the Surgeon General's Conference.*

48. Robert Goerge, Cheryl Smithgall, Roopa Seshadri, and Peter Ballard, "Illinois Families and Their Use of Multiple Service Systems," Chapin Hall at the University of Chicago, 2010, www.chapinhall.org/wp-content/uploads/Goerge_Illinois-Families-Their-Use_Brief _2010.pdf.

9. Making a Difference: Rebuilding the Village

1. "City of Chicago's Youth Violence Prevention Plan," Youth.gov, accessed September 20, 2018, https://youth.gov/youth-topics/preventing-youth-violence/forum-communities/chicago/brief.

2. "City of Chicago's Youth Violence Prevention Plan."

3. Dexter Voisin, Kathryn Berringer, Lois Takahashi, Sean Burr, and Jessica Kuhnen, "No Safe Havens: Protective Parenting Strategies for Black Youth Living in Violent Communities," *Violence and Victims* 31, no. 3 (2016): 523–36.

4. "City of Chicago's Youth Violence Prevention Plan."

5. Wesley G. Skogan, Susan M. Hartnett, Natalie Bump, and Jill Dubois, "Evaluation of CeaseFire-Chicago," March 19, 2009, www.skogan.org/files/Evaluation_of_CeaseFire-Chicago_Main_Report.03-2009.pdf.

6. Mitchell Armentrout, "Chicago Homicides Down Sharply in 2017, Still Over 650 Slain," *Chicago Sun-Times*, December 31, 2017, https://chicago.suntimes.com/news/chicago-murders-homicides-2017-steep-decline/.

7. Associated Press, "Chicago Group Fights Growing Street Violence with Yoga Classes," *People*, July 5, 2014, https://people.com/human-interest/englewood-chicago-using-yoga-classes-to-fight-violence-and-gun-crimes/.

8. James Baldwin, "The Negro Child—His Self-Image," *Saturday Review*, December 21, 1963, 42–44, published as "A Talk to Teachers," in *Child Development and Learning*, ed. William C. Johnson (New York: MSS Information, 1973), 8.

INDEX

Index

Index

Index